Why Taiwan Matters

Why Taiwan Matters

Small Island, Global Powerhouse

Updated Edition

Shelley Rigger

ROWMAN & LITTLEFIELD PUBLISHERS, INC.
Lanham • Boulder • New York • Toronto • Plymouth, UK

Published by Rowman & Littlefield
4501 Forbes Boulevard, Suite 200, Lanham, Maryland 20706
www.rowman.com

10 Thornbury Road, Plymouth PL6 7PP, United Kingdom

British Library Cataloguing in Publication Information Available

The hardback edition of this book was previously cataloged by the Library of
Congress as follows:

Rigger, Shelley, 1962-
  Why Taiwan matters : small island, global powerhouse / Shelley Rigger.
      p. cm.
  Includes bibliographical references and index.
  1. Taiwan—Foreign relations—21st century. 2. Taiwan—Foreign relations—
United States. 3. United States—Foreign relations—Taiwan. 4. Taiwan—Foreign
relations—China. 5. China—Foreign relations—Taiwan. 6. Taiwan—Economic
conditions—21st century. I. Title.
  DS799.625.R54 2011
  951.24'905—dc22

                                                               2010051417

ISBN 978-1-4422-0479-9 (cloth : alk. paper)
ISBN 978-1-4422-0480-5 (pbk. : alk. paper)
ISBN 978-1-4422-0481-2 (electronic)

♾️™ The paper used in this publication meets the minimum requirements of
American National Standard for Information Sciences—Permanence of Paper for
Printed Library Materials, ANSI/NISO Z39.48-1992.

Printed in the United States of America

Contents

Preface

Why Taiwan Matters is a book I have wanted to write for a long time. It answers the two questions I am asked most often about my work: What makes Taiwan so interesting to you? And, why is Taiwan such a big deal in U.S.-China relations?

I hope when you finish reading the book the first question will be answered. My goal is to give you an inkling of the excitement I feel every time I step off a plane at the Taoyuan International Airport. I felt that excitement for the first time in 1983 when I was a twenty-one-year-old college student embarking on a summer research project. I will never forget how bewildering, terrifying, and exhilarating it was to find myself standing alone with my suitcase on a hot, dusty sidewalk in Taipei, armed with nothing more than an envelope of traveler's checks, a couple of telephone numbers, and four semesters of Chinese language instruction. Today, arriving in Taipei feels like returning to a second home—but it is a home where time accelerates and people cram three days of living into every twenty-four hours.

The second question—why does Taiwan matter so much to U.S.-China relations?—is more complicated. Taiwan matters to the United States and other countries because it is an economic powerhouse that supplies much of our information-technology equipment and because it occupies a strategic niche in the Western Pacific. It is unique in the world in having all the attributes of a state—territory, population, government—except recognition by others. The People's Republic of China insists that history makes Taiwan part of China, and because the government in Beijing is the recognized Chinese state, it should rule the island. Few Taiwanese share that view, but there is a lively debate about how to fend off Beijing's attentions. Navigating between the two sides—developing amicable relations with

China while supporting a democratic Taiwan—is a challenging assignment for leaders in the United States and other countries.

Still, I hope to convince you that Taiwan is more than just a "problem." Taiwan also matters because its history makes it a test case for values Americans and many others claim to cherish. For centuries, powerful countries treated Taiwan as war booty, an afterthought. In the past half century, Taiwan's people rejected that status and stood up for themselves. In their determination to claim a better future, they created one of the world's most successful economies and vibrant democracies. The United States has long encouraged free markets and democratic politics, both as a matter of national interest and as a reflection of its national values. Taiwan proves it is possible to achieve those ends peacefully, and to do so in a way that respects and enhances its turbocharged culture. For that, it matters.

Why Taiwan Matters is the culmination of all the work, all the reading, all the trips, all the interviews and encounters I've had in nearly thirty years of traveling to Taiwan. Throughout the text, I include many quotations from people I've talked to over the years, including hundreds of formal interviews and informal conversations. No one gets to know a place well without lots of help, but the student of Taiwan is especially blessed because hospitality, generosity, and conversation are (along with baseball and eating) national pastimes.

Thanking everyone who has helped me get to know Taiwan over the past thirty years would make the book unconscionably long, but there are a handful of people who have provided extraordinary support, encouragement, and information over the years. Chen Chu, the mayor of Kaohsiung, was the first public figure I met in Taiwan. Without her help, my efforts to learn about Taiwan politics would have come to nothing. Scores of Taiwanese, American and PRC officials, politicians, and activists have talked to me over the years, on and off the record. Those conversations shaped my views fundamentally. I also owe an enormous debt to my fellow political scientists, especially those in Taiwan, whose patience with a foreign scholar's efforts to understand their homeland is humbling.

I have benefited from the scholarship of researchers in Taiwan, the PRC, the United States, Canada, Australia, and Europe, nine of whom rendered especially generous (and timely) service to this book at a critical moment: Richard Bush, Tun-jen Cheng, Dafydd Fell, Sara Friedman, Steven Phillips, Michael Szonyi, Alan Wachman, Vincent Wang, and Joseph Wong. And I thank my friend, guide, mentor, and confidant Fan Meei-yuan for making time for me in every visit.

Funding from the Smith Richardson Foundation made my work on this and other books possible, and I thank the foundation most sincerely. I have also received funding, administrative help, and bounteous encouragement from Davidson College. Thanks also to my research assistants: Shuo-ting Chen, August Ho, Yi-long Huang, and Aaron Saltzman.

Finally, I thank my traveling companions: David, Emma, and Tilly Boraks. You make every day an adventure.

Because Chinese is not a phonetic language, there is no one-to-one correspondence between Chinese characters and Roman letters. Spelling out Chinese words is a matter of deciding how they sound and writing down that sound as best we can. There are a number of systems for spelling Chinese words; the most popular is the pinyin system used in the People's Republic of China. That's the system that gives us "Beijing" instead of the old "Peking." Unfortunately, Taiwanese don't use any particular system consistently. As in so many realms of life, Romanization in Taiwan is, shall we say, democratic. In this book, I have not attempted to impose any order on the chaos of Taiwanese spelling, but instead have used the most popular spelling of each word. For place names I use the most familiar form; for personal names, I use the spelling preferred by the individual in question.

1

The World's Tallest Building

Taipei 101, the blue-green glass tower that reigned for six years as the world's tallest building, is everywhere in Taiwan. Its image appears on advertisements, magazine covers, brochures, guidebooks, and billboards; the soaring structure itself is visible from nearly everywhere in Taipei City. As ubiquitous as Shanghai's Oriental Pearl TV tower—and considerably more graceful—Taipei 101 has become the iconic image of contemporary Taiwan. *On cover of book*

Patterned on the tiered design of traditional pagodas, the 101-story tower consists of eight cubical sections with gently sloping sides rising out of a massive 20-story base (a less generous description: a stack of Chinese take-out containers). The topmost floors and spire take the shape of a stupa, a Buddhist monument, and the building is decorated with traditional motifs symbolizing fulfillment and health. Taipei 101 is an engineering marvel, the world's tallest building—built atop a tectonic fault, stabilized by a massive, gilded sphere perched on giant pistons twelve hundred feet above the ground. According to C. Y. Lee, the architect who designed it, Taipei 101 blends recognizably Chinese elements with cutting-edge global aesthetic and technical standards. In his words, the building embodies "Oriental philosophy and Western technology."

Lee's magnificent building is beautiful from any angle—from any angle, because Taipei 101 stands completely alone. Unlike skyscrapers in Shanghai, Hong Kong, and New York, Taipei 101 does not compete for sunlight with a forest of similar buildings. It was constructed at the edge of Taipei as part of a redevelopment scheme to update a sleepy residential neighborhood. The next tallest building in the city is less than half its height, and three miles away. Taipei 101 thus stands absolutely alone; no man-made

1

object obstructs the views from its eighty-ninth and ninety-first floor observation decks. On a clear day, one can see the point where Taiwan disappears into the Taiwan Strait to the west and the East China Sea to the north.

When he accepted the commission, architect Lee knew he was designing a building that would embody Taiwan's grandest aspirations. Originally envisioned as a typical office complex—a sixty-six-story tower flanked by two smaller buildings—investors and politicians talked themselves into something far more ambitious. Given the mandate to design the world's tallest building in a city in which fifty stories had seemed massive just a decade before, Lee predicted, "The location and height will reshape the Taipei skyline. The impact will be enormous; it will be [an] icon not only for Taiwan but to the world as well."

C. Y. Lee accomplished his mission: Taipei 101 is a magnificent building, an icon, unquestionably. But does Taipei need an iconic building? Did it make sense to spend almost two billion dollars constructing this behemoth in a city with plenty of office space? Why expend vast resources engineering solutions to typhoon winds and frequent earthquakes when there was ample vacant land nearby? What does it say about Taiwan that the island would become the home of a project so expensive, so hubristic, so gratuitous and disproportionate?

It is easy to dismiss Taipei 101 as the product of an overeager society of strivers with a serious inferiority complex—and that possibility is not lost on the building's neighbors. Taiwanese are proud of the achievement, but not too proud to make fun of the building and criticize everything about it—from its architecture to its feng shui. As a symbol of contemporary Taiwan, Taipei 101 cuts two ways. It captures Taiwan's vitality and optimism; the fact that Taiwanese could finance such an undertaking reflects the island's extraordinary economic dynamism. At the same time, the building's solitary profile parallels Taiwan's isolation. From a distance, it can look fragile, lonely, and exposed.

Taipei 101 may be a vanity project, but if ever there were a country that could be forgiven such a folly, it is Taiwan. For centuries, even as its economy and culture flourished, the island was regarded as a political sideshow, the object of other nations' attention, never as the subject of its own history. Taiwan and its people have been traded back and forth among great powers, their fate decided in distant capitals, their voices absent from the negotiations.

Since World War II, however, the island has developed an identity and aspirations of its own. Its people have resisted outsiders' efforts to absorb, subjugate, and marginalize their homeland. Keeping Taiwan alive as an autonomous actor in international politics and economics requires determination and energy. It also requires creativity, as Taiwan has been forced to work outside the world's conventional structures and practices. The qualities that made Taipei 101 possible—ambition, invention, perseverance, and a strong tolerance for risk—are the same qualities that allow Taiwan to survive and prosper as a major global player.

The purpose of this book is to explain what it is about Taiwan—an island slightly larger than Belgium with a population a little less than Ghana's—that has won it such a prominent role in global economics and politics. To understand why Taiwan matters we will explore how the people living there built a society capable of economic and political feats so astonishing that scholars call them "miracles." We will also consider the unique international predicament that compels Taiwan to seek the global limelight and that powers its domestic politics. We will see that Taiwan matters for practical reasons (its companies make most of our notebook computers and flat-screen devices) and moral ones: Taiwan proves that a determined nation can attain democracy, freedom, and prosperity peacefully. And I will try to persuade you that Taiwan matters for a more fundamental reason: it matters because its people, like all people, are ends in themselves, not mere instruments of someone else's destiny.

Taipei 101 is at the eastern terminus of Hsinyi Road. At the western end stands a tall building from another era, Taiwan's presidential office. In its day, it too was a skyscraper, with a two-hundred-foot tower rising above a magnificent marble entrance flanked by massive, elaborately decorated six-story wings. The building was completed in 1919 as a headquarters for the governors-general who ruled Taiwan for fifty years on behalf of the empire of Japan. In 1895 the Qing Dynasty ceded the island to Japan in the Treaty of Shimonoseki—a treaty whose legitimacy Chinese nationalists deny. Japan viewed the island as an opportunity to prove its bona fides as a rival to imperialist powers in Europe. Within a decade, Tokyo was ready to declare its Taiwanese colony a success, and in 1906 it invited its best architects to submit designs for a government building capable of crowning its achievements.

The winning design took years to build, but the result was the imposing, ornate building that still stands today. It was badly damaged by U.S. bombing during World War II, when Taiwan served the Japanese empire as a source of food and soldiers. After their surrender in 1945, the Japanese cleared out and, following renovations, new occupants moved in. The flag they hoisted atop the tower belonged to the Republic of China.

The ROC had been established in 1912 after Chinese revolutionaries striving for democracy and development overthrew the Qing Dynasty. From the beginning, the Republic faced profound challenges. Warlords—independent military leaders loyal only to themselves—controlled much of China. Differences in political ideology and personal loyalties drove vicious infighting within and between the two main political camps, the Nationalist Party, or Kuomintang (KMT), and the Chinese Communist Party (CCP).

In the 1930s, Japanese expansionism deepened the crisis facing the struggling ROC state, forcing Chinese of all political stripes to concentrate their energies on resisting Japan's occupation of eastern China. But when World War II ended, conflict between the KMT and CCP reignited and the Chinese Civil War began. Four years later, in 1949, the Communists proclaimed a new Chinese state, the People's Republic of China (PRC), and the defeated ROC government fled to Taiwan. Its president, Chiang Kai-shek, moved into the building at the west end of Hsinyi Road.

For the ROC government and the 1.5 million refugees who joined the exodus to Taiwan, the island was not a homeland but a place of exile. For the next forty years they devoted themselves to the task of keeping the Republic of China alive in the hope that it might someday return to the mainland in triumph, drive the Communists from power, and restore itself as the reigning Chinese state. To this end, they built Taiwan into a launching pad from which to mount their campaign to "recover the mainland."

The 6 million people already living in Taiwan when the refugees arrived had a very different view. For them, Taiwan was the only homeland they had ever known. Though their ancestors had lived in Taiwan for centuries, most families could trace their origins to the mainland, and many had been eager to see the end of Japanese colonialism. Still, the ROC's policies reduced Taiwan to a pawn in a fight between the Kuomintang and the Communist Party—two entities whose goals and aspirations had little relation to those of ordinary Taiwanese.

The Kuomintang's driving ambition was to recover mainland China, but the economic policies it adopted in pursuit of that goal were transformative. Under the protection of the United States, which regarded Taiwan as a crucial bulwark against Communist expansion, the KMT adopted a state-led economic development plan that soon put Taiwan on the road to prosperity. As chapter 3 details, the little island was a global leader in light manufacturing by the 1970s. It continued to clamber up the value chain in the 1980s and 1990s to take its place as a leading high-tech center, a story I tell in chapter 6.

Economic growth did not bring political reform, at least not right away. As the likelihood of an ROC return to the mainland diminished, more and more Taiwanese began to question—at first in secret, and then more openly—the ROC's determination to prioritize its mainland recovery project ahead of the island's social and political modernization. Some—nearly all of them living outside Taiwan, beyond the reach of Chiang Kai-shek's secret police—even went so far as to advocate making a clean break, that is, declaring Taiwan independent, not just of the PRC or the ROC, but of China itself.

In the 1980s and 1990s, Taiwan's political system evolved from single-party authoritarianism under the KMT to multiparty democracy, and the debate over how Taiwan should view its relationship with the mainland emerged into the open. Many longtime residents believed that decades of subjugation to the KMT's "mission" had prevented Taiwan from developing its own sense of nationhood and pursuing its own destiny, while those who subscribed to the KMT's view feared that allowing Taiwan to claim a status separate from China would foreclose forever the possibility of a non-Communist China. When the People's Republic of China weighed in with its preferences, it became clear that redefining Taiwan's identity could also bring it into a potentially catastrophic confrontation with Beijing.

The PRC maintains that Taiwan has been Chinese territory for centuries, so it is Chinese territory today. Beijing does not recognize the ROC's legitimacy; in its view, the Communists' victory in 1949 extinguished the Republic, leaving the PRC as the only state representing the Chinese nation. The fact that the Chinese government does not currently rule Taiwan is a historical anomaly that must be rectified.

For decades, the PRC's position was the inverse of the ROC's: it swore to "liberate" Taiwan, to annex it to the PRC by force. In 1979, a new generation of PRC leaders, determined to open China to the world, traded in that policy for a less bellicose objective: "peaceful unification." Since the early 2000s, Beijing has emphasized patience, arguing that unification need not come soon. Still, its bottom line is firm: Taiwan must not renounce unification. If it does, say PRC leaders, China's sacred territory will be severed, and that is an outcome they refuse to accept. As Premier Wen Jiabao put it in a 2003 interview with the *Washington Post*, "The Chinese people will pay any price to safeguard the unity of the motherland." Myriad policy statements and comments from Chinese leaders leave no room for doubt: the price they are willing to pay includes war.

Taiwanese see the situation very differently. They are at best deeply ambivalent about unification. The reasons for Taiwanese people's reluctance to unify with the PRC have changed since the 1940s, but the fact of that reluctance has not. In the early decades, Taiwan's government taught its people to resist the PRC out of loyalty to the ROC; it was the PRC, not China, that was to be rejected. Over time, though, the appeal of "China" has faded.

As the island's democracy grew and deepened, the political gulf between Taiwan and the mainland widened. Today, many Taiwanese resist the PRC because they value the political and economic freedom they enjoy as citizens of an ROC whose jurisdiction is limited to Taiwan. They still oppose folding Taiwan into the PRC, but they now see little benefit in giving up what they have to become part of *any* Chinese state headquartered on the mainland—even a non-Communist one. "Little Taiwan" is enough for them, not least because 1.3 billion mainland people and their leaders inevitably would dominate a unified Chinese state.

If few Taiwanese are ready to risk losing their way of life for an abstract notion like the territorial integrity of China, there is little more enthusiasm for putting that way of life at risk for a different abstract notion, Taiwan independence. In the parlance of pollsters, the mainstream preference, one shared by three-fourths of Taiwanese, is to "maintain the status quo." The Chinese phrase used in surveys translates as "preserve the way things are now," and that captures well what most Taiwanese hope to do, recognizing that "the way things are now" includes not foreclosing the possibility of unification someday and continuing to fly the Republic of China flag today. As U.S. Senator James Leach has said, Taiwan can have democracy or independence, but not both. Increasingly, too, Taiwan's economic prosperity rests on maintaining cooperative relations with China, which is its top target for trade and investment.

This, then, is the central dilemma facing Taiwan: how to live both freely and at peace. The PRC insists that if Taiwan does not at least pay lip service to unification, war is inevitable, but the vast majority of Taiwanese prefer to avoid unification as long as they can. Navigating this narrow passage is the central challenge facing Taiwan's leaders and voters. The high stakes and limited options help to explain why Taiwanese pursue politics with such uncommon passion.

Charles Kao, the founder and head of Commonwealth Publishing, one of Taiwan's most important news organizations, had that passion in mind when he observed, "If you don't read newspapers or watch TV, Taipei is the most beautiful place to live in the world. If you *do* read newspapers and watch TV, it's the worst!" Politics is at once Taiwan's national sport and its national shame. Taiwanese love to criticize their boisterous politicians, and most seem genuinely embarrassed when their lawmakers pummel each other or hurl their lunches across hearing rooms. Still, those same Taiwanese are the audience that sustains twenty-four-hour news talk shows and nonstop partisan combat.

Part of the reason politics is so exciting in Taiwan is that democracy is still relatively new there, and it is very much a spectator sport in a country small enough that anyone who wants one can have a ringside seat. Still, what makes politics so relentless in Taiwan is the need to manage an exceptionally difficult problem: balancing Taiwan citizens' desire to maintain, even enrich, the benefits they enjoy as a self-governing democracy with the need to pacify, or at least keep at bay, the PRC's demand for unification. Differences of opinion about precisely what Taiwan should be striving for and how to achieve it are at the heart of the island's political life.

Taiwan's twenty-first-century presidents exemplify the predominant viewpoints on these questions. The president elected in 2008, Ma Ying-jeou, believes Taiwan's best hope for maintaining the status quo—de facto separation, albeit short of full independence—is to cultivate friendly ties with the mainland. In his view, Taiwan must persuade the PRC that allowing Taiwanese to run their own affairs for the foreseeable future will not undermine Beijing's long-term goals or violate its short-term interests.

Taiwan's economic prosperity, too, rests on maintaining a cordial relationship with the PRC, an economic and military powerhouse just one hundred miles away. Moreover, he argues, reducing tensions between the two sides might induce China to lift its embargo on Taiwan's participation in international institutions, a necessary step if Taiwan is to be fully incorporated into a rapidly integrating global economy.

Ma's approach reflects his party's preference for cooperation with the mainland. As inheritors of a tradition that stresses mainland recovery and Chinese nationalism (the party's official English name is the Chinese Nationalist Party), it is hard for today's KMT politicians to abandon unification as a goal. At the same time, however, they well know that unification has little appeal for Taiwanese voters—and the PRC's Communist system has been anathema to their party for decades. The way they square this circle is by holding out the hope that the two sides might someday sit down and negotiate to create a united, non-Communist Chinese nation attractive enough to win over Taiwan.

While it refuses to rule out the possibility of unification in the future—both for ideological and strategic reasons—the KMT is in no hurry to bring it about. Ma himself has repeatedly said that it will not happen while he is president, and he has set democratization of the mainland as a precondition for starting any kind of unification process. His party appears willing to prolong the status quo indefinitely. Needless to say, Ma's counterparts in Beijing find his preferences far from ideal—they would like to see movement toward unification now, and they scoff at his advice regarding political reform—but they find him infinitely preferable to the alternative.

That alternative would be a president representing the Democratic Progressive Party (DPP), the political party that grew out of Taiwan's pro-democracy movement. A Democratic Progressive held the presidency from 2000 to 2008, and those years confirmed Beijing's darkest fears about what a DPP government would be like. President Chen Shui-bian's policies aimed to maximize the psychological distance between Taiwan and the mainland. While Chen was careful to maintain plausible deniability on claims that he was trying to engineer permanent independence for Taiwan, the PRC was convinced that was his aim—as were many Taiwanese and Americans.

Given Beijing's determination to "pay any price" to stop Taiwan from becoming independent, it is hard to imagine how Chen could have pulled off such a feat, especially in a democratic nation in which his political opponents controlled the legislature and the vast majority of voters opposed taking such a risk. But whether or not he spent his presidency scheming, as Beijing put it, to "split China," there is no question he devoted himself to making unification more difficult.

For eight years, direct communication between the two sides stalled because Chen refused to meet Beijing's preconditions for talks. First among these was the PRC requirement that Chen accept the principle that Taiwan and the mainland are part of "one China." That alone was a deal killer for Chen, above all because the PRC's "one China" principle also states that the Beijing government is the sole legal authority over all of China. To Chen—and many others—Beijing's precondition looked a lot like surrender. The PRC relaxed its stance when President Ma came into office, and talks resumed without Taiwan ever explicitly accepting Beijing's One China Principle.

With cross-Strait talks suspended, Chen's domestic policies aimed to reinforce Taiwan people's sense of themselves as separate and different from mainland Chinese. His government revised textbooks to emphasize Taiwan's history and geography. It rebranded numerous state-owned corporations, replacing "China" in their names with "Taiwan," and it tried, with little success, to stem the flow of Taiwanese business to the mainland. Some of Taiwan's most famous landmarks got makeovers. The Chiang Kai-shek Memorial—a massive, sepulchral white marble pyramid that houses a thirty-three-foot bronze statue of Chiang Kai-shek upstairs and an exhibit of his effects (including his armored limousine) below—was renamed the "National Taiwan Democracy Memorial Hall."

The episode degenerated into farce. The Chen administration downgraded the site's landmark status so it could seize jurisdiction over it from Taipei City, at which point the Ministry of Education hastily unveiled new placards and closed off Chiang's statue. Meanwhile, the KMT-led Taipei City government and legislature scrambled to undo the changes. Chen's move was not only calculated to impress his political base, it was also part of a larger effort to encourage Taiwanese to relinquish the pro-China, pro-unification mentality Chiang and his party had inculcated and embrace a more DPP-friendly, Taiwanese-only identity.

The most enthusiastic audience for Chen's policies were people known as "Deep Greens"—folks with a fondness for Taiwan independence and a bred-in-the-bone antipathy to the KMT. In their view, even Chen Shui-bian was disappointingly moderate. The Deep Greens do not accept that formal independence is unattainable. If the PRC collapses, economically or politically, they argue, Taiwan should be able to wriggle free—if it's prepared. Another scenario they imagine is that Taiwan's timid public might grow bolder and unite behind a gesture that would force the world to recognize the Taiwan people's will for independence. In that case, they believe, other nations—mainly the United States—would step in to help the newly independent Taiwan survive the PRC's punishment.

Even the most fervent independence supporters acknowledge these scenarios are unlikely in the near term, but they are not ready to give up hope that things may change in the future. Chen's determination to put as much distance between Taiwan and China as possible reflected their logic even if he was never able to go as far as they would have liked. His policies also appealed to the so-called "Light Greens"—Taiwanese who recognize the risks of independence, but are wary of too much contact with the mainland—and even to some "Light Blues"—centrist Taiwanese who lean toward the KMT, but not strongly.

It may seem odd that Taiwan politics is so passionate when—with the exception of the Deep Greens—most people agree that, one way or another, the best option is to preserve the status quo. Paradoxically, though, it is precisely because the goal is clear, but still very hard to attain, that the fight over how best to pursue it has become so intense. For example, President Ma's approach undoubtedly protects Taiwan in the short run. It minimizes the chances of conflict with the PRC, it maximizes mutually beneficial cooperation between the two sides, and it does not rule out any possibility in the long term. But there is risk in this approach. Interdependence constrains the PRC, but it constrains Taiwan, too, and many Taiwanese worry that being the small player in this game puts Taiwan at particular risk. Today's cooperative engagement can become tomorrow's coercive leverage, and China is vastly larger and insists it will sacrifice its people's short-term interests to achieve its strategic goals.

Another force driving Taiwan's politics is a debate over the country's international status. In the Deep Greens' view, Taiwan leaders' refusal to challenge the PRC too overtly inhibits Taiwan from becoming a "normal country." To survive as an autonomous political entity, Taiwan has accepted a compromise. It cannot call itself the Republic of Taiwan, but it can and does assert the statehood of the Republic of China, a state once universally recognized, now reduced in territory but still robust within its own jurisdiction. That compromise satisfies everyone, and it satisfies no one. It allows the KMT to hold its head up before its founding fathers, and it allows the PRC to claim Taiwan still calls itself "Chinese." It allows the DPP to ferment the wine of an independent Taiwan within the bottle of the ROC. But none of the three sees itself drawing closer to its ultimate goal.

Taipei 101 is modern, sleek, and impressive; it celebrates Taiwan's economic success, including its high-tech ascendancy and extraordinary growth. But the real reason it so quickly became not just *an* icon, but *the* icon of contemporary Taiwan, is that unlike every other symbol the island can muster, Taipei 101 bears no political coloration. The tourist bureau favorites—the Chiang Kai-shek Memorial, the Longshan (Dragon Mountain) Temple, the presidential office building, even the Grand Hotel—are freighted with history and politics, too controversial to represent a nation still struggling for consensus about its own past and future. Only Taipei 101 stands above the political fray, evoking economics, technology, global business—the only languages Taiwanese seem able to speak without arguing.

It is in these realms that Taiwan has succeeded in becoming not an object but a subject; not a means to an end—the renaissance of Chinese civilization—but an end in itself. Politics is much more difficult. That is not to say that Taipei and Beijing are destined to fight. Taiwan's people have shown themselves willing to accept a diminished status if doing so will allow them to continue to enjoy de facto independence—including a democratic political system. It is not their first choice, but it is a compromise most can live with, so long as they can be, for themselves, the end, and not the means.

A harder question to answer is whether the People's Republic of China will make a similar compromise by relinquishing its demand for effective sovereignty over Taiwan in exchange for a peaceful, stable, and cooperative relationship between the two sides—including a promise that Taiwan will not challenge China's ultimate claim. If the two sides can build such a relationship and avoid conflict, their economic and political systems might someday converge, creating an opportunity for mutually acceptable political integration. But that is a process that cannot be rushed. In the meantime, it is enough to "preserve the way things are now."

2

Building Taiwan

Cold, misty rain is falling but the ground is boiling under the feet of twenty third-graders milling around a platform on Seven Stars Mountain. They are less than an hour's drive from their elementary school on the opposite slope of the basin cradling Taipei City, but they might imagine they are on another planet. Above them, peaks cloaked in head-high grasses disappear into the clouds; at 2,624 feet above sea level, the children are above the tree line, but the mountain towers over them. They hold their noses and squint into billows of sulfurous steam hissing out of yellowed crevasses in the heat-softened mountainside. Squatting to warm their hands at the edge of the massive fumarole—a volcanic vent that releases heat, gas, and minerals from deep within the earth—these Taiwanese schoolchildren can feel their island home exhaling.

Taiwan is a link in the chain of volcanic islands known as the Pacific Ring of Fire, and here at the fumarole that geologic fact impresses itself on all five senses. Volcanic eruptions and their aftereffects built an island of fourteen thousand square miles (thirty-six thousand square km), about the size of Maryland and Delaware combined. Shaped like a leaf, Taiwan is dominated by high, rugged mountains. Its tallest peak, Mount Jade, towers more than thirteen thousand feet above sea level. The earth's restless activity continues to reshape the landscape. An earthquake in September 1999 sliced the tops off some mountains and thrust others up. The summit of Mount Jade vaulted several meters in the 1999 quake.

Except for the Taipei basin and neighboring alluvial plains, mountainous terrain dominates the island's north, east, and center. The rugged mountains create countless distinct ecological zones, giving Taiwan extraordinary biodiversity, including 338 bird species and more than 400 butterfly species.

11

In sections of the northeast coast, stone cliffs fall more than three thousand feet, their descent from mountain peaks to the Pacific Ocean broken only by a narrow notch where engineers blasted a road into the rock face in the 1920s. Southeastern Taiwan has a narrow rift valley, beautiful and fertile, but remote from population centers. That leaves the island's broad western plain as the homeland for almost 90 percent of Taiwan's 23 million people, making it one of the world's most densely populated places.

The Tropic of Cancer cuts through Taiwan, and the climate and vegetation are just what one would expect on a tropical island. Despite the dense human settlement, with endless apartment blocks, miles of asphalt highways, and massive landfills full of plastic refuse, nature is rarely far away. Urban neighborhoods end abruptly at near-vertical mountainsides thick with forests; trees grow from rooftops and sprouts erupt from cracked pavement. Debris left along the roads—including wrecked cars and motorcycles—quickly disappears under tangles of vines. On Roosevelt Road in downtown Taipei, a house has been built around an enormous tree. The tree begins in the sidewalk, grows through the house, and spreads its canopy over a rooftop terrace. At Kaohsiung City's Sun Yat-sen University, students must lock their dorm room windows to keep food-stealing monkeys from the nearby jungle from breaking in.

Given this verdant land, it is no surprise that agriculture has thrived in Taiwan for centuries. As early as the 1600s, Taiwan was exporting rice, sugar, and indigo-dyed cloth to mainland China. According to early nineteenth-century reports, Xiamen (Amoy), Fujian province's largest city, depended on Taiwanese rice for most of its food supply. The island is less well-endowed when it comes to the natural resources needed for modern industry. In the seventeenth century, explorers from China collected sulfur from the Taipei basin fumaroles to manufacture gunpowder, and the Japanese colonial government that ruled Taiwan in the early twentieth century placed a high value on its massive camphor trees, but the island's lack of fossil fuel and ore deposits forces Taiwanese to rely on imports for industrial raw materials.

Water can be a problem, too. Taiwan has ample rainfall, but much of it comes in heavy storms and the sharp changes in elevation make flash floods, runoff, and erosion a challenge. Visitors often puzzle over the tiny streams trickling through wide, rocky riverbeds. During a summer afternoon storm or one of Taiwan's violent typhoons, these waterways become dangerous torrents; in 2009, Typhoon Morakot dumped more than one hundred inches of rain on parts of Taiwan in just four days. Even with hundreds of dams channeling water into reservoirs, hydroelectric plants, and irrigation facilities, maintaining a consistent flow is a constant challenge. Summer water shortages have become the norm, especially in southern Taiwan.

In addition to the main island, which lies about 75 miles (120 kilometers) off mainland China's southeastern coast, Taiwan's political jurisdiction extends to numerous smaller islands. The largest island group is the Penghu Islands (Pescadores), halfway between western Taiwan and the mainland. Off the east coast lie Orchid Island and Green Island, which once sported a prison where political dissidents were locked away. Nestled near the mainland coast are two heavily militarized "frontline islands," Jinmen (Quemoy) and Mazu (Matsu). In the 1950s, Taiwanese forces on Jinmen and Mazu exchanged fire with their counterparts on the mainland; eventually the Chinese Communist troops settled into a pattern of shelling Jinmen on alternate days. The Taiwanese used the frontline islands to launch propaganda messages encouraging resistance to the Communist Party; they blasted away with loudspeakers and lofted balloons laden with anti-Communist messages into westbound winds. But relations have improved in recent years. In 2001, Taiwan opened direct travel links between Jinmen and Mazu and mainland China, making the frontline islanders the first Taiwanese in half a century to travel directly from one side to the other.

The north-south mountain spine and shortage of navigable east-west rivers make overland transportation difficult, and the island's population is clustered near its coasts, so Taiwan's culture has a strong maritime flavor. Most of the island's major cities—past (Tainan, Lukang, Tamsui) and present (Kaohsiung, Taichung, Keelung, Hualien)—are ports. Taiwan's position on the trade routes connecting Northeast Asia and Southeast Asia gives it a critical role in global shipping and it is an important player in the international fishing industry and its regulatory organizations. Taiwanese boats take about 13 percent of the global tuna catch, for example. Even religion reveals this maritime orientation: Taiwan's largest popular religious sect is the cult of Mazu, the patron deity of seafarers. Mazu was born in Fujian province in 960; she became a deity when she was credited with miraculous rescues at sea.

EARLY SETTLEMENT

The sea also brought Taiwan its human inhabitants, beginning with the ancestors of the island's Austronesian people. Today's Austronesians can be traced to Austronesian-speaking settlers who began living in Taiwan about four thousand years ago. Over the centuries, these early islanders developed distinct languages and cultures. Taiwan's government recognizes twelve groups: Atayal, Amis, Bunun, Kavalan, Paiwan, Pingpu, Puyuma, Rukai, Saisiyat, Tao, Thao, and Tsou. The earliest Austronesian settlements were located in the coastal plains, but some Austronesian groups adapted to life in the high mountains. The arts and culture of the different groups reflect their economic and social conditions. The east-coast Bunun and Amis communities are famous for polyphonic choral singing to celebrate harvests, while the mountain-dwelling Paiwan are known for carving wild boars and "thousand pacer" snakes into slate and wood ("thousand pacers" because if one bites you, you can walk a thousand paces before you die). The Atayals are famous for hunting and warfare; their distinctive facial tattoos celebrated success killing animals—and men. The Tao, the Austronesian occupants of Orchid Island, carve magnificent seagoing canoes to catch flying fish. Approximately 450,000 Austronesian people live in Taiwan today, most in urban areas. The tribal groups continue to struggle for legal recognition, environmental protection, and the restoration of their ancestral lands. Austronesian individuals often face discrimination and prejudice.

In 1544, a Portuguese vessel passed by Taiwan, and one of its passengers called it "Ilha Formosa," beautiful island. The sailors recorded the remark in their ship's log, giving the island the name by which the West has known it ever since. As exploration gave way to trade and colonization, Europeans took note of Formosa's location on trade routes, near (but not yet occupied by) China and Japan. In 1623, Dutch traders established a settlement at Anping, near present-day Tainan, on the southwest coast. Under the protection of Fort Zeelandia and Fort Provintia, the Dutch East India Company set about building a commercial colony in southern Taiwan, exporting deer meat and skins bartered from Austronesian hunters as well as rice and sugarcane raised by migrants from the Chinese mainland.

Three years later, Spanish settlers took up residence in the northern part of the island, establishing Fort San Salvador at Keelung in 1626 and Fort San Domingo at Tamsui in 1628. (The Chinese called San Domingo the Red Hair Fort in honor of the Europeans' exotic appearance. At least it wasn't Fort Big Nose, another Chinese slang term for Europeans.) The European settlements coexisted for over a decade. In 1638 the Spanish abandoned the Red Hair Fort; the Dutch later built their own fort on the site. Four years later, Dutch forces teamed up with Austronesian fighters to drive the Spanish out of Keelung, leaving the Dutch East India Company as the sole authority on Taiwan.

A major challenge for Taiwan's European and Chinese residents was the extreme difficulty of north-south navigation. Taiwan's west coast has only two natural harbors, Kaohsiung in the far south and Tamsui in the far north. The Taiwan Strait is shallow and stormy. Approaches to the island from the west are difficult, with innumerable constantly shifting shoals and islands. The island's rivers are impossible to navigate except in very small boats. Chinese plied coastal waters in small flat-bottomed junks with retractable rudders, but even these craft ran aground frequently, leaving seagoing bamboo rafts with extremely shallow draft to ferry cargo to shore while the junks moored outside the hazardous shoals.

Prior to the Europeans' arrival, a few Chinese already were using Taiwan as a base for fishing, smuggling, and piracy. When the Dutch and Spanish constructed forts and began trading with local hunters and farmers, the pace of Chinese settlement accelerated. Under the protection of the European settlements, Taiwan began to look like a good option for poor farmers in crowded Fujian. The Dutch opened farmland and provided some education and order. They retained ownership of the land but allowed Chinese farmers considerable autonomy and local self-government. Although most early migrants probably did not intend to settle permanently on the island—few brought wives with them—it was not long before permanent settlements sprang up.

By the mid-1600s, Taiwan had several significant Chinese towns populated by three distinct groups. Most settlers were Hokkien-speakers from the Quanzhou and Zhangzhou regions of Fujian. Their origins and dialects were similar, but not similar enough to keep the two groups from seeing one another as competitors, at times even enemies. More different yet were the Hakka, a Chinese minority scattered throughout southern China. Hakka, many of whom had been forcibly transported from Guangzhou province to Taiwan, tended to settle in fortified villages in hard-to-reach areas near the mountains; they frequently clashed with Hokkien and Austronesian neighbors.

Hokkien-Austronesian relations were tense as well. Over time, Chinese settlements displaced or absorbed many of the Austronesian communities in the western plain. Some Austronesian people moved into the mountains to avoid extinction, and communities in the far south and east retained more of their traditional cultures and identities. The Dutch encouraged these interethnic conflicts; in particular, they used Austronesian people as fighters to put down Hokkien revolts. The casualty count in the largest of these, a rebellion in Tainan in 1650, was eight thousand.

The sources of conflict were many: Dutch and Spanish divide-and-conquer tactics, economic competition, ethnic rivalry, and land disputes. Over time, some of these disputes ripened into full-on feuds, with adjacent villages carrying on vendettas for generations, long after the original causes were forgotten. In one coastal city, clan rivalries played out in a bloody—but all-in-good-fun—annual ritual: the Lukang Rock Fight. Every year until the mid-twentieth century, the men of Lukang would gather outside town on a spring day, line up with their kinsmen and throw rocks at the other clans. When the supply of rocks dwindled, the combatants closed in for hand-to-hand fighting with sticks and fists. Women, children, and the aged stood around the fringes of the mayhem cheering their favorites and snacking on street food. An anthropologist who visited Lukang inquired about the motivation for the fight, only to learn that townspeople were "superstitious" in the old days. They thought a little bloodshed around the

New Year would bring good luck. And anyway, no one ever *died*, so what was the harm?

The seventeenth-century European demand for labor and export goods attracted Chinese migrants to Taiwan's shores. At the same time, deteriorating conditions on the mainland propelled Chinese out of Fujian. When severe famine hit the province in the 1620s, the warlord Zheng Zhilong suggested to the governor that he pay farmers to migrate to Taiwan. Zheng was the boss of a pirate fleet whose ships patrolled the sea from Japan to Vietnam. When the Dutch expelled him from his base in Taiwan, Zheng put his pirate armada in the service of the Ming empire, earning the title "Admiral of the Coastal Sea." Zheng Zhilong's son Zheng Chenggong also earned an honorary surname from the Ming emperor, leading to his nickname "Guoxingye" or "the old man with the national surname." Rendered as "Koxinga," that nickname provided the moniker under which Zheng Chenggong is known to Western historians.

Zheng Zhilong, perhaps revealing his pirate instincts, betrayed his Ming patron during the Manchu invasion that overthrew the Ming Dynasty in 1644. He allowed the Manchus to enter his territory without resistance. His son, however, remained loyal to the Ming. In 1659, Zheng Chenggong led troops on the mainland against the young Qing Dynasty. When the venture failed, he withdrew to Taiwan, and in 1661 drove the Dutch off the island. He vowed to fight on and restore the Ming.

Zheng's actions made him a hero to Chinese nationalists three centuries later. Some credit him with leading an anti-imperialist struggle, while others lionize Zheng for holding out against what he saw as an illegitimate government. Others view him as an opportunist. In any case, the two decades when Zheng and his descendants governed Taiwan was a period of relative prosperity. The Zhengs promoted agricultural development and continued the Dutch policy of keeping most farmland in government hands. Between battles they kept their soldiers busy opening new areas to farming. They also promoted education and Confucian ritual—the first concentrated effort to bring Chinese elite culture to Taiwan. The Zheng family's effort to keep the Ming Dynasty alive was long remembered but short-lived: in 1683, the Qing admiral Shi Lang defeated Ming-loyalist forces led by Zheng Chenggong's grandson. For the first time in history, a government seated in the mainland capital had secured effective control over Taiwan.

THE QING DYNASTY

The Qing empire incorporated Taiwan as a prefecture within Fujian Province. The island's lowly status reflected its marginal position in the empire, as a "place beyond civilization." Inhabited by Austronesians and rough-

and-ready Chinese of questionable loyalty and limited economic value, Taiwan received little attention from the Manchu court—except when there was trouble. But trouble was frequent: a Qing-era proverb says of Taiwan, "There is a major rebellion every five years, a minor rebellion every three." Conflict among the various groups on the island continued, and as the Chinese population grew, new sources of antagonism—such as competition between clans and lineages—emerged. The Qing tried to restrict migration to the island, but the Chinese population grew steadily. Trade was also controlled—for much of the Qing period, the law permitted vessels to cross at only one location, Xiamen to Tainan—but enforcing this restriction was difficult.

As one Taiwanese historian has written, the Qing governed Taiwan "preventively, indirectly and incompletely." Its main concern was not to direct the course of Taiwan's development or provide administrative benefits comparable to those on the mainland, but simply to suppress rebellions before they could threaten Qing control, and even this was difficult. In one illustrative (but not unique) example, a loosely organized group calling itself the Heaven and Earth Society carried out a series of violent revolts in central Taiwan in the 1700s and 1800s. The group slaughtered one city's entire cadre of Qing officials in 1787, then murdered their replacements eight years later. In the 1860s, a *new* Heaven and Earth Society was killing officials in the same region.

Taiwan's economy flourished under the Qing's light hand. By the mid-1700s, the island was exporting rice and sugar in quantity. In 1719, a huge water works project sponsored by a Quanzhou merchant began carrying water from the Choshui River to irrigate a massive section of central Taiwan. Irrigation opened the Changhua plain for intensive rice cultivation, making the region a key source of rice imports to Fujian. Rice, sugar and tea, indigo-dyed cloth, preserved fish and timber—all these products flowed west to the mainland. More complex manufactures made the return trip. As exports increased and prosperity grew, Taiwan became home to merchants, tradespeople and guilds, but the society remained predominantly agricultural, structured around a chain of relatively isolated settlements that often enjoyed stronger links to the mainland than to their northern and southern neighbors on the island.

The nineteenth century again brought Europeans to China's shores, but these visitors were different from the Spanish and Dutch traders two centuries earlier. They were not satisfied to perch on unwanted spits of land, conducting small-scale trade with willing partners. The foreigners who came to China in the 1800s—Britons, Americans, Germans, French, even Japanese—were more assertive in their demands. When the Qing court rejected their requests to trade, the British forced their way in, bartering opium grown in their South Asian colonies for Chinese tea and porcelain.

In the 1840s and 1850s, Great Britain and China fought two wars over trade. In defeat, China was forced to open its markets and turn over territory—including Hong Kong—to the British. In a practice called "most favored nation status," other foreign powers were guaranteed the same access to the Chinese market that Britain enjoyed. Britain also demanded reparations—cash payments to compensate its losses in the war. To ensure they would be paid, the British took over tariff collection from the Qing.

Perched on a high cliff above the mouth of the Kaohsiung harbor is a graceful brick building: the British consulate. The building (the last in a series of increasingly grand structures housing the consulate) has a commanding view of the harbor. The good views allowed a succession of late-nineteenth-century British officials to track maritime traffic and assess taxes on trade. As in the rest of China, the British first paid themselves their reparations then forwarded what was left to the Qing court. Today the consulate houses a popular teahouse; its terraces are perfect for watching container ships steaming off into splendid sunsets. Another popular feature is the dungeon—a maze of rooms and passages just high enough for children to wander upright. Today the basement rooms are dry and well lit, but they carry whispers of a harder time when Taiwanese and Chinese traders who ran afoul of the British were locked away in a dank, cramped labyrinth. A similar building—with a similar coffee shop and a similar history—stands above downtown Tamsui, nineteenth-century Taiwan's major northern port.

The influx of Western economic and military power exacerbated domestic problems brewing in Qing China. Rebellions devastated large sections of the country. The worst of these was the Taiping Rebellion. It scorched China's Yangtze River region in the 1850s and 1860s and caused between 20 and 30 million deaths as well as massive economic destruction. To defend the empire against these threats, the Qing court was forced to give local military leaders unprecedented power and autonomy—including the right to collect taxes. Liberated from the central government's fiscal control, some became warlords, laws unto themselves in vast regions of what was nominally Qing territory. The court's hold on power grew ever more tenuous, even as it upgraded Taiwan's status to a province in 1885 in the hope of promoting modernization and a more effective defense.

Just outside its borders, the Qing faced threats from Japan and on the Korean peninsula. Korea had long been under Chinese influence, but Japan's newly installed Meiji government was bent on modernizing that country, including its military forces, and expanding its influence. Korea was the venue for a series of skirmishes between the declining Qing and rising Meiji in the 1870s and 1880s; in 1894, the smoldering conflict erupted into a full-scale war. China's military was fragmented and exhausted; it proved no match for Japan's modern forces. Among the spoils Japan demanded to end the war were cash reparations, access to trade, the Liaodong Peninsula—and the island of Taiwan.

THE EMPIRE OF JAPAN

On April 17, 1895, Chinese representatives signed the Treaty of Shimono-seki, ceding Taiwan to the empire of Japan. Acquiring colonies was a crucial element in Meiji Japan's strategy of defensive modernization. Japan was desperate to prove to the West that it was a modern state—a colonizer, not a territory eligible for colonization by others. Taiwan was not Japan's only colony, but it had a special purpose in the empire. It was to be a model colony, a massive demonstration project where the Meiji state would show off its military, economic, and administrative prowess. It also gave Japan unprecedented access to mainland China.

For Taiwanese, colonization brought a mixture of benefits and losses. Its model colony status made it a target for all sorts of development projects. To make Taiwan a more efficient and productive source of agricultural exports, the Japanese built an extensive transportation infrastructure, including a railroad along the western plain that connected the island from north to south for the first time. The island's first modern industries were agricultural processing businesses developed under Japanese rule. The Japanese also built roads, power plants, an electric power grid, irrigation projects, and dams. By the end of the colonial era, 58 percent of the adult population was literate in Japanese, and three-fourths of school-aged children attended school. Colonial authorities implemented detailed city plans for Kaohsiung and Taipei. To this day, the broad, tree-lined avenues, majestic traffic circles and charming parks in the two cities' old downtowns are a welcome contrast to the cramped, narrow streets of Taiwan's other cities—towns where Japanese urban planners never ventured.

One of the toughest challenges for the colonial government was subduing the Austronesian peoples. The Qing had never asserted its authority beyond the western plain, but the Japanese were determined to bring the entire island under central authority. Some of Taiwan's most valuable resources—including camphor trees, which supply a chemical used in medicine and other products—were found in the high-altitude forests where the least assimilated Austronesian groups lived. Japanese historical records document a long and violent struggle between Austronesian fighters and Japanese soldiers and police. The Japanese used warships, poison gas, and aircraft as well as conventional military methods (including divide-and-rule political tactics) to bring the groups under government control. They drew a boundary around the Austronesian areas and forbade non-Austronesian Taiwanese to enter. Japanese troops were dispatched into this "reservation" to subdue Austronesian communities—especially Atayal and Bunun—and resettle them in villages near police stations where they could be monitored and controlled.

Resettlement profoundly disrupted the Austronesian people's economic, social, and religious life. It tore them away from villages, hunting grounds, and sacred sites. They were often forced to labor for Japanese firms for meager wages, and when the police confiscated their hunting rifles, life became even grimmer. Some Austronesian communities fought back; in 1930, a group of Atayal killed 134 Japanese at an athletic meet. The Japanese responded with a force of more than 2,000 men. The Atayal rebels and their families were wiped out; those who survived the Japanese reprisals committed mass suicide. Their leader, Mona Rudao, a sophisticated man who had visited Japan in 1911, went deep into the forest to die, hoping to prevent the Japanese from taking his head as a trophy. Three years later, Japanese stumbled across what they believed was his skeleton. As he had feared, the remains were displayed before the public; it was not until 1974 that Mona Rudao's bones were returned to the Atayal people.

Managing the Chinese-speaking population posed a different set of challenges. As Japan and China were preparing to sign the Treaty of Shimonoseki, a handful of Taiwanese tried to fend off Japanese colonial rule by setting up a "Republic of Formosa"—a Taiwanese state independent of both China and Japan. They failed, but their failure did not end local resistance to Japanese control. The familiar pattern of rebellions, uprisings, and local conflicts continued. The Japanese borrowed the Qing strategy (called the *baojia* system) of grouping ten or so households into a ward (*bao*), and every ten or so wards into a larger administrative unit (*jia*). Each ward was responsible for the actions of its member households, and households were responsible for the individuals within them. Goto Shimpei, a deputy governor who designed many Japanese colonial institutions, took his cues from the *Complete Book on Benevolence*, a Chinese classic describing the operation of the baojia system. He had the book translated into Japanese and its principles written into legislation. The baojia system handled civic education, law enforcement, surveillance, and even militia functions for the Japanese colonial administration. Unlike their Qing-era counterparts, Japanese officials made sure not to let local elites gain control of the system for their own purposes. By 1902, Taiwanese resistance to Japanese control had evaporated.

The heads of bao and jia were elected. Over time, Taiwanese participation in local governance increased; by the 1930s, property-owning Taiwanese were electing representatives to local councils whose powers, while limited, were real: they reviewed local budgets and kept an eye on local administrators. In 1920, the colonial administration set up assemblies throughout Taiwan to advise local executives. Although the members were appointed—

and most were Japanese colonists—the assemblies did give Taiwanese some voice in local decision making. In 1921, the governor appointed nine Taiwanese to his own personal consultative council.

A decade later the Japanese government decided to allow Taiwanese to partially elect the advisory assemblies. The electoral process used a single-vote system in multimember districts, so that in a six-seat district, each voter would choose one candidate, and the top six vote-getters would be elected. These rules are still used in Taiwanese local council elections today. The purpose of the reforms was political: they were designed to encourage Taiwanese to identify with Japan and give up any residual loyalty to China—a goal made more urgent by Japan's decision to invade China in the early 1930s. There was never any question that real power belonged to the governor-general, who answered only to Tokyo. Whatever rights the Taiwanese enjoyed were subject to his approval and could be revoked at any time.

As of 1935, there were 172 members in Taiwan's assemblies: 109 Japanese (49 of them elected) and 63 Taiwanese (37 elected). Although the franchise was limited (fewer than 5 percent of Taiwanese were eligible to vote above the baojia level) and elected officials had only advisory authority, Taiwan's early elections were meaningful. They helped quell the demand for self-government among Taiwanese, they focused attention on local issues, and they encouraged local elites to emphasize electoral competition rather than banding together against the Japanese. In the long run, they also built a foundation of political participation among Taiwanese. By 1939, almost 300,000 Taiwanese were registered to vote, and more than 3,000 had been elected to public office. The American diplomat George Kerr later wrote, "The Formosans . . . were becoming familiar with all the devices of political campaigns and electioneering . . . elements of training and experience that ultimately were to form a frame of reference for future (post-Surrender) demands and expectations."

The colonial regime's social and cultural policies toward the island's Chinese-speaking majority reflected Japan's ambivalent attitude toward its new territories. On the one hand, Japanese leaders believed it was necessary to inculcate a Japanese identity in their subject peoples. At the same time, Japanese in the home islands resisted the integration of people they saw as non-Japanese. Taiwanese became, in the words of historian Wu Rweiren "Japanese that were not Japanese." They received a Japanese education (although many wealthy families continued to give their sons a traditional Confucian education at home in addition to their modern Japanese schooling), and they were encouraged to dress, eat, and live as Japanese—even to adopt Japanese surnames. The elite could send sons to universities in Japan for higher education—but once they were there, their options were limited. Taiwanese students were steered toward "practical" disciplines, such as medicine and engineering, and away from "dangerous" areas of knowledge like philosophy.

The government's caution on this point was well-placed. Even after decades of Japanese rule, many Taiwanese still resented their colonial status and by the 1920s, a self-conscious Taiwanese identity was emerging. While Taiwan itself was tightly controlled, Taiwanese students in Japan enjoyed considerable freedom. It was among this group that a movement for home rule for Taiwan began. Proponents were inspired by U.S. President Woodrow Wilson's post–World War I campaign promoting national self-determination and human rights. Many Japanese politicians, too, used these ideas to promote their country's status in the world. In 1921, a group of Taiwanese living in Japan founded the Taiwan Culture Society. They called for a Taiwanese parliament to balance the colonial governor and they asked for Taiwanese representation in Japan's national legislature, the Diet. Thousands of Taiwanese signed petitions in support of their cause. The Taiwan Culture Society activists saw the creation of elected assemblies in the mid-1930s as a partial success for their cause, and some members even became candidates in local elections.

Forty years into the colonial experiment, it was clear that while the Japanese were proud to claim Taiwan, they had not yet fully integrated Taiwanese into Japan. The effort to assimilate Taiwanese accelerated after Japan invaded China in 1931. To ensure the loyalty of colonial populations—whose men were needed as soldiers—Japan redoubled its efforts to "Japanize" its colonies. This was especially important in Taiwan, where most people still recognized China as their ancestral homeland. In 1940, the colonial government decreed that all Taiwanese must take Japanese names. As the war continued, the Japanese Imperial Army even exploited the Austronesian peoples for their fighting spirit and knowledge of mountainous terrain. Japan recruited as many as eight thousand Austronesian men for guerrilla fighting in the jungles of Southeast Asia. Several thousand Taiwanese—both Austronesian and Chinese—are honored at the Yasukuni Shrine in Tokyo, the controversial shrine to Japan's war dead. Had Japan's efforts continued longer, the war-era fast-track to "Japanization" might have succeeded. Instead, the war ended, and Taiwanese found themselves facing a new identity crisis. The "Orphan of Asia" was once again adrift.

"RETROCESSION"

Seventeen years after it ceded Taiwan to the Japanese empire, the Qing Dynasty collapsed under the combined weight of foreign pressure, economic crisis, domestic rebellion, and internal rot. The immediate cause was an uprising that had its first success on October 10, 1911: rebels seized a munitions depot in Wuchang, a city in central China. When the Chinese political activist Sun Yat-sen, who was on a fund-raising trip in the United States, heard the news he rushed back to China to help set up a new Chinese state based on democratic principles. On January 1, 1912, Sun declared the founding of the Republic of China, or ROC. A month later, the Qing emperor abdicated the throne, although it was decades before the ROC managed to bring all the former Qing territories under its effective control.

Sun was interested in both sides of the nation-building process, ideology and institutions. His ideology centered on a reinterpretation of Abraham Lincoln's "government of the people, by the people and for the people." In Sun's "Three Principles of the People" "of the people" was rendered as nationalism (*minzu*), "by the people" as democracy (*minquan*), and "for the people" as livelihood, or socialism (*minsheng*). Institutionally, Sun promoted a Chinese reinterpretation of the American system in which five branches of government, or *yuan*, would check and balance one another. In addition to the American executive, legislative, and judicial branches, Sun added two traditional Chinese government functions: control (to supervise and impeach officials) and examination (to manage civil service examinations).

Implementing these ideas in a divided and chaotic nation proved nearly impossible. The ROC was deeply fragmented; cutthroat political combat was the norm; assassinations were common. Nonetheless, the ROC state gradually consolidated its authority and extended its reach. In the 1920s, the Chinese Nationalist Party, or Kuomintang (KMT) headed by Chiang Kai-shek (Jiang Jieshi) became the leading force in ROC politics. In June 1928 the KMT captured the capital, Beijing. While the Northeast still was only nominally attached, Chiang declared military unification complete and the ROC ready to advance to a new stage in its development: political tutelage. Once the Chinese people had been schooled in the ways of democracy, the KMT leader said, the nation would advance to a third and final stage: constitutional democracy.

Tragically, mainland unification was short-lived. In 1931, Japan invaded northeastern China, the region known as Manchuria. The following year, Japan set up a puppet state in the region and installed the deposed Qing emperor as its nominal head. In 1937, it invaded the rest of China and drove the young ROC out of its own heartland. With the fall of the ROC capital at Nanjing imminent, the KMT and its forces fled up the Yangtze River to Chongqing, in Sichuan province. It was there, bombarded from the air but unreachable by land, that the Republic of China government (sometimes called the Nationalist government) survived eight horrifying years of siege warfare.

Japan's surrender in 1945 brought new hope to China. In November 1943, Chiang Kai-shek met with British Prime Minister Winston Churchill and U.S. President Franklin Roosevelt in Cairo to discuss the Allied nations' plans for a postwar settlement in Asia. Their joint declaration promised to strip Japan of all territories seized since 1914, and it specified that "all the territories Japan has stolen from the Chinese, such as Manchuria, Formosa and the Pescadores (Penghu Islands), shall be restored to the Republic of China." To Korea, they promised independence. The Cairo Declaration was a simple statement of intent, but its provisions gained legal weight when they were referenced in more formal documents, including the Japanese Instrument of Surrender. When the Japanese emperor accepted the terms of surrender on August 15, 1945, Taiwan officially became part of the Republic of China.

For Taiwanese, the return to Chinese control was simultaneously a very natural event—after all, with the exception of the Austronesian people, they were Chinese in language, culture, and ancestry—and a worrisome change. Very few could remember the Qing era that had ended fifty years earlier. Japanese colonial administration was the only government they had ever known. Also, Taiwan and mainland China had grown very far apart during those five decades of separation. Until the war brought privation and military regimentation, Taiwan had flourished under a stable and largely benevolent colonial regime. Meanwhile, the Chinese mainland was being torn apart by revolution, foreign invasion, and war.

In Taiwan, "nationalism" was a vague notion: a half-finished project half-heartedly undertaken in the waning years of the colonial era. In mainland China, nationalism was the fuel powering half a century of suffering and resistance. National unification, national defense, national liberation, national development—these were the guiding passions of generations of Chinese patriots. Taiwanese were about to become Chinese again, but they were Chinese Rip van Winkles: they had missed the cataclysmic process that forged the modern Chinese nation they were about to join.

The ROC government officially took the reins on October 25, a date that is celebrated today as "Retrocession Day." The Chinese term—*Guangfu Jie*—is not as dry as the English. In Chinese, the phrase evokes the glory of restoring lost territory, and that was how the ROC government and the KMT politicians who led it viewed the day. Taiwanese, too, welcomed the event. According to observers, some three hundred thousand people turned out to greet troops entering Taipei, although the "lonely" atmosphere in which the first contingent of Chinese troops arrived at Keelung on October 17 revealed a degree of ambivalence—even anxiety—among Taiwanese.

Retrocession introduced a new social division to Taiwan. There were now "Taiwanese," those whose families had been living on the island anywhere between fifty and three hundred years (known in Chinese as *benshengren,* people of this province) and "Mainlanders," people who arrived in the wake of Retrocession (*waishengren,* people from outside provinces). The two groups held very different visions of how Taiwan should be incorporated into the Republic.

Taiwanese believed their island was more advanced and cosmopolitan than most areas of China, and they did not want to be drawn into the economic and political miseries plaguing the mainland. Taiwanese elites, in particular, thought Taiwan should be allowed to govern itself; at the very least, the ROC should permit Taiwanese the same role in government that the Japanese colonial administration had allowed. Mainlanders took the opposite view. ROC leaders thought Taiwan was *less* suited to self-government than other provinces. They felt it was tainted by long association with the Japanese empire; everywhere they looked they saw evidence of collaborationism and disloyalty. In their view, what Taiwan needed was comprehensive reeducation and indoctrination in Chinese nationalism—not self-government.

Debates over Taiwan's political future attracted elites, but for ordinary Taiwanese, Retrocession brought more immediate problems. The island's economy had suffered heavy damage during the war, including destruction wrought by U.S. bombers targeting its industrial and transportation infrastructure. Japanese colonists (including some who had been born and raised in Taiwan) were repatriated, leaving Taiwanese to repair the damage by themselves. Shortages of food and other goods were widespread. Unemployment skyrocketed, especially after thousands of men began returning from deployments overseas. Economic conditions in the mainland were even worse, but Taiwan's KMT governor, Chen Yi, encouraged economic integration between the two sides of the Strait. Taiwan was soon infected with the same uncontrolled inflation and corruption that were sapping the mainland economy.

Chen Yi favored nationalization for ideological reasons, but his policies became a cover for ROC officials to confiscate property from departing Japanese, and from Taiwanese owners and claimants. While Taiwanese had once complained of Japan's iron-fisted approach to law enforcement, the new government's failure to stem the explosion in bribery, corruption, theft of public (and private) property, arbitrary law enforcement, and other abuses produced nostalgia for the Japanese era. As a popular saying put it, "The dogs are gone; the pigs have arrived."

On February 27, 1947, a police officer in Taipei City struck a woman he was arresting for selling cigarettes illegally (tobacco was a state monopoly). A crowd gathered to confront the police; one officer fired his weapon, killing a bystander. The next day Taiwanese held protests at the Monopoly Bureau Headquarters and the governor's office. Another killing late in the day sparked a wave of violent uprisings that swept through the island. In city after city, Taiwanese attacked police stations, military installations, and government offices. They met surprisingly weak resistance; mainland troops and officials mostly folded in the face of the angry mobs. They hid at home, or took refuge in military outposts. After a few days, the fighting subsided. Taiwanese had effectively taken over the island.

With ROC officials unable to assert their authority, Taiwanese elites stepped in. Within days, they had restored order and restarted basic transport and communications services. Their larger goal was to craft a resolution to the crisis, but they were stymied by the lack of consensus among Taiwanese about goals and strategy. Some Taiwanese simply wanted the ROC government to admit its mistakes and promise to do a better job in the future. Others were looking for more local self-government. The most extreme demand, articulated by only a small minority, was for an independent Taiwan separated from the Chinese Republic. At first, ROC officials including Governor Chen Yi tried to work with Taiwan's de facto leaders to resolve the crisis. As the list of Taiwanese demands lengthened, the ROC government became impatient. The Nationalists had not expected to need an occupation force in Taiwan, but that did not mean they were incapable of mounting one. They had dealt with similar situations on the mainland, and their response to the crisis on Taiwan was boilerplate.

On March 8, 9, and 10, the ROC landed troops in Keelung and Kaohsiung. They used deadly force to cow the population, and quickly restored ROC government control. On March 10, the governor declared the groups helping to resolve the crisis illegal; negotiations were over, and the ROC government was dictating terms. ROC forces used the uprising as a justification to round up political dissidents and local elites of all stripes. Many were murdered on the spot; others were executed after cursory trials. Historians believed close to twenty thousand Taiwanese were killed and an even larger number injured as the military reestablished control. Knowing exactly how many died is difficult, but as the historian Steven Phillips writes, "Knowing who was killed helps make clear the incident's effect on later political activity. As soldiers spread terror through the island, they crushed the Taiwanese as a political force able to advocate change outside the Nationalist state or [KMT] party structure."

The events of February and March 1947, which are known today as the 2-28 (February 28) Incident, set the course of Taiwan's history for decades to come. After Retrocession, Taiwanese and Mainlanders needed to negotiate a way of living together as equals. The 2-28 Incident aborted that process. The ROC government saw those weeks' events as proof that Taiwanese were disloyal, a threat to the nation. Beset by civil war, besieged on all sides, the KMT leadership decided to crush the one threat it could. The crackdown continued in a less virulent form for decades, and came to be known as the White Terror. The 2-28 Incident and the White Terror that followed convinced Taiwanese that the Mainlanders were determined to occupy Taiwan and impose their will—by force if necessary. There was to be no negotiation, no coexistence, no marriage of equals, only the Republic of China government ruling Taiwan from its capital, Nanjing.

THE REPUBLIC OF CHINA ON TAIWAN

From 1945 to 1949, Taiwan was a sideshow for the KMT politicians leading the Republic of China. Their overwhelming preoccupation was to avoid losing power in mainland China. The ink on the Japanese surrender was barely dry when a new threat—one the KMT leadership had long anticipated—arose: Communism. Within a few months of the Japanese surrender, troops loyal to the KMT were fighting Communist Party forces for control of ever-larger chunks of Chinese territory. The Nationalists had been at war for decades; their troops were exhausted. Economic crisis and social unrest gripped KMT-controlled areas of China. The Communists, for their part, were winning converts with aggressive land reform and other economic policies that seemed to offer relief from the spiraling inflation and other economic hardships plaguing KMT-ruled areas.

By 1948, both momentum and morale favored the Communists, and in early 1949, Communist troops crossed the Yangtze River. Nationalist forces lost more and more ground until only Taiwan and its outlying islands remained in KMT hands. On October 1, Communist Party leader Mao Zedong declared the birth of the People's Republic of China. As far as the PRC was concerned, the Republic of China ceased to exist; the PRC had superseded it, and all of its territories—including Taiwan—now belonged to the new state.

The Nationalists' defeat transformed Taiwan's status. Suddenly, the marginal territory had become the last refuge of a state that had lost its nation. In an uncanny twist of history, Taiwan was once again—as it had been under Zheng Chenggong—the holdout against a new mainland regime. Like Zheng trying to restore the Ming Dynasty, Chiang Kai-shek spent the rest of his life trying to win back the mainland for the Republic of China. For Chiang, the Republic of China, despite its limited jurisdiction, still defined "real" China.

In 1949, the most immediate challenge facing Taiwan was to absorb one-and-a-half-million Mainlander refugees. The island's economic recovery was progressing slowly and the sudden addition of so many mouths to feed and hands to employ made the task even harder. Taiwan's existing population was about 6 million, so the influx of Mainlanders prompted a significant jump in competition for resources of every kind, from jobs to food to housing. Economic competition was not the only source of tension between Mainlanders and Taiwanese. Cultural, social, and political differences also existed.

The vast majority of Mainlanders who came to Taiwan between 1945 and 1949 were both Chinese nationalists and Chinese Nationalists, members of the Nationalist Party, or KMT. They believed the Chinese mainland was trapped under the boot heel of un-Chinese, tyrannical outlaws, and it was the sacred responsibility of all Chinese, including the Chinese on Taiwan, to rescue their motherland from Communism. Their vision for Taiwan was clear: it must be built into a bastion of Chinese nationalism from which the campaign to recover the mainland could be mounted. To accomplish that vision they believed it was necessary to enforce political conformity, inculcate nationalist zeal, rebuild economic prosperity, and acquire military might. Those four tasks were the pillars on which the Republic of China on Taiwan was built.

CREATING A COMMUNITY OF SHARED FATE

Taiwan's history made it a melting pot shared by Austronesian peoples, Hokkien-speaking migrants arriving from various regions of Fujian at various times, Hakkas driven out of southern China, and Mainlanders from all corners of China who became Taiwanese by accident. The island's modern history began with a tragic collision of these groups. But Taiwan's recent history is a chronicle of reconciliation, as these different groups have grown together, become intertwined, and gradually come to recognize their shared fate as citizens of a thriving but imperiled country.

This reconciliation took place against a background of profound political change. In the early decades after Retrocession, the KMT operated a single-party authoritarian state with few individual or civil rights, but over the course of the 1980s and 1990s, the system was transformed into a fully democratic state. We record the story of that metamorphosis in another chapter; it is enough for now to know that Taiwan's ethnic rapprochement took place in an era of political rebirth.

The first marker of membership in one of Taiwan's ethnic communities is language. Almost 90 percent of Taiwan's 6 million occupants at the end of World War II spoke Hokkien. Their ancestors had come to Taiwan from Fujian, and while they carried the accents of northern and southern Fujian, their language was the same. Hokkien, like all Chinese dialects, is written using Chinese characters. Characters convey ideas, not sounds, so words are written identically, no matter how differently they may be pronounced from one place to another. The two characters that form the word "China," for example, mean "middle" and "kingdom." In Hokkien, they are pronounced "tiong-kok." In Mandarin, the northern Chinese dialect chosen as the ROC's official medium of spoken communication, the two characters are pronounced "zhongguo." A Hokkien speaker and a Mandarin speaker cannot understand one another when they talk, but they can read the same newspapers and books. Hakka is also a dialect of Chinese; Hakka speech is unintelligible to Hokkien and Mandarin speakers, but Hakka people, too, write their language using Chinese characters.

During the Japanese colonial period, Taiwanese were educated in Japanese (which also uses Chinese characters, as well as alphabetic symbols unique to Japan), but they continued to speak their mother tongues—Hokkien, Hakka, and Austronesian languages—in everyday life. After the Japanese surrender, one of the ways Taiwanese prepared themselves for the new regime was to study Mandarin. One of the surprises Retrocession delivered was the profusion of dialects spoken by the new arrivals. Most Mainlanders were not officials, but soldiers. Many were conscripts with little or no education; their hometown dialects were as different from Mandarin as Hokkien and Hakka. In the early years of the ROC, Taiwan was like Babel, with dozens of different dialect and language groups communicating in broken Mandarin. Language was a source of tension and an important marker of group identity. In *Cities of Sadness*, Hou Hsiao-hsien's classic 1989 film about the 2-28 Incident, a deaf Taiwanese is nearly killed by an anti-Mainlander mob because his deafness prevents him from speaking Taiwanese fluently.

Language was a top concern for the ROC government. After Retrocession, officials on Taiwan were preoccupied with integrating Taiwan into the Chinese nation. Making Mandarin the lingua franca for the island was an important step in replacing Japanese, Hokkien, Hakka, and Austronesian identities with a unified Chinese identity. It was also important because the island needed a common language to facilitate communication among the different ethnic communities. Even though Hokkien was the mother tongue for the great majority of Taiwan's people, the ROC leadership never considered making it the island's official language. Taiwan was a province of the Republic of China; the ROC's official language was Mandarin. Joining the Chinese nation meant shedding other identities. Taiwanese would learn Mandarin, which the Nationalists called *guoyu*, the national language.

Language policy did not change when the mainland fell to the Communists—far from it. The mainland was in the hands of a Communist Party the Nationalists believed would wipe out traditional Chinese culture. To fulfill its role as the launching pad for mainland recovery, Taiwan would need to be fully dedicated to rescuing the Chinese nation—including its cultural heritage. (In some cases, this "rescue" was literal: the most precious treasures of China's imperial past were boxed up and transported to Taiwan where they are stored inside a mountain. The stars of the collection are displayed in Taipei's National Palace Museum.) In the eyes of its leaders, Taiwan had a historic mission, to save China from Communism. All other goals, including the parochial demands of Taiwan's Hokkien and Hakka communities, were subordinated to this grand destiny.

To carry out its cultural project, the KMT government turned to education and mass media. Radio (and, later, television) programming in Hokkien was limited to a few hours a day. Most programming was in Mandarin, and the proportion of Mandarin grew over time. Mandarin replaced Japanese as the language of instruction in public schools, and because few Taiwanese children or parents spoke Mandarin, elementary school became a sink-or-swim immersion in a strange language. Many Taiwanese have bitter memories of sitting in first-grade classrooms in which they understood little and were fined for speaking their mother tongues. For some Taiwanese, the language barrier compounded other problems and caused them to cut their education short. Others mastered Mandarin, even as they continued to speak Hokkien or Hakka at home. In the 1980s, local government offices had signs on the walls urging employees (with little apparent effect) to "Speak Mandarin on the Telephone!" Mandarin spread, but Hokkien persisted, and Taiwan today is a multilingual society, with Hokkien, Hakka, and some Austronesian languages spoken alongside Mandarin.

For Mainlanders, especially those who had Mandarin as their mother tongue, the government's decision to make Mandarin the national language conferred significant benefits. They entered nearly every realm of life at an instant advantage. They learned more quickly in school because they were being taught in a language they understood, and by the time their Taiwanese classmates had mastered the language, they already were ahead in their studies. The government reinforced this advantage by making Mandarin proficiency a criterion for educational and career advancement. The state-owned companies that dominated major industries were led by Mandarin-speaking executives, while Taiwanese military conscripts were commanded by an overwhelmingly Mainlander officer corps. Informal factors like personal connections and formal perks such as civil service quotas (the law said provincial representation in national government offices should be proportional to provincial population) added to the Mainlanders' linguistic and educational advantages. The combined effect of these "neutral" policies was to severely limit Taiwanese people's employment opportunities, especially in the public sector.

As one would expect, these policy decisions deepened the social divide between Taiwanese and Mainlanders. Taiwanese felt like second-class citizens in their own homeland. It was not only language; other aspects of traditional Taiwanese life were also targets of discrimination. The state defined the cultural practices of ordinary Taiwanese as inferior to those of the Mandarin-speaking, Confucian-spouting elite. Taiwanese religious practices, which centered on an eclectic mélange of local cults, Mazu worship, Buddhist orthodoxy, and Taoist mysticism, were dismissed as low-class superstitions unworthy of a modern Chinese nation. At school, Taiwanese memorized endless minutiae about Chinese history and geography, but learned next to nothing about Taiwan itself. The government hoped to mold Taiwanese into the kind of Chinese Mainlander elites imagined themselves to be: modern, rational, cosmopolitan, and nationalistic. But by defining "Chineseness" in a way that marginalized and denigrated Taiwan's indigenous social and cultural practices, the ROC's cultural policies had the perverse effect of making many Taiwanese doubt whether they were Chinese at all.

From the perspective of Hokkien Taiwanese, the system seemed rigged in favor of the Mainlanders. Mandarin-speakers who had arrived in the 1940s enjoyed special treatment in politics, education, culture, and government. They lived in subsidized housing called "military dependents' villages" (*juancun*), often in former Japanese quarters; they were favored for admission to the military and civil service; when they got old or sick, they were cared for in veterans' homes the Chinese called "Homes for Men of Honor" (*rongmin zhi jia*).

To Mainlanders, the picture looked quite different. For the elite, their material life in Taiwan was good, but they longed to return home. For the majority of Mainlanders—those in more humble stations—material comforts were few. The military dependents' villages were more like isolated ghettos than exclusive enclaves. While government jobs provided a steady income, wages were modest. Private business offered better returns, but it was not easy for Mainlanders to work in Taiwan's Hokkien-dominated private economy. All too often, the veterans' homes were little more than grim warehouses where friendless old men, their health ruined by years of soldiering and physical labor, lived out their lives in lonely confinement. Hokkien residents of Hualien City used to complain about Mainlanders being given houses where Japanese officers had lived before the war. Their street even had its own private bomb shelter! But for the Mainlander families living in those houses, the experience was isolating and sad. Their homes were owned by the state, and they were never renovated, not least because renovations might betray a lack of faith in Chiang's promise that they would soon "return home." Forty years after Retrocession, the houses were crumbling and primitive, but still a source of envy and ill will among Hokkien.

For ordinary Mainlander soldiers and low-level civil servants, life in Taiwan was difficult. In most cases, their families were gone, including mothers and fathers, but often wives and children as well. A few had managed to bring their families to Taiwan before the Communist victory cut off travel between the two sides. The lucky ones married (or remarried) in Taiwan, but many Hokkien families refused to marry their daughters to Mainlanders.

Nor did ordinary Mainlanders enjoy more freedom than their Taiwanese neighbors. The KMT's deepest fear was that Communist subversion would bring down the ROC in its last redoubt. Communist infiltration was likeliest among Mainlanders, many of whom had worked side by side with Communists on the mainland and had relatives still living there. As a result the KMT kept Mainlanders under constant surveillance. In the 1970s, one old soldier disappeared without warning. After a long delay, his family learned he had been arrested on political charges, but they never were told what he was alleged to have done. On this flimsy premise, he spent eleven years in prison. In the 1990s, when democracy was taking hold in Taiwan, the prisoner's daughter went to work for Chen Chu, a Taiwanese political prisoner and human rights activist. Across the ethnic divide, two victims of the White Terror worked together for justice.

Mainlander life was also hierarchical, reflecting the influence of the military. A young Taiwanese diplomat officer tells the story of his grandparents, a low-ranking Mainlander officer and his wife. They worshipped the Chiang family, and Madame Chiang Kai-shek's pet project, the Grand Hotel, was their temple. The Grand Hotel is a massive imperial-style building with a gold-tiled roof nestled into a verdant mountainside overlooking downtown Taipei. The diplomat was raised on tales of its magnificent rooms and five-star restaurants, and, above all, Madame Chiang's favorite delicacy, fancy red bean cakes. His grandparents never actually ate the cakes; they only dreamed of them. But times have changed. Although their grandson finds the Grand Hotel stuffy and threadbare, and its restaurants overpriced, he likes to order Madame Chiang's cakes from time to time, because, unlike his grandparents, he can.

For Hakka and Austronesian Taiwanese, ethnic politics after Retrocession were tricky. They were ineligible for the benefits provided to Mainlanders, but Retrocession did not put an end to the long-simmering tensions between them and the Hokkien majority. In many cases, they cast their lot with the KMT and the Mainlanders, whom they viewed as less threatening than their Hokkien neighbors. Given the poverty and isolation of most Austronesian and many Hakka communities, the KMT was able to win their support at a pitifully low price. For Austronesian communities driven into the high mountains or confined to guarded villages during the Japanese colonial period, a cluster of concrete houses a few hours' walk from a paved road was a huge boon. Keeping Hokkien visitors out of Austronesian villages not only helped prevent exploitation and conflict but also minimized political resistance. Both the Austronesian and Hakka peoples became fierce supporters of the KMT—even today, Austronesian and Hakka voters are among the KMT's most loyal constituents.

In the decades after the 2-28 Incident, few Taiwanese dared to voice their resentments about how Retrocession had changed their lives. The KMT made it clear that Taiwanese were expected to throw themselves whole-heartedly into the campaign to recover the mainland. Those who suggested Taiwan might be an end in itself, with a history worth learning and a culture worth celebrating, were excoriated for their failure to embrace the national project. Reveling in Taiwanese identity marked an islander as either embarrassingly uncouth or downright subversive. And under Chiang's rule, being labeled "subversive" could bring harassment, arrest, or worse.

In the 1970s, things began to change. Taiwanese began standing up for their culture and demanding recognition. The transformation began with a literary movement known as "Hometown Literature." In novels and short stories, Taiwanese authors explored everyday life in Taiwan. The social milieu their work described was uniquely Taiwanese; it could not be separated from the island's physical and social landscape. The Hometown writers tried to capture their mother tongues' syntax and word choice in their writing, using Chinese characters to directly transcribe the local idiom, rather than "translating" Hokkien and Hakka thoughts into Mandarin. Before long, visual artists and musicians were introducing ideas from Hometown Literature into their work.

Hometown Literature and art transformed Taiwan's view of itself. They awakened a sense of pride in Taiwanese traditions. They also helped bring into the open an idea that had been hidden since 1947, that Taiwan's own aspirations need not be subjugated to Chinese nationalism. Taiwan was valuable in its own right, with or without the Chinese mainland. These revolutionary ideas brought a new willingness to practice a specifically Taiwanese way of life, to speak Hokkien without shame, to worship Mazu without apology, to eat the foods that flourished in Taiwan's rich volcanic soil without embarrassment. The political atmosphere was changing at the same time, and the two trends reinforced one another.

By the late 1980s, the Taiwan culture movement had developed into a craze for all things Taiwanese. Restaurants specializing in home-style favorites like salted-turnip omelets and three-cups frog appeared in Taipei's toniest neighborhoods. Publishers churned out thousands of books on Taiwan history, geography, and folkways. Traditional art forms such as puppet theater and Hokkien operas—art forms that had once seemed on the verge of dying out—were revived. Even the Austronesian peoples became fashionable (at least in the abstract) as a symbol of Taiwan's pre-Chinese roots. Taiwanese began to integrate Austronesian art, literature, and history into their understanding of Taiwan's culture and history. Eventually the term "Original Inhabitants" (*yuanzhumin*) replaced the derogatory and inaccurate words others had long used to name the Austronesian peoples.

After 2000, Taiwanese youth even took on one of the most painful images of the past, the *"Taike"* or Taiwanese bumpkin stereotype. "Taike" was a taunt that captured stereotypes of Taiwanese as backward and *déclassé*, something like the American term "redneck." According to the stereotype, the garishly dressed Taike cruised the main streets of small towns on a cheap, tricked-out motorbike, intensifying his ridiculousness by imagining himself stylish and *soigné*, too clueless to recognize his own cluelessness. Young Taiwanese erased Taike's power to hurt by embracing the slur and turning it into a source of fun. Taike parties became popular on university campuses. A young woman quoted in the book *Call Me Taike!* captured the new spirit: "I think *Taike* is a born-here, raised-here Taiwan thing; you can't see it anywhere else in the world. It's an important part of what makes Taiwanese culture so rich and riotous."

In the 1990s, activists introduced the terms "Taiwan subjectivity" (*Taiwan zhutixing*) and "Taiwan-centric consciousness" (*Taiwan zhuti yishi*). The new phrases expressed the idea that Taiwan should be the subject of its own story, not the object of others' desires, and that it should determine its own fate in accordance with its interests, not allow itself to become a sideshow in someone else's history. Taiwan-centric consciousness does not deny that Taiwan's culture and heritage include Chinese elements, but, to use Dan Lynch's clever formulation, it views China as part of Taiwan, rather than Taiwan as part of China. It also highlights unique cultural influences that differentiate Taiwan from the Chinese mainland.

For Mainlanders—and many Hakkas and Austronesian people as well— the flowering of Hokkien pride was a troubling trend. Pride easily slipped into chauvinism, and chauvinism was used to justify prejudice. Speaking "Taiwanese," which really meant Hokkien, became a marker of belonging, and Mainlanders and even some Hakkas began to doubt whether they were welcome in Taiwan. Many Mainlanders—including those born in Taiwan to Mainlander parents—felt tainted by their family origins. Suddenly, it was Mainlanders who felt they were second-class citizens. In 1990, a young Mainlander told the Taiwanese newspaper *Liberty Times*, "Overseas, no one thought we were Chinese; they said we were Taiwanese. In Taiwan, no one thought we were Taiwanese; they said we were Mainlanders. In the mainland, no one thought we were part of them; they said we were Taiwan compatriots (*Taibao*). We wandered around through all these different statuses and titles in all these different regions and places, and felt we were always at a crossroads. We were like homeless orphans; we ourselves didn't know what we were."

In the mid-1990s, Lee Teng-hui, Taiwan's Japanese-educated, Hokkien-speaking president, began to mend the rift between Taiwan's different ethnic groups. He used the term "New Taiwanese" to redefine Mainlanders as belonging to and in Taiwan. After fifty years of living together, he argued, it was time for islanders to look past the different paths they had traveled to reach the island, and recognize that all were members of a "community of shared fate." Taiwan, he said, would survive and flourish only if all her people stood together. In 1999, Lee outlined his ideas in an article in *Foreign Policy* magazine: "To convey a sense of the popular will on Taiwan today, I now refer to my fellow citizens as 'New Taiwanese,' meaning those who are willing to fight for the prosperity and survival of their country, regardless of when they or their forebears arrived on Taiwan and regardless of their provincial heritage or native language. This fresh national identity based on the New Taiwanese consciousness, holding that Taiwan's interests should be foremost and that the people of Taiwan all share a common destiny, has gradually harmonized the populace and provided a stable middle ground for Taiwan's political development."

Lee used the bully pulpit of his presidency to introduce the "New Taiwanese" concept, but the idea did not immediately take hold. For many Hokkien people, the scars left by the White Terror and decades of China-centric cultural policies were too fresh. They weren't ready to merge their newfound Hokkien pride into a post-ethnic identity, and they didn't trust the KMT to put Taiwan's interests ahead of Chinese nationalism—whatever Lee Teng-hui said. The cultural policies advocated by Lee's successor, President Chen Shui-bian, reflected this skepticism. The Chen administration pressed for cultural and educational reforms that critics said were aimed at "de-Sinicization," or gouging out Chinese elements from Taiwanese life—from revising textbooks to de-emphasize Taiwan's Chinese origins to removing the word "China" from the names of public utilities.

For eight years, the Chen administration worked to inculcate the notion that Taiwan is a Creole society in which Austronesian, Chinese, Hokkien, Hakka, Japanese—even Spanish and Portuguese—elements are melded together. It placed enormous emphasis on the Austronesian peoples' contributions to Taiwanese culture. Chen renamed the street in front of Taiwan's presidential office "Ketagalan Boulevard" after an early Austronesian group. In 2004, his Democratic Progressive Party produced a calendar entitled "The Twelve Months of President A-bian and the Austronesian Peoples" ("A-bian" is Chen's nickname). Each month was illustrated with a photo of the president garbed in a different Austronesian outfit. On the cover, he wrote a message to the Austronesian people: "People of the Southern Isle, let's come together with diligence and enthusiasm. Set out with A-bian, with Ketagalan Boulevard as our stepping off point, to find our roots, and the beauty of our homeland. Let's return to the land bestowed upon us by the spirits of our ancestors to shout and sing: We are the masters of Taiwan!"

Where Lee Teng-hui's concept of Taiwanese identity was essentially political—he argued for a separate, independent Taiwanese *state*—Chen Shui-bian's concept was cultural—it posited Taiwan as a *nation*. In the lingo of political science, Lee was advocating civic nationalism—nationalism based on the shared experience of democratic self-government—while Chen promoted *ethno-nationalism*—nationalism based on an ethnic bond. Promoters of ethno-nationalism in Taiwan claim that Taiwan is not only politically separate from mainland China, but it is also ethnically different, with a culture, history—even bloodlines—all its own.

Ethno-nationalism, it turns out, is a hard sell on Taiwan. With the exception of the Austronesian people, who make up less than 2 percent of Taiwan's population, all Taiwanese are of Chinese ancestry, and many of them would prefer not to choose between the Taiwanese and Chinese elements of their identity. For almost twenty years, pollsters have been asking Taiwanese "Do you think of yourself as Taiwanese, Chinese or both?" Back in the early 1990s, when education and mass media were still pushing the Chinese nationalist agenda, about a quarter of the people said "Chinese," and about 45 percent said "both." Since then, the proportion of people who call themselves "Chinese" has plummeted to about 5 percent, and the share of those who say they are "Taiwanese" has risen from the high teens to more than 40 percent. The percentage claiming to be "both Taiwanese and Chinese" remained remarkably consistent, at around 45 percent, although in some of the most recent polls, "Taiwanese" has surpassed 50 percent.

In late 2005, more than a thousand university students took an informal survey in their classes. The poll asked what the students were thinking about when they answered the "Chinese, Taiwanese or Both?" question. There was a strong connection between how they interpreted the question, and the answers they gave. Those who thought the question was asking about "where I was born and raised" tended to choose "Taiwanese," while those who interpreted the question to refer to "my historical and cultural background" tended to choose "both Taiwanese and Chinese." That finding suggests that while many Taiwanese recognize their Chinese cultural heritage, their geographical (and by extension political) connection is to Taiwan. Meanwhile, the PRC's rising prominence—both internationally and in Taiwan's economic life—has strengthened the association between "China" and "People's Republic of China" and made it even less likely that Taiwanese will claim a "Chinese" identity.

During the Chen years, the government worked hard to persuade citizens to adopt its ethno-national view of Taiwanese identity. Lin Chia-lung, one of Chen Shui-bian's close advisors, told me: "I think we should try to persuade people of our values, to influence them to agree with us, not just follow behind the voters. You need to have values and ideals. At the same time, if we are not able to persuade people, we need to respect their decisions. This is democracy." Ultimately, it was democracy that ended both parties' practice of using the powers of government to promote ethno-nationalism.

In 2008, President Chen's Democratic Progressive Party suffered two huge electoral setbacks. In January, legislative elections left the KMT with more than 70 percent of the seats; in March, the KMT recaptured the presidency. The new president, Ma Ying-jeou, is the KMT politician for whom Lee Teng-hui invented the term "New Taiwanese." Ma is a Mainlander, born in Hong Kong in 1949, who has lived his entire life in Taiwan. He embraces the idea of Taiwan-centric consciousness, but he is not a Taiwanese ethno-nationalist. His 58 percent vote share proved that ethnicity is not the driving factor for mainstream Taiwanese voters.

The ethnic fault lines in Taiwan's society still are visible. Older people, in particular, still care about whether someone is Hokkien, Mainlander, Hakka, or Austronesian. But for younger Taiwanese, these categories mean little. Sixty years ago, many Taiwanese vehemently opposed intermarriage between Taiwanese and Mainlanders. As one woman quoted in a documentary film put it, in the 1950s, if a Hokkien woman married a Mainlander, her family would want to "chop her up and feed her to the pigs." Even in the 1980s, marrying across ethnic lines was controversial, although attitudes were changing fast. By 1991, only 7.5 percent of college students said they would consider ethnic background in choosing a marriage partner. Today, with as many as a quarter of all marriages in Taiwan involving a spouse born *outside Taiwan*, "intermarriage" has an entirely new meaning.

Language still matters—people worry that Hokkien, Hakka, and Austronesian languages may be dying out—but Mandarin is accepted as a tool of communication shared by all. Much like British and American English, the mainland's *"putonghua"* and Taiwan's "Taiwanese Mandarin" (*Taiwan guoyu*) are similar, but not identical. Taiwanese have a distinct accent (one that fashionable young people in mainland China sometimes copy), and their choice of words is different. Young Taiwanese mix Hokkien and Mandarin (sometimes in the same sentence—often with an English word or two thrown in) and they choose different languages for different purposes—Mandarin for school, Hokkien for hanging out with friends. Some young Taiwanese even see a gender difference—Mandarin for girls, Hokkien for boys.

Young people chafe at the suggestion that their affection for and loyalty to Taiwan are revealed in their language choices. To them, language is a tool for communication, not a marker of ethnic solidarity. A college student expressed his generation's cynicism about the language wars when he said, "Even my dad says Hokkien has become a political commodity. It's just a device politicians use to get votes." One of the newest languages in Taiwan is "Martian"—a user-friendly shorthand to use in text messaging. Martian relies on roman letters to convey a mélange of Chinese and English words: 3Q (pronounced *"san* Q") means "thank you"; 88 (*ba ba*) means "bye bye."

Refusing to be dragged into their grandparents' culture wars doesn't mean young Taiwanese don't love their country. On the contrary, claiming a Taiwanese identity is natural for them. At the same time, their Taiwanese identity does not come at the expense of a growing interest in China. They see the mainland as not only a different country—young Taiwanese routinely use the phrase "going abroad" (*chuguo*) to describe trips to China—but also a special one. Unlike their elders, who grew up hating and fearing the mainland, young Taiwanese cannot remember a time when people did not travel freely back and forth for business and pleasure.

Taiwan once was dominated by a single social cleavage: Mainlanders versus Taiwanese. While those categories still matter, they matter less than they once did. At the same time, new categories and identities are coming to the fore. Hakka people are demanding that their unique culture and heritage be recognized and celebrated alongside Hokkien culture; they refuse to be absorbed into a Hokkien identity that monopolizes "Taiwaneseness." Austronesian people, too, are demanding recognition of their distinct cultures—and protection of their land. Taiwan has a long history of feminist organizations promoting identification among women. In the 1990s, the island brought forth a thriving gay culture, complete with annual gay pride parades since 2003. Taiwan's gay and lesbian people have chosen an ironic nickname for themselves: "comrades" (*tongzhi*). The term is borrowed from Chinese Communist parlance, and its use in the new context is at once apt, humorous, playful, and subversive.

The journey from White Terror to gay pride parade has been long and difficult. In traveling that distance, Taiwan has melted what began as diverse and hostile groups into a society that disagrees on many things, but is united around one fact: Taiwan is their home, and they will chart her course together.

SOURCES

When I first tried to write about Taiwan's early history, back in the 1980s, I found few sources in Chinese or English. The picture is very different today, as historians in Taiwan and overseas are quickly filling in the details of Taiwan's past. Historical sources consulted for this chapter include books by Emma Jinhua Teng (*Taiwan's Imagined Geography: Chinese Colonial Travel Writing and Pictures, 1683–1895*); Tonio Andrade (*How Taiwan Became Chinese: Dutch, Spanish, and Han Colonization in the Seventeenth Century*); Leo Ching (*Becoming Japanese: Colonial Taiwan and the Politics of Identity Formation*); Melissa Brown (*Is Taiwan Chinese?*); Macabe Keliher (*Out of China: A History of 17th Century Taiwan*); Murray Rubenstein (ed.) (*Taiwan: A New History*); and others. The information about Lukang comes from Donald R. DeGlopper's book *Lukang: Commerce and Community in a Chinese City*. The description of Taiwan's government under the Qing as "preventive, indirect, incomplete" comes from Wu Rwei-ren's article "Fragment of/f Empires: The Peripheral Formation of Taiwanese Nationalism," *Social Science Japan* (December 2004).

Details about Japanese-era governance are drawn mainly from work by Chen Ming-tong and Lin Jih-wen, published in Chinese in a volume entitled *Basic Level Elections and Socio-Political Change on Both Sides of the Strait.* Efforts to win more rights for Taiwanese within the Japanese empire are detailed in American diplomat George H. Kerr's *Formosa: Licensed Revolution and the Home Rule Movement, 1895–1945.* Kerr also published a firsthand account of the early postwar era, including the 2-28 Incident, *Formosa Betrayed,* in 1965.

The most complete histories of the postwar era and the 2-28 Incident in English are found in Steven E. Phillip's book *Between Assimilation and Independence: The Taiwanese Encounter Nationalist China, 1945–1950* and a study by Lai Tse-han, Ramon Myers, and Wei Wou entitled *A Tragic Beginning: The Taiwan Uprising of February 28, 1947.* The description of Taiwan's atmosphere in the 1940s as "lonely" comes from a KMT official quoted in Li Hsiao-feng's very important study (in Chinese) *Forty Years of Taiwan's Democratic Movement.*

Dan Lynch wrote about "Mr. Ma's Taiwanese Identity" in the *Far Eastern Economic Review* in March 2008. Information about ethnicity and marriage comes from Chen Wen-chun's article entitled "The Political Culture of Taiwanese Students: High School and University Students' Attitudes and the Future of Taiwan's Democratization," in the spring 1998 issue of *Guoli Zhongshan Daxue Shehui Kexue Jikan.*

3

From Farmers to Manufacturers

Taiwan is a small country, but it plays an outsized role in the global economy. It's one of the world's top fifteen trading nations, and its companies manufacture a huge share of the information technology that keeps modern societies going: 98 percent of computer motherboards, 90 percent of notebook PCs, 65 percent or more of thin-film transistor–liquid-crystal display (TFT-LCD) screens. A single Taiwanese company—Taiwan Semiconductor Manufacturing Corporation—makes more than half the world's computer chips, while Acer, Taiwan's first global computer brand, edged past U.S.-based Dell Computer in 2009 to become the world's second-largest seller of notebook PCs.

The story of how this tiny island—endowed with few natural resources and a small population—became a global economic powerhouse brings together politics, culture, economics . . . and a little luck. Together, Taiwan's government and people—its workers, entrepreneurs, farmers, engineers, merchants, and students—earned for their nation the title "Taiwan Miracle." They did it by looking outward toward world markets and by staying light on their feet, adjusting constantly to new technologies, new products, new demand. In less than half a century they built a war-torn agrarian backwater into a high-tech superpower.

The roots of Taiwan's global outlook run deep. The island's earliest export was a classic specialty product: deer antlers. According to Chinese medical theory, deer antlers cure diseases of the bones, joints, and blood. As early as the 1600s, Austronesian hunters were harvesting wild deer in Taiwan and exchanging them for salt with Chinese traders who delivered them to the mainland as medicine and meat. These earliest Chinese residents lived in the shallow coves and harbors along the island's west coast;

their business model included smuggling and piracy—raiding boats in the Taiwan Strait—as well as trading antlers and deer meat.

The Dutch and Portuguese travelers who first described the island to European audiences recognized Taiwan's economic potential. A Dutch account from 1624 called Taiwan "a very beautiful and fertile land. It is full of game like deer, pigs, serows [goats], pigeons, partridges, pheasants, and the like. And the waters teem with fish." When agents of the Dutch East India Company set up their trading colony at Anping in 1623, they upgraded the deer-products trade, using their superior trade connections and transportation technology to expand the market. Antlers and meat went to China, while deer hides were sold to Japanese artisans who crafted them into samurai armor. At the height of Dutch colonization, Taiwan's deer hide exports averaged over sixty thousand per year. The Dutch East India Company also encouraged Chinese farmers to settle the island; within a few years, they had added sugar to the list of Taiwanese exports. In just five years, the number of acres under sugar cultivation increased sixfold.

The pirate king Zheng Chenggong (Koxinga) expelled the Dutch from Taiwan in 1661, but he retained many of their economic practices. He, too, relied on agriculture for revenue, which gave him a strong incentive to promote farming and immigration. Zheng commanded a powerful military force loyal to the deposed Ming Dynasty, and during breaks in warfare his soldiers cleared and farmed new land in Taiwan. That reclaimed farmland was a major draw for settlers from crowded Fujian Province, just opposite Taiwan on the Chinese coast, and Zheng encouraged immigrants to come. The trade in deer products continued under Zheng, and with Taiwan at war with the Qing, smuggling flourished.

The Qing Dynasty defeated Zheng's forces and took nominal control of the island in 1683, but the change of government did little to alter Taiwan's economic patterns. The Qing leadership preferred to minimize its expenditures on the island, and Beijing left day-to-day management of Taiwanese affairs to local strongmen. Under the Qing's light hand, Taiwan's agriculture flourished. With rice and sugar exports expanding, ports and towns also grew, including the leading Qing-era port, Lukang (Deer Harbor).

In Lukang, today's visitor can sense the atmosphere of a wealthy Taiwanese trading center at the height of the Qing. Tucked between modern buildings are remnants of a bustling, fashionable city of grand houses and public spaces, including Taiwan's most architecturally significant temple, the Lungshan (Dragon Mountain) Temple. Narrow cobbled alleys wind through the town, offering protection from the weather to the porters who carried goods from the harbor to the shops and warehouses in town. One local dignitary designed his courtyard so that his well could be accessed from both sides of the wall, making water available to his less fortunate neighbors. Changes in shipping eventually made Lukang's shallow harbor obsolete, preserving both its architecture and its traditional way of life; today, it is a center for the production of handcrafted ritual objects. Sadly, the rock-fighting grounds mentioned in chapter 2 were not preserved.

The first attempt to exploit Taiwan as a source of strategic minerals came in 1696 when the Qing armory at Fuzhou, Fujian, exploded, destroying the province's supply of gunpowder. Fujian's governor appointed the explorer Yu Yonghe to travel to Taiwan and collect sulfur—an ingredient in explosives—from the volcanoes around the Taipei basin. His detailed account of his journey, beautifully rendered into English in Macabe Keliher's *Out of China: Yu Yonghe's Tales of Formosa*, sketches an island that is terrifyingly wild and fantastically beautiful, where the line between man and beast can barely be discerned and travelers climb to dizzying heights to see the underworld open directly into the clouds. Yu Yonghe's diary is a powerful statement of how far outside the pale of Chinese civilization Taiwan lay in the seventeenth century.

While Taiwan relied on agriculture throughout the Qing era, its economy had a significant outward focus even then. The island prospered by exporting commercial crops (rice, sugar, indigo dyes) and natural resources (timber, fish, deer products, camphor). Western interest in the island resumed in the mid-nineteenth century, when European and American governments began pressing China and Japan to open their countries to global trade. In 1860, China and Britain signed the Treaty of Tianjin (one of the so-called unequal treaties), forcing China to give foreign traders free access to Taiwan's ports. The return of European buyers promoted a new crop: tea. By the end of the century, tea was the island's biggest export.

In response to the increasing importance of maritime activity—both economic and military—and Taiwan's strategic location, the Qing tightened its control over the island. In 1885, Beijing upgraded Taiwan to provincial status. General Liu Ming-ch'uan, Taiwan's first provincial governor, began a process of administrative modernization, conducting a census, restructuring the tax system, expanding infrastructure, and intensifying land reclamation efforts.

General Liu's efforts to improve Taiwan's economic performance had little time to bear fruit. Just a decade after it made Taiwan a province, the Qing ceded the island to the empire of Japan in another "unequal treaty"—the settlement ending the Sino-Japanese War. In the 1890s, Japan was governed by a team of ambitious, development-oriented politicians determined to match the Western powers in military and economic might. They envisioned Taiwan as a model colony—a laboratory for demonstrating Japan's parity with other modern imperial states. They also recognized Taiwan's capacity to contribute to Japan's own economic development.

To realize the island's potential, the Japanese government emphasized agriculture. Taiwan quickly became a source of sugar, rice, camphor oil, and fruit for Japan's home islands and an important market for Japanese manufactures. Japanese governors dispatched to the island actively encouraged its integration into the imperial economy. They introduced new production technologies in synch with the island's development. To increase productivity, the colonial government developed both hard infrastructure—roads, railroads, electrification, telegraph services—and soft infrastructure—education, banking, legal reform, civic associations. It completed the north-south railway in 1907 and dredged the ports at Keelung and Kaohsiung. Those projects connected the west coast by land from top to bottom and provided maritime trade access at each end. By 1905, only ten years after colonization, Taiwan was self-supporting; its contributions to imperial revenues exceeded Japan's administrative expenditures.

As the island (and the Japanese homeland) grew wealthier, opportunities for higher-level economic activities increased. The first wave of industrialization was limited to agricultural processing, but as Japan's needs and capacities changed, the empire looked to Taiwan to manufacture a larger range of goods. Japanese entrepreneurs and state agencies took the lead in Taiwan's industrialization, but over time, some Taiwanese accumulated the skills and capital to compete in business. In the 1920s, the colonial government changed the law to open nonagricultural business activities to Taiwanese.

Invading China in 1931 increased Japan's need for industrial goods, and Tokyo turned to Taiwan to meet that demand. By the 1940s, Taiwan was developing heavy industry and consumer manufacturing, both to enable the island to play a larger role in the wartime supply chain and to decrease its dependence on Japan. Under the auspices of the state-owned Taiwan Development Company, Japanese firms introduced a wide range of industries, from chemicals to machine tools to textiles.

From a breadbasket servicing the Japanese home islands' need for food and markets, Taiwan had, by end of World War II, blossomed into an economy of eager and capable workers and entrepreneurs experienced in external trade, familiar with industrial processes and well-served by modern infrastructure. These features stood in conspicuous contrast to Taiwan's war-ravaged neighbors—including China—and they helped set the stage for the successes to come. Still, despite these advantages, the transition from Japanese colony to "miracle economy" was rocky, thanks to the political crisis in the Chinese mainland.

The unconditional surrender that ended Japan's participation in World War II restored the island to Chinese sovereignty. At the time, the Allied powers recognized the Republic of China led by Chiang Kai-shek's Nationalist (KMT) Party as the Chinese state, and it was to the ROC that Japanese colonial administrators handed over the island. The ROC government's economic record on the mainland was dismal. During the devastating eight-year Japanese occupation of China's coastal cities, corruption and inflation in the areas under ROC control sapped the state's legitimacy. After Japan's surrender, the ROC still faced massive economic problems—and a political crisis that tilted into full-scale civil war in 1946. Rebuilding Taiwan's economy was a low priority.

When ROC administrators moved to Taiwan in 1945, the gap in expectations between Taiwanese and the new arrivals was enormous. For Taiwanese, China was a dimly remembered homeland wrapped in misty nostalgia and high expectations. For the mainland Chinese, Taiwan was a sideshow, a symbol of China's humiliation by Japan. Its residents were suspect: they had lived for fifty years under China's archenemy, and many of them, if their Japanese mannerisms, diet, dress, and speech were any indication, seemed to have adapted alarmingly well to colonization. As ROC soldiers and administrators entered Taiwan, their first priority was to stabilize the island and wipe out any lingering Japanese sympathy or subversion. Their second was to put the island's economy to work—for the Republic of China.

Taiwan's first postwar governor, Chen Yi, was committed to both of these goals. His security policy resulted in the tragic 2-28 Incident; his economic policy was little better. Chen's approach emphasized public ownership of the "four pillars" of the economy: production, transport, trade, and finance. A substantial portion of Taiwan's wartime economy had been owned by either the colonial government or Japanese corporations. Rather than turning those enterprises over to the private sector, the ROC state took ownership of most of them, while the Kuomintang acquired others. In their desperation to save the mainland, ROC leaders pillaged Taiwan's economic assets, dismantling whole factories and sending their equipment across the Strait. Ravaged by war and instability, and with some of its most valuable industrial assets spirited off to China, Taiwan's industrial output in 1945 was only a third of its prewar peak. By 1948, inflation had soared to more than 1000 percent.

Between 1945 and 1949, Taiwan's economy suffered enormous setbacks but the collapse of ROC power on the mainland in 1949 marked a turning point. Suddenly, the ROC's survival no longer rested on mobilizing Taiwan's economy in service to the mainland; now the ROC would survive only if it could build Taiwan's economic and military power *independent* of the mainland. And it would have to do this without assistance from the United States, which had withdrawn its support (temporarily, as it turned out) after the mainland fell. Recognizing his dilemma, Chiang Kai-shek launched a thoroughgoing overhaul of the ROC's economic policies guided by the "whatsoever principle": whatsoever was required to preserve security and stabilize the economy should be done.

Chiang and his advisors' most inspired decision was to empower able technocrats to make and execute economic policy. Most governments leave economic decision making to politicians—or at least give them veto power over it—but the ROC authorized officials chosen for their technical abilities to create national economic policy based on their best judgment, then insulated those technocrats from outside pressure. The most famous technocrats were K. Y. Yin, who took the leading role until his death in 1963, and his successor, K. T. Li, who led Taiwan's economic policy making through the 1980s. The two men served in a variety of formal posts, but their real influence came from the respect and confidence afforded them by Presidents Chiang Kai-shek and Chiang Ching-kuo. Their decisions were guided by careful research and sound judgment, and a deep sense of responsibility to Taiwan and to the ROC. Ezra Vogel calls Yin and Li "Super-Technocrats," and indeed they were, but they also staffed the ROC's government agencies and commissions with ordinary technocrats of extraordinary quality.

The first round of measures aimed at rescuing Taiwan's economy included setting up the Taiwan Production Board to oversee state-owned firms, establishing a new currency (the New Taiwan Dollar, or NT), and undertaking an ambitious land reform. The land reform was risky, but it promised a high return if it succeeded. Many experts believed the KMT's failure to reform the land tenure system on the mainland had been a key factor in its loss of popularity to Mao's Communist Party. Land reform stumbled in the mainland because the ruling party was unable to act against the interests of the politically powerful land-owning class. In Taiwan, the recently transplanted KMT was not beholden to local social forces—least of all landlords, whose cooperation with the Japanese colonial regime and participation in the anti-KMT agitation of 1947 made them particularly vulnerable. The fragmented, terrorized landlord class offered little resistance when the government launched its reform plans.

In the first phase of land reform, undertaken in 1949, the state ordered farm rents reduced from a standard 50 percent of the harvest to 37.5 percent. Almost three hundred thousand rural families benefited from the program, which boosted their income instantly. That same year, the state sold off publicly owned land to the farmers who worked it, setting the price at two and a half years' harvest, payable in kind over ten years. Two years later, the ROC began phasing in the second stage of land reform, "Land to the Tiller." This program rested on the belief that family farming was more efficient and productive than tenant farming. Under the reform, landlords were required to sell land in excess of about nine acres to the government in exchange for land bonds and shares in publicly owned firms. The state then sold family-sized parcels to the landlords' tenants. The terms of purchase—thirty-year loans at a low interest rate—enabled tenant farmers to become independent landowners, so that by 1960, the percentage of land cultivated by the people who owned it was twice what it had been twenty years earlier. The land reform also incorporated programs to help the newly independent farmers succeed, including farmers associations, extension services, and marketing assistance. The U.S. government backed the land reform with technical assistance and financial aid.

The land reform brought both economic and political benefits to Taiwan. Economically, it boosted agricultural investment and productivity; between 1951 and 1961, per-acre rice yields increased by 37 percent. In that same period, the amount of land devoted to rice cultivation declined as farmers diversified into more profitable crops. Reducing farmers' land costs, increasing productivity, and improving farmer education combined to significantly increase farm incomes, reduce income inequality, and boost farmers' assets. Land reform's political benefits flowed directly from its economic merits. The policy transformed several hundred thousand landless peasants into independent farmers. It raised their incomes, improved their social status, and integrated them into empowering organizations. Not surprisingly, most Taiwanese viewed the land reform as a positive development, and they gave much of the credit to the ROC state, especially its local representatives. Thanks to the land reform, rural Taiwanese came to see the ROC government as more than an alien, occupying force.

Unleashing Taiwan's agricultural productivity was an important step in promoting economic development, but ROC leaders understood that it was only a first step. To build Taiwan into a base capable of propelling the ROC back to mainland China would require industrialization, so the KMT turned its attention inward, purging corrupt officials and promoting a new cadre of economic policy makers dedicated to developing the island's economy. To jump-start industrialization, economic bureaucrats adopted policies aimed at substituting locally made goods for imports. Import-substitution industrialization is powerful medicine; many countries have become addicted to its protectionism and subsidies. But Taiwan's leaders believed they could kick the habit when the drug lost its effectiveness.

International forces also helped boost Taiwan's industrialization. Japan adopted a strategy very similar to Taiwan's, but earlier, which gave ROC policy makers the opportunity to learn from Tokyo's successes—and avoid its mistakes. Even more importantly, the onset of the Korean War reversed Washington's direction. With international Communism apparently "on the march" in Northeast Asia, Washington was keen to reinforce non-Communist states, including the ROC. It restarted the aid program it had suspended when the mainland fell, and Taiwan became a major target for U.S. development assistance. Between 1950 and 1965, when the aid program ended, the United States provided over $100 million in nonmilitary aid to Taiwan.

In the early 1950s, the KMT used a wide range of policy tools—finance, foreign exchange controls, administrative guidance, tax and tariff policies—to encourage light industry in markets with strong consumer demand, including textiles and food processing. Where private capital was reluctant to enter, the state used publicly owned enterprises. The public sector led the manufacturing boom in the early 1950s, but because it filled gaps in the supply chain, it boosted private sector growth at the same time (encouraging private enterprise also was a high priority for the influential U.S. aid officials advising the ROC government). Domestic production benefited, too, from high tariff walls and import restrictions that allowed infant industries to gain a foothold.

At first, only the state could provide heavy industry on a scale that would support consumer-oriented manufacturing, but Taiwan's economic policy gurus left room in the economy for private firms to grow into that niche. The most famous example of this public-private competitive synergy is the petrochemical industry. The state-owned China Petroleum Corporation dominated Taiwan's oil and gas market from the beginning of ROC rule in Taiwan. The CPC is involved in every stage of the petroleum industry, from exploration to marketing. Given its massive competitive advantage in the 1950s, it could have extended its monopoly beyond petrochemical fuels to plastics—but it didn't.

Despite its initial advantage—and strong state support—CPC is not Taiwan's major plastics producer. That honor belongs to a built-from-scratch private firm, Formosa Plastics. Today, the Formosa Plastics Group is a massive global conglomerate with twenty-two companies in Taiwan and six overseas, but it grew from the humblest of roots. Its founder Wang Yung-ching was born into a peasant family in 1917. His formal education was brief, but he was a tenacious entrepreneur. He opened a rice store at the age of sixteen; decades later he recalled beating the competition by staying open later and skimping on luxuries—like hot bathwater.

In 1954 Wang secured an $800,000 loan from a U.S. development assistance program to produce polyvinyl chloride resin, which he delivered in ox carts. The market for raw PVC proved limited, so in 1958 Wang founded Nan Ya Plastics Processing Corporation. From there Wang's enterprises grew to be one of the largest chemical conglomerates in the world, rivaling Dow Chemical and DuPont. Under its founder's hands-on leadership, Formosa Plastics diversified into a dizzying variety of businesses, from carpets to biotechnology to organic fertilizers composted from kitchen waste. Wang also founded charities, including hospitals, a nursing school, and technology institutes. The nursing school includes a subsidized training course to help Austronesian women escape poverty and avoid prostitution.

When Wang Yung-ching died in 2008, he was among the world's wealthiest individuals—and one of Taiwan's most admired heroes. Nor is his thrilling rags-to-riches story unique. A number of well-known Taiwanese entrepreneurs built global enterprises from scratch during the rapid-development decades. Wang and others like him are folk heroes in Taiwan, beloved for their success—and for their sometimes offbeat philanthropic activities. Wang's Formosa Plastics Group Museum includes a faux New Zealand rain forest and Wang family history dioramas. The family-owned appliance manufacturer Tatung Corporation built a university to train its engineers, and on its downtown Taipei campus constructed a full-sized white brick replica of Thomas Jefferson's Rotunda at the University of Virginia. Lin Yi-shou, the head of the E-United Group (core business: steel) built a full-service university to, as the university Web site puts it, "commemorate his mother and benefit the villages and towns where he grew up." These entrepreneurs' successes reflect their hard work and brilliance, but they could not have succeeded had Taiwan's economic policy makers not taken a balanced, pragmatic approach that allowed public and private enterprises to coexist in a competitive symbiosis.

By the mid-1950s, Taiwan's market for domestically produced goods was saturated. Growth was slowing, and more than 85 percent of Taiwan's exports were still coming from the agricultural sector. To survive, the island's nascent industries needed additional demand; to thrive they needed competition. The "medicine" of import substitution had achieved its aim, and the time had come to wean the patient. That meant shifting from import substitution to export-oriented industrialization. If infusions of cash and technical guidance from the United States were critical to the success of the import substitution model, Washington's willingness to keep U.S. markets open to Taiwanese manufactures—so long as Taiwan continued to move toward a market-oriented economy—was an equally important boon as it shifted its economy toward exports.

Taiwan's economic bureaucrats signaled the shift toward export-oriented manufacturing in 1960 when they unveiled the Nineteen Point Program for Economic and Financial Reform. The plan—which liberalized trade, expanded the role of the private sector, and encouraged savings and investment—smelled strongly of Washington, but it served the needs of Taiwan's manufacturing sector, too. Under the plan, the state expanded access to capital by reactivating banks, liberalizing access to foreign currency, and creating a stock exchange. It also implemented generous tax rules for industrial companies and their investors.

In 1958, Taiwan's government hired consultants from the Stanford Research Institute to recommend industries that would suit the island's comparative advantages. The consultants advised Taiwan to stress plastics, synthetic fibers, and electronic components—all of which soon became staple exports. Industry also benefited from the ready supply of labor in Taiwan. After the post–land reform growth spurt productivity gains in agriculture had leveled off, leaving a large rural population eager for industrial work. Although industrialization raised incomes, wage increases trailed productivity growth for several decades, thanks to an abundant labor supply, a weak labor movement, and an explosion in small, family-owned businesses.

Taiwan's innovative economic planners also invented economic processing zones—industrial parks in which firms were exempt from many taxes and regulations. The first EPZ opened in Kaohsiung in 1966. It attracted strong interest from international investors, especially manufacturers from the United States and Japan. Within two years, it had met its targets for investment, export value, and employment, prompting the state to construct EPZs in several other cities. Other government policies, including hefty spending on education, reinforced Taiwan's export expansion and helped push overall economic growth to an average annual rate of 10 percent in the 1960s and 1970s.

Large corporations, many of them state owned, provided a steady supply of industrial raw materials—energy, plastic, steel, cement—to Taiwan's export manufacturers. The export sector, in contrast, was dominated by small and medium-sized enterprises (SMEs). That pattern is another fascinating chapter in Taiwan's economic success story. Taiwan's economic divide reflected the division in the society between Taiwanese and Mainlanders. Both the education system and the structures for civil service promotion were biased in favor of Mainlanders, who were overrepresented in the military, government, and state-owned firms. As a side effect, the export-heavy private sector belonged to the Taiwanese.

Taiwan's generous investment incentives and low labor costs attracted "sunset" industries from the United States and Japan, where rising labor costs and environmental restrictions were driving out many manufacturing firms. They also attracted ethnic Chinese investors from around the world. While some foreign companies established subsidiaries in Taiwan, a more typical pattern was to contract with local firms to produce goods according to the foreign company's designs and specifications. This process—known as contract manufacturing—allowed Taiwanese firms to build their manufacturing capacity and absorb new technologies and know-how without taking on the burdens of brand building and marketing.

"It's better to be a chicken's head than an ox's ass"—so say Taiwan's entrepreneurs. The colorful idiom captures the essence of Taiwan's business culture, and it goes a long way toward explaining why SMEs play such a huge role in the island's economy—almost 80 percent of employment and 50 percent of exports. The government policies that favored state-owned firms in large-scale and heavy industry limited the growth of private firms and ensured a steady supply of industrial inputs. The state's relaxed approach to new business creation reinforced the cultural preference for being one's own boss. Together these policies allowed Taiwan's small-scale manufacturing to become the most vibrant, competitive, and successful in the world.

The "Made in Taiwan" label was as ubiquitous in the 1960s and 1970s as "Made in China" is today, and it was found on many of the same products.

Shoes, apparel, toys, small appliances, consumer electronics—these were the export goods that put Taiwan on the map. Whatever brand name they bore, they were almost always manufactured in small, family-owned factories linked together in production networks clustered around dusty village crossroads. The owners of these factories rarely had engineering degrees or MBAs; they learned their businesses by working as laborers, machinists, and apprentices. Once they'd acquired the skills they wanted, they struck out on their own, earning them the nickname "black-hand bosses"—entrepreneurs who'd gotten their hands dirty on the way up and weren't squeamish about pitching in on the factory floor.

Generations of Americans grew up with Christmas trees strung with two-inch colored-glass light bulbs on heavy wire—a classic "Made in Taiwan" product. Glass Christmas lights are as good an example as any of how Taiwan's SMEs kept the world supplied with consumer products. Making the lights and stringing them on the wire is not a high-tech process; it requires coloring, cutting, and shaping glass tubes; inserting filaments and fitting metal bases to the bulbs; attaching sockets and plugs to coated wire; and assembling and packaging the finished strands.

The Taiwanese approach to manufacturing such a product was to break down the production process and have individual firms make each piece: the metal base, the glass bulb, the wire. To maximize efficiency, factories would set up close together. Taiwan had few zoning or land-use regulations, so manufacturers were free to locate in rural areas and small towns where land and labor were cheap, but reliable transport was never far away; in our Christmas light cluster, the glass cutting and wire shops might be on either side of a banana grove or rice paddy. Any land that wasn't needed for the factory was cultivated, with agriculture supplying a small but reliable supplementary income.

Firms were family owned, and family members provided much of the labor. When orders were strong, factories ran 24/7, pulling in youngsters and relatives from the countryside to work. When business was slack, the children concentrated on school, and the relatives returned to farming or trade. Instead of paying wages to family members employed in a business, families treated factory profits as collective household income. The "Boss Wife" (*laobanniang*) was a key player in these businesses—serving multiple management functions, and pitching in when necessary on the factory floor. Involving women (and children) in production was nothing new. Whether they were farmers, artisans, or merchants, Taiwanese families had long expected all their members to contribute economically. This patriarchal form of corporate organization predominated into the 1980s, when generational and technological turnover gradually introduced professional management to Taiwan.

Clustering small firms for joint manufacturing promoted cooperation among relatives, schoolmates, and friends. It also promoted flexibility and minimized marketing costs. SMEs learned to retool quickly to meet the demand for new products. Often, a whole cluster could get by with sending one representative to trade shows to collect orders from foreign buyers. By keeping their business within close-knit networks, Taiwanese entrepreneurs were able to minimize risk while sharing know-how and capital.

Capital was especially precious in Taiwan's SME economy, because small firms' access to formal credit was minimal. Banking and finance were weak points in the ROC economy, and government credit policy favored large companies. It was nearly impossible for SMEs to borrow money in conventional ways, so they turned to informal sources of capital, including mutual aid societies, or *hui*.

Hui are a fascinating solution to the shortage of credit in developing economies; they resemble microloans, but require no outside sponsor. If a Taiwanese wants to assemble a hui, he or she (hui are very common among women) invites friends, relatives, coworkers, and business associates to join. The duration of the hui typically is one month per member; they tend to last between one and three years. The first month, each member contributes a set amount of money, and the founder takes the whole kitty. Thereafter, everyone (including the founder) continues to pay in the same monthly contribution, but the other members bid for the kitty. The winning bid is, in effect, interest paid to the remaining members. Each member gets to "buy" the kitty one time; the longer you wait, the more interest you can earn.

Today, Taiwan is saturated with formal credit, as the ubiquitous credit card ads in the Taipei subway attest. But many Taiwanese still participate in hui—and some participate in many hui at the same time. Hui do not require a credit record, documentation of income, or really any paperwork at all. A skillful player can balance interest paid and interest earned and schedule payouts when they're most needed. Of course, hui have one serious drawback: cheating. They are not legally binding, so there's little protection if a member decides to stop paying in once the member has taken his or her money out.

What makes hui possible is the dense network of relationships in which they are embedded. If a coworker asks you to join a hui to help raise a down payment for an apartment, you know that coworker will see you at work every day until that hui has played out. If the coworker disappears, that coworker knows you will find him or her (or at the very least the coworker will never work in *this town* again); 23 million people are fewer than you'd think when they're squeezed together on an island the size of Denmark. And few tears are shed for those who lose money by joining hui with strangers, because everyone understands that absolute trust is an absolute requirement for joining hui.

The era of rapid export growth provided the ideal environment for hui: dense social networks of people living close together and working in interlocking businesses. Lending money to one another to invest in their SMEs served everyone's interests; like nearly everything else the SMEs did, it concentrated resources for mutual benefit. Small-scale factories were not particularly safe or pleasant places to work. Their environmental practices did no favors to the natural world or human health. And many, many SMEs were losers in the ruthless competition for orders. Nonetheless, small and medium-sized enterprises were the foundation of Taiwan's export-led development. Like coral polyps building up a reef, thousands of tiny businesses powered by millions of small, unsecured loans built one of the world's largest trading economies.

Small and medium sized firms are the bedrock of Taiwan's economy, but a handful of consumer-oriented manufacturers did manage to get large. Tatung Corporation is to Taiwanese what GE and Ford are to Americans: a company everyone grew up with. Women of a certain age get misty remembering their first Tatung rice cooker (introduced in 1960); folks in their forties can sing the Tatung advertising jingle they watched on their first TV (black-and-white, 1964; color, 1969) with its classic import substitution tagline: "Tatung! Tatung! Local products are the best!" Tatung products brought electric power into millions of homes (generators, transformers, cable) and helped relieve the misery of long tropical summers (electric fans, 1949; air conditioners, 1964). In many ways, Tatung is an exception to the pattern of Taiwanese manufacturing: a large, consumer-oriented company producing for the domestic market. But in other ways, it's a typical family-owned company—just one that happened to get very, very big.

Tatung Corporation is the successor to Xie Zhi Business Enterprise, founded by Lin Shang-Zhi in 1918. In the early years, the company's main line of business was construction; it built the Executive Yuan complex, one of the largest Japanese-era buildings still in use today. In 1939, the company went into iron and steel manufacturing as Tatung Iron Works. It began mass production of electrical motors and appliances a decade later. In 1962 it was listed on the Taiwan Stock Exchange. In 1969 the company adopted a mascot, Tatung Boy.

Tatung Boy is a strapping, round-faced lad dressed in rugby gear, rugby ball tucked under one arm. He's cheerful and cute, but he was designed to deliver some stern lessons. To begin with, there's a slot in his head to put money in, because, as the company founder famously stated, "Entrepreneurship starts with the saving of one dollar." His extra-large head and eyes reflect the importance of staying smart and keeping an eye on consumer trends; his oversized feet reflect Tatung's pioneering spirit. The rugby outfit symbolizes teamwork.

Tatung is one of Taiwan's oldest, largest, and most successful businesses, but it remains true to its founder's penny-pinching ethic and traditional approach to business. The current chairman, Mr. W. S. Lin, is the grandson of the founder. He welcomes visitors in an old-fashioned reception room in the company's Taipei headquarters, a green-tiled first-generation office building that looks a little dowdy compared to Taipei 101. A huge, low table covered with trophies, prizes, awards, and gifts from dignitaries fills much of the room; Mr. Lin provides a quick tour of the highlights. Tatung Boy is everywhere.

It is clear from Mr. Lin's comments that Tatung's leaders credit the company founder's hands-on leadership and resolute focus on production for its success. The company doesn't spend money on fancy buildings for its executives, but it built a university to train its engineers. During the import substitution era, the Tatung brand became hugely popular, but as the economy shifted toward export-oriented development, Tatung played it safe. It sold Tatung-branded products in Southeast Asia, but its market was limited outside Taiwan. Like many smaller companies, it turned to contract manufacturing. Tatung moved into information technology (IT) in the early 1970s, making television picture tubes. Since then it has tracked technological changes closely, manufacturing computer mother boards, monitors, televisions, telephones, and other IT items for global companies. Tatung never established its own high-tech brand, but with profit margins in high-tech contract manufacturing slim and shrinking, it recently undertook a new push to internationalize its brand—a move that required breaking with the company's long tradition.

Tatung's recent history highlights another important dimension of Taiwan's economic "miracle," the shift from traditional manufacturing to high-tech production. Between 1990 and 2000, electrical products' share of Taiwan's exports doubled, to more than 20 percent. Today, Taiwan is a global leader in IT manufacturing. Its companies have a huge market share in critical IT products, and it is constantly moving forward with cutting-edge technologies, including nanotechnology and biotechnology. These developments are explored more fully in chapter 6, but the roots of Taiwan's technological leadership reach all the way back to the era of export-oriented industrialization.

The shift from import substitution to an export-based economy was not seamless. By the late 1960s, it was becoming clear that Taiwan needed to keep moving to stay ahead of its competitors. Competition from other low-cost manufacturers already was cutting into its market share. Trade restrictions and exchange-rate volatility brought further risk. The oil crisis of 1973 threw Taiwan's energy-dependent economy into turmoil. The ROC government decided to shift Taiwan's economy away from low-cost manufacturing with foreign technology. Instead, it sought to make Taiwan's manufacturing independent, with an emphasis on using technology—rather than cheap labor—to create value. To do so, it invested, too, in human capital, extending free compulsory education to the junior high school level in the mid-1960s.

To accomplish these goals, Taipei unveiled another stage in its industrial upgrading plans. The Ten Major Development Projects used government resources to build capacity in heavy industry. The private sector needed steady supplies of strategic inputs. Rather than depending on foreign suppliers, the ROC undertook a new phase of import substitution, setting up its own facilities in petrochemicals, steel, shipbuilding, automobiles, and electronics. The Ten Major Development Projects also aimed at breaking through infrastructure bottlenecks that were limiting growth. Some industries succeeded; others, notably shipbuilding and autos, failed, but the shift toward high-technology, low-energy industries that began in the 1970s kept Taiwan's economy moving forward, toward the information age.

When the KMT first arrived in Taiwan, its ambition for science and technology was limited. Until the mid-1960s the ROC government was content to allow Taiwanese manufacturers to license the technologies they needed; developing new products and patents was not a high priority. Taipei's interest in science and technology jumped abruptly when the PRC exploded a nuclear weapon in 1964. The successful nuclear test was incontrovertible evidence that Taiwan would never conquer the mainland with conventional military force and raised frightening questions about the ROC's very survival. It prompted a reexamination of science and technology policy.

In 1969 the ROC government created the high-level Committee for Science Development. Its members included some of the government's most powerful men: Minister of Economic Affairs K. T. Li, Minister of Education C. H. Yen, and Minister of National Defense (and future president) Chiang Ching-kuo. The members recognized that industrial upgrading was critical to Taiwan's security and economic health. They were charged with developing a comprehensive, long-term science and technology policy that would integrate progress in academic research, industrial development, and military innovation. They were determined to connect manufacturing with advances in academic science and develop a full spectrum of technical talent—from basic scientists to engineers to technicians. The Committee for Science Development invited science and technology experts from the United States to offer advice. The consultants—who shared their findings with President Chiang Kai-shek at the end of their visit—reinforced and legitimized the committee's efforts. Promoting science and technology became a national priority.

The new emphasis on technology got a boost from the oil crisis. Taiwan's economic analysts believed oil prices would continue to climb, and they were determined to find ways to insulate the island's economy against future price shocks. The U.S. decision to recognize the People's Republic of China and drop diplomatic ties with Taipei in 1972 reinforced Taipei's determination to become more independent. Throughout the 1970s and 1980s, Taiwan's government actively promoted scientific and technological development, including basic research and industrial application.

In 1973, the ROC merged three government research institutes to form the Industrial Technology Research Institute (ITRI). ITRI's charge was to develop new industrial technology and upgrade industrial techniques in the private sector, and it has been spectacularly successful. In 1976 ITRI used technology licensed from RCA to begin semiconductor research; three years later, it spun off United Microelectronics (UMC). UMC was Taiwan's first semiconductor manufacturer, and it is one of the world's leading makers of integrated circuits (IC) today. In 1987 ITRI birthed another IC giant, Taiwan Semiconductor (TSMC). In 1985 it collaborated with Giant Bicycle Inc. to develop carbon-fiber materials that allowed Giant to enter the top ranks of high-end bicycle manufacturing. Tens of thousands of ITRI "alumni" are working in Taiwan's industrial firms today.

In addition to ITRI, Taipei poured money into scientific research and education at all levels. It developed flagship research institutes, such as Academia Sinica (home of Nobel prize–winning chemist Lee Yuan-tseh), National Taiwan University, Tsinghua University, and technical high schools that prepared huge numbers of workers for skilled industrial work. It built science-based industrial parks to encourage cooperation between scientists and manufacturers. The most famous of these is the Hsinchu Science-based Industrial Park, founded in 1980, which houses more than four hundred high-tech companies in industries ranging from telecommunications to optoelectronics. In all of these endeavors, the ROC government invited private business to participate in making science policy.

The decision to promote strategic industries helped Taiwan's information technology industry flourish in the 1980s. At the same time, however, the island's rapid economic growth produced massive trade surpluses and a spike in savings. To pacify its trade partners—including the United States—Taiwan followed Japan's lead in the mid 1980s. It dropped protectionist trade barriers and allowed its currency to rise in value. These liberalizing reforms were necessary, but they raised the price of Taiwan's exports. The traditional industries that had moved to Taiwan two decades before—textiles, toys, shoes—were sunset industries once again. But this time, the sun was setting on Taiwan. For those industries, the next phase of Taiwan's economic miracle would play out in a very different venue: the Chinese mainland.

One of Formosa Plastics founder Wang Yung-ching's famous aphorisms was "develop manufacturing; don't play money games." His single-minded focus on manufacturing reflects the attitude and priorities that brought Taiwan dizzying growth rates through the 1980s. Taiwan's ambitious, hands-on entrepreneurs seized opportunities created by the development-oriented state to expand the private sector. And by the 1980s, some of the largest private firms were overtaking their state-owned competitors. In 2000, Wang's Formosa Petrochemical Company opened a refinery to compete with the China Petroleum Corporation; in 2001, the Taiwan legislature passed a bill to privatize the state-owned oil giant.

Just as Wang Yung-ching's private venture caught up with its state-owned competitor, the service sector eventually overtook manufacturing. Industry's contribution to Taiwan's economy peaked around 1980, when it constituted almost half of GDP. Since then, services have grown to occupy about three-fourths of Taiwan's economy. Agriculture—the leading sector just sixty years ago—now accounts for less than 2 percent of the island's GDP. These changes were painful for many individual Taiwanese, but the country as a whole benefited from them. Guided by technocrats and powered by the boundless energy of its high-achieving entrepreneurs and workers, Taiwan managed to stay ahead of global economic trends through the second half of the twentieth century. As the economists Hsueh, Hsu, and Perkins put it, "one of the most important lessons one can learn from Taiwan's development experience is that rapid growth requires equally rapid changes in approach."

SOURCES

Taiwan's economy has attracted intense scholarly interest and attention. Some of the most important studies—all of which I rely on heavily in this chapter—include Thomas Gold's classic book *State and Society in the Taiwan Miracle*; Li-min Hsueh, Chen-kuo Hsu, and Dwight H. Perkins' *Industrialization and the State: The Changing Role of the Taiwan Government in the Economy, 1945–1998*; Ezra Vogel's *The Four Little Dragons*; Robert Wade's *Governing the Market*; and *The Key to the Asian Miracle: Making Shared Growth Credible* by Jose Edgardo Campos and Hilton L. Root.

The Dutch description of Taiwan in the 1600s comes from Macabe Keliher's history, *Out of China: Yu Yonghe's Tales of Formosa*; and data about rice production during the land reform come from Chien-chung Chiu, "The Improvement and Production of Rice in Taiwan," *Taizhongqu Nongye Gailiangchang Yanjiu Huibao*, no. 5, 1981. Details about the role of SMEs in Taiwan's economy are drawn from Rong-I Wu and Chung-Che Huang's report for the Mansfield Foundation, "Entrepreneurship in Taiwan: Turning Point to Restart" (available online at www.mansfieldfdn.org/programs/program_pdfs/ent_taiwan.pdf). Megan Greene's book, *The Origins of the Developmental State in Taiwan*, is an excellent source of information on Taiwan's science and technology policy.

4

From "Free China" to Democratic Taiwan

To their political supporters they have little in common beyond wide smiles set in round faces. One is a Hokkien-speaking Taiwanese who has devoted her life to bringing Taiwan out of China's shadow. A political outsider, she fought her way into leadership with courage, hard work, and charisma. The other is a Mainlander, born into the Republic of China's political elite. The party he has served all his life calls itself the Chinese Nationalist Party, and its aspiration has always been to merge Taiwan and the Chinese mainland. But from a distance, these two politicians—Kaohsiung Mayor Chen Chu and Taichung Mayor Jason Hu—bear a surprising resemblance. Both are politicians whose deepest joy comes from being among the people. Both are workaholics who have suffered strokes while in office—but refused to resign—and fully recovered. Both have pressed through great personal hardship—Chen Chu early in her career, when she went to prison for her political views, Hu late in his, when he stayed in politics after profound personal losses.

Chen and Hu have something else in common, too: They are the ambitious mayors of large, complex communities whose interests and needs cannot be captured in a partisan sound bite. The mayors struggle every day with the practical challenges of governing; their careers span a time when adjusting to the changing environment has required tremendous flexibility. For Hu, that has meant accommodating the popular preference for a Taiwan separate from China; for Chen, it has meant learning to live with—and even promote—a degree of integration between Taiwan and China far beyond her expectations only a decade ago. Their histories, including those adjustments, track the development of Taiwan's democratic politics, a process so rapid, comprehensive, and peaceful that it has earned the label "political miracle."

In August 1947, a few months after the bloody 2-28 Incident, General Albert C. Wedemeyer submitted a sobering report to U.S. Secretary of State George Marshall. A recent fact-finding mission had found the situation in China grim, and nowhere more so than in Taiwan:

> The Administration of the former Governor Chen Yi has alienated the people from the Central Government. . . . The Central Government lost a fine opportunity to indicate to the Chinese people and to the world at large its capability to provide honest and efficient administration. They cannot attribute their failure to the activities of the Communists or of dissident elements. The people anticipated sincerely and enthusiastically deliverance from the Japanese yoke. However, Chen Yi and his henchmen ruthlessly, corruptly, and avariciously imposed their regime upon a happy and amenable population. The Army conducted themselves as conquerors. Secret police operated freely to intimidate and to facilitate exploitation by Central Government officials. . . . There were indications that Formosans would be receptive toward United States guardianship and United Nations trusteeship. They fear that the Central Government contemplates bleeding their island to support the tottering and corrupt Nanking machine, and I think their fears well founded.

It is hard to imagine a less promising beginning. The 2-28 Incident and the tensions that sparked it marred the Republic of China government's early days in Taiwan. Then, less than two years after Wedemeyer delivered his dreary report, Mao Zedong's Red Army drove the ROC off the mainland, leaving Taiwan's poisoned political landscape as its only refuge. The psychological and social consequences of those disastrous early encounters—distrust, anger, fear—lingered for decades, reinforced by the ROC's institutions and practices. An authoritarian mentality pervaded nearly every realm, from popular culture and education to high politics. It was only in the 1970s that Taiwanese began to resist the state in significant numbers, to demand their freedom. But when they did, they discovered an unlikely resource to support their claims: the ROC Constitution.

Although it didn't look that way in the 1950s and 1960s, the ROC state was not built on an authoritarian foundation. The constitution adopted in 1947 is a democratic document; it rests on the ideas of Sun Yat-sen, a man whose impulses—if not always his actions—leaned toward democracy. Sun's political philosophy was rooted in his "Three Principles of the People": nationalism, democracy, and well-being. His Chinese approximation of Lincoln's "government of the people, by the people and for the people" carried the same democratic promise that Lincoln had in mind when he spoke those memorable words.

Although the ROC state incorporated many compromises aimed at accommodating the political realities of early twentieth-century China, it took the three principles as the basis of its legitimacy. But democracy was not its only value—or even its primary one—for the ROC also was a nationalist state. For the ROC government, the survival of the Chinese nation was a precondition for democratization. Achieving that goal was a daunting task in a China wracked by internal division and foreign aggression. To reconcile democracy and nationalism, Sun prescribed a three-stage process. In the first phase, a military government would unite China, fulfilling the nationalist mission and establishing a foundation for democracy. During the second phase—which Sun called "political tutelage"—a provisional government would rule the nation while the Chinese people learned the skills of democratic citizenship through local self-government. Only after these two phases were completed would China enter the third and final phase—constitutional government.

Sun Yat-sen imagined the first two phases might take ten years, but as it turned out, uniting China and repelling Japanese invaders took more than three decades. In 1947 the ROC at last was able to implement the final phase. A new constitution came into effect, followed by elections throughout China that staffed local governments and two national representative bodies, the National Assembly and Legislative Yuan. The Legislative Yuan made ROC law; the National Assembly's responsibilities included naming a president, and in 1948 its members elected Chiang Kai-shek.

As the ROC entered the era of constitutional government, its political system was shot through with contradictions. It was based on democratic concepts, but rarely lived up to its founders' lofty promises. The Nationalist Party, or Kuomintang (KMT), had squeezed out nearly all of its political competitors, and Chinese politics had hardened into a violent competition between the KMT and the Chinese Communist Party. Their hot war ended when the Nationalists fled to Taiwan, but the animosity lasted for decades, and distrust between the two sides is palpable even today.

Stranded on Taiwan in 1949, the ROC government and its ruling party faced conditions as dire as any they had encountered on the mainland. Any liberal impulses they might have had were swamped by a torrent of crises, and the political institutions they set up on Taiwan overrode and invalidated most of the constitution's democratic precepts. Martial law provisions imposed in the wake of the 2-28 uprising criminalized most political debate. They empowered a military agency—the Taiwan Garrison Command—to enforce a ban on any activity that challenged the KMT's dominance. Other measures effectively suspended ROC citizens' political rights, walling off the national government from popular participation.

Despite these limitations, the constitution remained the source of the ROC state's legitimacy. Under the logic of the Cold War, the ROC carried the sobriquet "Free China." The label seemed a cruel joke to many Taiwanese, but its designation as part of the "Free World" forced the KMT-led government to justify the glaring discrepancies between its democratic promises and authoritarian practices.

The Cold War itself provided the most potent rationale for the ROC's retreat from constitutional government: rescuing mainland China from the clutches of the "Communist bandits" (*gongfei*) who had seized the motherland. From the moment he set foot on Taiwan, Chiang's battle cry was "Fight back to the mainland!" For the 2 million Chinese soldiers, officials, and refugees who moved to Taiwan from the mainland, recovering the mainland was a personal mission as well as a political mandate. They had left behind their homeland, their families, their property, their ancestors' bones. Recovering the mainland was a matter of desperate urgency.

The newcomers were mostly men, including thousands of soldiers, but there were women and children, too. One tiny refugee, born in Beijing less than a year before the Communist victory, was Jason Hu. The second son of a mid-ranking military officer, Hu grew up in Taichung. A shy boy with a slight stammer, he was one of thousands of Mainlander youths who grew up surrounded by reminders that the mainland—not Taiwan—was their true home. Theirs was a life of privileged isolation that brought many opportunities, but also cut them off from the everyday life around them.

The logic of segregation was rooted in history. The wave of Mainlanders arriving in Taiwan in 1945 came not to settle, but to reincorporate the island into the Chinese nation. They were soldiers and administrators— agents of a government headquartered on the mainland. Their job was to rule the local people, not to integrate with them. When the mainland fell, a second wave of Mainlanders arrived who were no more interested in becoming "Taiwanese" than were the first. Mainlanders were planning to go home; relationships with Taiwanese would only complicate their eventual departure. Nor were many Taiwanese enthusiastic about assimilating the Mainlanders. Both groups saw the other as far too alien to be absorbed.

Growing up on the Taiwanese side of this social divide was a little girl named Chen Chu, born in 1950 to a large farming family in Ilan County. Ilan is on Taiwan's northeast coast; as the crow flies, it is not far from Taipei, but until recently it was remote and rural. High mountains cut Ilan off from Taipei and the broad western plain where most Taiwanese live; it would take a very high-altitude crow to make that direct flight. Ilan's remoteness preserved its wild natural beauty and rich Hokkien culture. Few Mainlanders ventured over the mountains to live there, and the young Chen Chu grew up immersed in her Hokkien heritage with its unique language, stories, beliefs, music, aromas, flavors, and outlook. Her grandfather was a traditional Taiwanese patriarch who maintained a household of up to forty people, but when Chen Chu was ready for school, he took a progressive view: Chen Chu was the first girl in her family to attend high school, and she graduated from a technical college in 1968.

Even in an era when it was dangerous to speak against the government, Ilan sheltered an abiding resentment of the KMT and the ROC government, whom many in the county saw as outsiders who had imposed themselves on Taiwan by force. Chen Chu's clan shared that tradition: one biographer calls the family "pioneers of the democratic movement." Her older brothers kept Chen Chu supplied with dissident literature from the big city while she was in school, stoking her passion for justice. When she was nineteen years old, Chen Chu went to work as a secretary to Ilan's most famous independent politician, Kuo Yu-hsin. Her life in politics had begun.

As far as the ROC government was concerned, segregating Mainlanders from Taiwanese was a matter of national destiny. The government that moved to Taiwan in 1949 never accepted defeat; it planned to continue the civil war until the ROC battled back to power in the mainland. It might be cut off from most of its territory, but the state itself was intact: the National Assembly and Legislative Yuan were meeting in Taipei, the ROC's bureaucratic agencies had set up shop in offices built for Japan's colonial officials, the armed forces were fortifying their defenses—and President Chiang Kai-shek oversaw it all from the grand Presidential Office at the west end of Hsinyi Road. As long as those institutions were operating, the Republic of China was alive, and Mainlanders were its leading citizens.

Taiwanese were citizens of the ROC too, of course, but in the regime's eyes, they were citizens of a single, Johnny-come-lately province. Mainlanders, in contrast, were a microcosm of Chinese society, including people from China's many provinces and ethnic minorities. They regarded themselves as the representatives of a past and future Chinese nation; they felt obligated to their compatriots in the mainland to preserve the diversity of China's population within the ROC state. To fulfill their duties to the Chinese nation, they held themselves apart, resisted the temptation to settle down in Taiwan, and took upon themselves the job of governing the nation.

What did these duties mean in practice? To begin with, ROC citizens were required to be vigilant about protecting their Chinese identity. The province of one's birth became a key demographic datum, recorded in household registries and on identity cards. Children born in Taiwan inherited their fathers' provincial origins, allowing diversity to survive through time and intermarriage. Even if they had never visited their erstwhile hometowns, Mainlander children were raised to think of themselves as "Hunanese" or "Shanghaiese" who shared their parents' responsibility to rescue the motherland from Communism. Their duty to govern the nation meant Mainlanders trained themselves and their children for government service. Preparing for government service was exactly how Jason Hu spent his youth. He attended National Chengchi University, a training ground for future KMT leaders, and graduated from its School of Diplomacy. From there he moved to England where he earned a PhD in international relations at Oxford. After teaching for a few years in Britain and Taiwan, Hu entered the ROC government.

For Taiwanese, the ROC government's efforts to reinforce Mainlanders' Chinese identity and sense of mission looked less like the selfless humanitarianism the Mainlanders imagined it to be and more like a cynical rationalization of the newcomers' power and privilege. It is not hard to see how the demographic category "provincial origin" could look to Taiwanese like a tool for entrenching discrimination. The expectation that Mainlander youth would take government positions meant Taiwanese were expected not to take them, while a quota system guaranteeing all provinces a share of state jobs limited the number of Taiwanese who could serve.

Nor did the state limit its nationalistic indoctrination to Mainlanders. The ROC government used education and popular culture to encourage all Taiwan residents to identify with China. At first, its efforts were directed to wiping out Japanese cultural influences, but over time the focus shifted to replacing Taiwanese identities—Hokkien, Hakka, and Austronesian—with a homogenized Chinese identity. Even though more than three-quarters of the people living in Taiwan in 1950 spoke Hokkien, the ROC government imposed Mandarin as the national language. School curricula stressed Chinese history and mainland geography; students learned exactly as much about Taiwan—the only "province" most would ever visit—as they did about each of the ROC's thirty-five other provinces.

The most consequential of all the measures the ROC government took to preserve its legitimacy as a government for all of China was to freeze the national representative bodies. In 1948, citizens throughout China elected representatives to the Legislative Yuan and National Assembly. By 1950, about half of those elected members had found their way to Taiwan, where they took their seats in parliamentary bodies representing their constituents on the mainland. When the time came for new elections a year later, the Judicial Yuan made a fateful decision: the legislators elected in 1948 would retain their seats until new elections could be held in the mainland. Electing new members from among the residents of Taiwan, the logic went, would disenfranchise voters in the rest of China and overbalance the parliamentary bodies in favor of a single province. Of course, holding new elections in the mainland was never possible. As years—then decades—passed and the prospects of mainland recovery dimmed, freezing the legislature increasingly seemed like a stratagem for denying democratic representation to the people who actually lived under the ROC state: the people of Taiwan.

STIRRINGS OF RESISTANCE

Taiwanese call the 1950s and 1960s the period of White Terror—a repressive era when the regime used martial law and political "necessity" to justify harsh violations of civil and human rights. At first, the government concentrated on consolidating support and rooting out Communist sympathizers in the Mainlander community, but crushing the legacy of the 2-28 rebellion was also a high priority. In particular, the regime sought to wipe out any thought that Taiwan might seek its destiny independent of China. Thousands of Taiwanese and Mainlanders were swept up by the White Terror, suffering imprisonment, torture, even execution.

Three high-profile White Terror cases, those of Peng Ming-min, Bo Yang, and Lei Chen, illustrate the regime's preoccupations. Peng was a Kaohsiung-born professor at National Taiwan University in the 1950s. Although he was Taiwanese and his father had narrowly escaped execution during the 2-28 Incident, Peng had good relations with the government. But the more he learned, the more he doubted the regime. In 1964 Peng and two colleagues composed a manifesto criticizing the ROC's authoritarianism and calling for reform—including rights for Taiwanese. The government viewed the document as an attack on its authority and despite pressure from the United States to be lenient, it convicted Peng and his confederates of inciting others to overthrow the ROC government. Recognizing the damage the case had done to Taipei's international reputation, Peng was soon released, but he left Taiwan in 1970 and became a leading figure in Taiwan's overseas dissident movement. Twenty-five years later he returned to Taiwan as a presidential candidate—and the standard-bearer for Taiwan independence.

Bo Yang and Lei Chen were Mainlander intellectuals who had come to Taiwan with the ROC government; both ended up in prison after publishing work critical of ROC leaders. Theirs were among the writings Chen Chu's young relatives brought home to Ilan. Bo Yang had already established himself as a leading ROC literary light—with a strong anti-Communist bent—under his real name, Guo Yidong, when he began publishing satirical essays under the name "Bo Yang." Satirical essays were a popular genre in the early decades of the ROC; social critics conducted important debates in the fleet-footed, sharp-tongued format. Bo Yang was one of the best, and his mordant criticisms of KMT politicians earned him powerful enemies. But it was Popeye, the spinach-loving cartoon character, who put Bo Yang behind bars.

One of Bo Yang's jobs was to receive the Popeye comic strip from its syndicator in New York and translate it for publication in a Taipei newspaper. In a series of strips Bo translated in early 1968, Popeye and his son were celebrating their newly acquired power as owners of an island. Bo's translation had them bragging about their status as president and crown prince of the island, and fighting over who would be elected president in this nation of two voters. Bo's enemies claimed Bo Yang was using the cartoon to make seditious fun of President Chiang Kai-shek and his son (and political heir apparent) Chiang Ching-kuo. The accusations mushroomed, and Bo eventually wrote an absurd, implausible confession. Although he later retracted it, he was convicted and sentenced to eighteen years in prison. He was pardoned after seven years in the Green Island Prison, and returned to writing. In the 1990s, Guo Yidong (alias Bo Yang) founded Taiwan's chapter of Amnesty International; after he died in 2008 his ashes were scattered on Green Island.

A third White Terror victim, Lei Chen, posed a genuine threat—not to the survival of the ROC, but to the KMT's political interests. Lei edited an important journal called *Free China Fortnightly*. The magazine took the word "Free" in "Free China" seriously; its founding principles, printed in every issue, were to promote democracy and democratic values, fight Communist expansion, and bring freedom to Chinese living under Communist rule. Although it received funding from the government and its publisher Hu Shih was the ROC's leading intellectual, the magazine frequently took positions that put it on the wrong side of the KMT. Lei attracted strong criticism in 1957 when *Free China* published an editorial that dared suggest the ROC was unlikely to return to China and advised the regime to set aside this unrealistic goal to focus on improving life in Taiwan. Before long, Lei's activism moved beyond rhetoric. He began looking for ways to press forward his program of democratization. One idea was to join forces with Taiwanese politicians who were using local elections as a forum to promote reform.

Local elections were a unique feature of KMT authoritarianism. Japan's colonial government had introduced limited elections in the 1920s, and the KMT deepened and expanded Taiwan's local democracy after 1945. By the 1950s, Taiwanese were going to the polls regularly to elect leaders in villages, townships, counties, and cities, as well as representatives to Taiwan's Provincial Assembly. Local elections carried risks for the ruling party, but their benefits outweighed those risks. To begin with, the ROC's claim to be "Free China" required at least a veneer of democracy to be persuasive to audiences at home and abroad. Local elections provided sound bites and photo-ops to make that case, from newspaper articles about hot contests in remote counties to grainy photos of candidates pressing the flesh in rural marketplaces.

Good propaganda was not local elections' only virtue. The 2-28 Incident taught KMT leaders that controlling Taiwan by force would be terribly costly. The loss of the mainland two years later reinforced that lesson: the ROC could not rebuild and regroup in a hostile land. Recovering the mainland would require enlisting all ROC citizens in a common project of national unification; to do that, the regime needed to assimilate Taiwanese into the ROC—including its ruling party and government. Local elections thus became a vehicle for enticing Taiwanese into the system. Most Taiwanese politicians began their careers as independents; the KMT recruited the successful ones into the party. Once enrolled, they received many benefits, including electoral support, help with local governance, and opportunities to enhance their status.

Local elections also reduced the national government's administrative burden. Governing every little town and village in Taiwan would have required an enormous commitment of manpower, and expecting Hokkien, Hakka, and Austronesian communities to accept Mandarin-speaking administrators dispatched from the center was unrealistic. A far more promising approach would be to identify authentic local leaders and co-opt them into the KMT-led state. And what better way to identify those leaders than competitive elections?

Taiwan's local elections were flawed in many ways. Under martial law, new political parties were prohibited, allowing the KMT to monopolize the electoral process. Non-KMT candidates could—and did—participate, but without the ruling party's vast financial and organizational resources, their chances were slim. Access to money was especially important because islanders expected their votes to confer concrete benefits. An incumbent might point to new construction or an economic development project in the village as proof of his competence, but the easiest way to reach voters was to hand them something of value. In the 1950s, these gifts were most often simple household items—a towel, a box of soap powder, a packet of cigarettes—but before long, cash payments to voters were the norm. Vote buying made political campaigns expensive and lengthened the KMT candidates' head start. On the rare occasion that its financial and organizational advantages fell short, the KMT sometimes intervened in the vote counting process to deny election to independent candidates. To protect its power further, the KMT made sure to limit elected local officials' influence. The important decisions—including decisions about money—were made in Taipei.

Despite their flaws, local elections inspired enthusiastic participation. They were a stage on which Taiwanese acted out conflicts and pursued ambitions. The personal stakes were high and the competition was often heated. Assembly and council elections took place in multimember constituencies that easily devolved into unpredictable free-for-alls in which all the top vote-getters—sometimes a half dozen or more—were winners. The complexity of multimember elections increased their excitement and uncertainty.

In most counties and cities, KMT-linked politicians formed factions within the party to help them manage the complicated electoral rules; before long, a pseudo-partisan competition evolved in which faction labels (White versus Red; Mountain versus Ocean; Lin versus Chen) supplanted the KMT party brand. The fact that all the candidates were members of the same party gave the KMT leadership some leverage, but factions could be feisty. Factionalism allowed groups in society to compete for resources and power within a system of rules and institutions defined by the central government.

It was this lively crowd of grassroots politicians sparring in a complex and competitive arena that *Free China* publisher Lei Chen hoped to harness to the cause of democratic reform. In 1957, several independent politicians joined forces to contest local and provincial elections. Under the name "*Dangwai* (Non-Party) Candidates' Alliance" they endorsed candidates in local races, sponsored public meetings and openly criticized the KMT's unfair election practices. Six of their recommended candidates were elected to the Provincial Assembly, where they advocated for democratic reform. *Free China* staffers met with Alliance leaders to discuss ways they could work together to advance a pro-democracy agenda. In 1960, Lei Chen's magazine published an article calling for a new political party, to be called the China Democratic Party.

The notion of popular, electable Taiwanese politicians joining forces with Mainlander reformers was a fearsome prospect for KMT leaders. The Taiwan Garrison Command—the military unit responsible for enforcing martial law—arrested Lei and accused him of spreading Communist propaganda. Efforts by well-placed Mainlanders to free him failed. When a KMT legislator questioned the government's actions on the floor of the Legislative Yuan, the party suspended his membership. Lei's collaborators tried to press forward with the new party, but it never got off the ground. Lei Chen spent ten years in prison.

One of the men who worked with Lei Chen to bridge the gap between Mainlander and Taiwanese reformers was Kao Yu-shu. Kao was one of the most successful independent politicians of his day; in 1954, he was elected mayor of Taipei City, Taiwan's largest municipality. When he sought a second term in 1957, the story made international headlines. A *Time* magazine article published in May described Kao as "no Kuomintang . . . party stalwart, but a hard-campaigning islander":

> Overruling the advice of old-line ward bosses (who wanted to gerrymander Taipei into an independent city and make its mayor a political appointee), Kuomintang reform politicians set out to defeat Independent Kao in the next election on his own terms. . . . Candidates toured their constituencies in open cars, sound trucks blared, backs were slapped, babies kissed. Nearly all Kuomintang candidates were Taiwanese. The new tactics paid off. In Taipei, where 82% of 376,870 voters cast their ballots in a hotly argued and cleanly fought campaign, the Kuomintang candidate, Formosa-born Huang Chi-jui, roundly trounced Independent Kao, despite the fact that Kao piled up 9,000 more votes than in 1954. Government party candidates, all native Taiwanese, took 46 of the Provincial Assembly's 66 seats, four of the island's five mayoralties and all 16 magistrate posts.

Kao's political career did not end in 1957. He was elected mayor twice more, beating KMT candidates both times. Finally, the "old-line ward bosses" got their way: to avoid yet another embarrassment, the regime elevated Taipei City to "special municipality status" with an appointed mayor in 1967. Cleverly, though, the central government gave Kao the position; later he was appointed to a cabinet post.

Arresting Lei and muzzling Kao broke up the collaboration between Mainlander intellectuals and Taiwanese politicians, but it did not silence the nascent opposition movement. Local politicians continued to use electoral campaign events as occasions for criticizing the regime; those who were successful took their message into municipal and provincial government chambers. And the size of their platform was about to expand.

The ROC government had been designed for the whole of China, so when its jurisdiction contracted to include only Taiwan and a few tiny islands, its institutions were an awkward fit. To cope, the regime walled off the national government, sharply limiting Taiwanese people's access to it. Provincial and local politics flourished, but national politics became ever more frozen and crabbed. Factions battled behind the scenes for power and favor within the ruling party while the national representative bodies atrophied. Fewer than half the members of the Legislative Yuan and National Assembly elected on the mainland in 1948 were still attending sessions a decade later. Many had never come to the island; many of those who did make the move were growing old and infirm. By the mid-1960s, the government faced a crisis.

In 1966 the National Assembly approved "supplementary" elections to replenish the national bodies' dwindling ranks. Three years later, Taiwanese elected fifteen new representatives to the National Assembly and eleven to the Legislative Yuan. All of the National Assembly members and eight of the new legislators were KMT members, and they represented a tiny portion—less than 3 percent—of all national representatives, so the elections posed no threat to the KMT's power. Nonetheless, the change was significant. All twenty-six new representatives were Taiwan born, and they won their seats in competitive elections. For the first time, the Taiwanese people had a voice in national institutions. The regime's decision to hold supplementary elections also represented a tacit acknowledgment that stabilizing the ROC's political future could not wait until the mainland was recovered.

As the 1970s dawned, the island seemed headed toward a political breakdown, but instead the decade saw a democratic breakthrough. The supplementary elections had not reversed the national institutions' decline, and Chiang Kai-shek's advancing age made the question of succession increasingly urgent. Taiwan's economy stumbled due to disrupted energy supplies and flagging global markets. At the same time, the People's Republic of China was recovering from its chaotic Cultural Revolution and establishing diplomatic ties with countries around the world, undercutting the KMT's hopes for mainland recovery and undermining Taiwan's international status. Worst of all, from the KMT's point of view, the United States, Taiwan's longtime ally, opened a dialogue with Beijing in 1971.

It was a perfect storm: political decline, economic troubles, and international isolation. Taiwan's leaders could have responded by tightening their grip and staying the course. But that is not what they did. Chiang Kai-shek's impending death was a taboo subject in public, but behind the scenes KMT leaders were smoothing the way for his son, Chiang Ching-kuo, to take his place. In 1972, the younger Chiang—known in the West by his initials, CCK—was appointed premier. After his father died in April 1975, CCK took over the all-important position of KMT party chair. He became president in 1978.

Chiang Ching-kuo's biography held little promise for his future as a reformer. From age fifteen to twenty-seven he lived in the Soviet Union, first as a student, then as a political hostage. He was allowed to return to China only after his father revived his alliance with the Chinese Communist Party when Japan invaded China. As an officer of the ROC government, CCK played many roles, but his image in Taiwan was shaped by his fifteen years heading the secret police. To many Taiwanese, his was the hand behind the widespread human rights abuses of the White Terror era.

As CCK ascended toward the presidency, however, he chose a different approach. As premier, he opened new opportunities for Taiwanese in government. While Mainlanders retained a disproportionate share of national bureaucratic positions, CCK promoted Taiwanese for provincial and local posts. He appointed the first Taiwanese provincial governor and vice premier. He also spearheaded efforts to increase Taiwanese participation in the KMT, both at the grassroots level and in the leadership: between 1973 and 1979, Taiwanese representation on the KMT central standing committee more than doubled. In 1982 Chiang surprised observers by naming Lee Teng-hui—a Taiwanese—to be his vice president (and, given CCK's failing health, his likely successor). The officials CCK patronized—Taiwanese and Mainlander alike—shared his reformist ideology. Under his leadership they worked to revitalize and rejuvenate the KMT, and to make elections an integral component of the KMT's legitimacy formula.

Chiang's reformist inclinations were real, but limited. His goal was to reinvigorate the regime; he had no interest in toppling it. As the American Taiwan-watcher Gerald McBeath wrote in early 1977, "The regime has clearly expressed the limitations on dissent. Those criticizing high officials, demanding the termination of martial law, or suggesting negotiations with China will be jailed; and electoral procedures will be bent to deny office to opposition candidates with a strong base of support." Opposing the KMT was a grueling proposition. In 1977, Chen Chu's boss, the dissident politician Kuo Yu-hsin, left Taiwan for good after years of surveillance and harassment.

Under Chiang Ching-kuo, the KMT cultivated a more professional, public-spirited image. In the 1960s, most political candidates were driven by ambition and opportunities for personal gain. Money flowed freely between the central government and elected officials; the temptation to redirect some of that cash into private hands was sometimes irresistible. To make matters worse, KMT leaders tended to use party resources to manipulate the KMT factions that dominated local politics, reinforcing the pervasive corruption.

CCK sought to change those dynamics by nominating well-qualified candidates in place of well-connected politicians in the 1972 municipal elections. Money kept mainstream politicians tethered to the ruling party to ensure their access to the spoils of office; the threat of losing important nominations kept them obedient. CCK's reforms angered many local politicians, who felt the party had violated its deal with the factions. The breach created an opportunity for Taiwan's growing opposition movement.

Provincial and municipal elections scheduled for December 1977 brought these trends to a head. Dissident politicians Huang Hsin-chieh and Kang Ning-hsiang organized candidates to contest the elections under the banner of a new Dangwai movement. Huang had dropped out of the KMT years earlier and had a successful career as an independent. He supported Taipei City mayor Kao Yu-shu and he won seats in the Taipei City Council and the Legislative Yuan. In 1969, Kang Ning-hsiang had acted as Huang's campaign manager during his successful legislative bid. The coordinated Dangwai strategy these two activists engineered threw a wild card into the electoral process.

The KMT's reform-minded leadership decided to repeat its strategy from 1972 and denied nominations to many candidates linked to local factions. This time, the local factions fought back. Rather than mobilize their networks of supporters behind the KMT nominees who had displaced them, factions in several localities provided tacit support to Dangwai candidates challenging KMT nominees. Dangwai politicians captured four municipal executive positions and fourteen Provincial Assembly seats—other non-KMT candidates captured another seven, leaving the KMT with less than three-quarters of a chamber it had once monopolized. In one locality, rioting broke out when Dangwai supporters suspected a fraudulent vote count was underway. The incident revealed the depth of public distrust toward the KMT—and the importance of elections to the ROC's legitimacy.

After the 1977 fiasco the KMT abandoned its plans to replace local factions with higher-brow politicians, but the change came too late to arrest the Dangwai's growing momentum. The next round of elections was scheduled for December 1978, and the opposition again coordinated a slate of candidates, this time under the banner of the Dangwai Campaign Assistance Group. Huang Hsin-chieh headed the group, with help from the activists Shih Ming-teh and Chen Chu. The Dangwai group spent months preparing for the elections, but just days before the balloting was to take place the U.S. government announced its intention to normalize relations with the People's Republic of China—and to break off diplomatic ties with Taiwan. Although Taiwanese leaders knew the move was coming, the announcement's stark finality traumatized Taipei. Fearing chaos, the government called off the elections.

Dangwai politicians and activists were divided over how to respond. Moderates believed the regime was justified in postponing the balloting, but the militants saw the move as an excuse to derail the Dangwai's growth. The disagreement reflected an underlying difference of opinion within the Dangwai group. Despite their successful collaboration, the Dangwai legislators Huang Hsin-chieh and Kang Ning-hsiang did not see eye to eye on every issue. Kang advocated "political kungfu," turning a stronger opponent's strength against him rather than trying to overpower him. Huang believed in using strong words and actions to win democratic reform. Their relationship characterized a pattern in Taiwan's opposition movement: moderate and militant groups working together despite tactical disagreements.

Another important Dangwai politician was Yu Teng-fa, father of a long-lasting political dynasty. Yu was elected Kaohsiung County executive in 1977 under the Dangwai umbrella. His political career had begun in the KMT, where Yu was affiliated with his county's Black faction. The Black faction existed to do battle with the White and Red factions, all of which got their start under the KMT banner. For Yu, joining the KMT was a pragmatic act, not a sign of ideological commitment. But as time passed, Yu found the KMT less supportive of his undertakings—and himself more at odds with its goals—so when the Dangwai came into being he attached himself and his faction—a small army of vote bosses and ward heelers—to the upstart political force. Yu Teng-fa called the government's decision to postpone the 1978 elections an unconstitutional act that exposed the KMT's "martial law mentality," and for that he was arrested. The arrest sparked protests in his home county. The authorities removed the Dangwai-linked Taoyuan County executive Hsu Hsin-liang from office after he joined demonstrations in support of Yu. The conflict between the regime and the militants was escalating.

Yu's arrest marked the beginning of a year of rising activism. Huang Hsin-chieh pulled together key players from the Dangwai Campaign Assistance Group for a new enterprise, a dissident magazine called *Formosa*. The magazine's staff included high-profile Dangwai politicians such as Hsu Hsin-liang and provincial assembly members Chang Chun-hung and Lin Yi-hsiung as well as full-time activists like Chen Chu, Shih Ming-teh, and women's rights crusader Annette Lu. *Formosa* was the militants' answer to Kang Ning-hsiang's moderate publication, *The Eighties*. Both magazines criticized the regime and called for democratic reforms, but while *The Eighties* advocated working within the system, *Formosa* called for direct action against the government. The *Formosa* group announced plans to open "service centers" around the island, creating a network of locally based activist headquarters. With publications, coordinated electoral campaigns, and plans for local branches, the Dangwai was fast becoming a political party in all but name.

The *Formosa* group decided to sponsor a rally in Kaohsiung City on December 10, 1979, to recognize International Human Rights Day. As demonstrators gathered outside the *Formosa* service center in Kaohsiung, police surrounded the group. According to the activists, riot police trapped the demonstrators, then advanced on them with tear gas, shields, and truncheons. Photos of the incident show demonstrators using their placards to fight the heavily armored officers; Dangwai activists insist the police sent agents provocateurs to start the violence. Some police and demonstrators were injured, none seriously.

The regime seized on the Kaohsiung Incident as an excuse to round up the opposition. Chen Chu was arrested on December 13 at the *Formosa Magazine* office in Taipei. The office was in an upper story of Dangwai provincial assembly member Lin Yi-hsiung's home. Chen Chu loved working and living at the Lins' house; she was especially fond of their twin daughters. They were too young for school, so even though they lived in the heart of Taipei, their Hokkien speech bore their parents' distinctive Ilan inflection. Listening to their childish chatter in her own local accent was a tonic to the hardworking young activist.

Chen Chu was seized in her pajamas—in their race to round up the Dangwai, the police would not pause even to let her dress. She and seven other members of the *Formosa* staff were tried in military courts on charges of subversion. Thirty-seven others faced civilian trials. Even though Hsu Hsin-liang was out of the country when the demonstration occurred, prosecutors blamed him for the violence and he took political asylum in Sweden. Fearing a "fatal accident" if he were captured, Shih Ming-teh slipped through the police dragnet and sought refuge with Reverend Kao Chun-ming, head of the Presbyterian Church in Taiwan. Kao eventually arranged for Shih's safe arrest, only to find himself facing a seven-year prison sentence for harboring a fugitive. Shih was given a life sentence. Chen Chu was sentenced to twelve years. The entire militant group, it seemed, was in prison or exile.

With the militants decimated, the moderates stepped up. Kang Ning-hsiang assembled a team of first-rate attorneys to defend his Dangwai comrades. Taking the case carried enormous risks for the lawyers. For Huang Hsin-chieh's defense, Kang called on Chen Shui-bian—a southerner who had overcome enormous odds to become one of Taiwan's leading young attorneys. In his autobiography, Chen wrote that when he was very young, his mother would put him in a hole near the fields where she worked as a tenant farmer so he would not wander off. From this poor-man's playpen, Chen worked his way to Taiwan's top university. He qualified as a lawyer three years into the standard five-year law course, joined the commercial practice at a top law firm and married into Taiwan's Hokkien elite. Chen had heard Huang Hsin-chieh speak years earlier, and the firebrand's bold oratory left him "impressed from the bottom of my heart." But when the call came, the up-and-coming young lawyer with everything to lose hesitated. It was only when his wife urged him to take the case that Chen agreed.

The Kaohsiung defendants' legal team included top talent, but few expected to win. The regime was determined, as the Chinese saying goes, to "kill chickens to scare monkeys." In making the Kaohsiung defendants pay a terrible price for challenging the regime, the state planned to silence them and cow their would-be supporters. But no one was prepared for just how far the nightmare would go.

On February 27, 1980, defendant Lin Yi-hsiung's wife visited him in jail. Lin, along with several other defendants, had been beaten. His wife saw his injuries and asked if he was being tortured. Lin, who says his captors had threatened to harm his family if he spoke of his treatment, did not deny her suspicions. The next day, while police had Lin's home under twenty-four-hour surveillance, someone broke in and stabbed his mother and seven-year-old twin daughters to death. His older daughter survived, with terrible injuries. Chen Chu got the news in her prison cell: the sweet, vivacious girls with their adorable Ilan accents were dead. It was the lowest moment of her six-year ordeal.

The crime—which has never been solved—horrified Taiwanese. Lin Yi-hsiung had played no role in the Human Rights Day demonstration; he had not even planned to attend, but was called to the rally late in the day to help calm the crowd. Yet he was in prison, his family slaughtered. The brutality of the attack was unprecedented, beyond comprehension, and there was no way the regime could escape blame. A political show trial designed to silence the Dangwai instead exposed the regime's merciless determination to crush the opposition.

The Kaohsiung Incident and its bloody aftermath marred the KMT's reputation. Even within the government, there were stirrings of resistance. In 1982 the Provincial Assembly defied the ruling party and passed a resolution seeking clemency for their colleague, Lin Yi-hsiung. In the three years following the trial, Taiwanese showed their sympathy for the defendants—and their outrage at the regime—by turning out in droves to support their wives and attorneys, several of whom ran for office. Electoral campaigns gave the dissidents a platform on which to speak, and their passion moved the nation. Members of the "wives and lawyers club" finished first in a number of districts in the 1983 legislative elections. Lin Yi-hsiung's wife—

the murdered children's mother—received the third largest vote total of any candidate in the country.

The Kaohsiung Incident also damaged the KMT's reputation abroad. For decades, Washington had overlooked its anti-Communist ally's human rights abuses, but by 1979, the United States had switched its allegiance to Beijing. Taipei had lost its privileged position and with it, protection against scrutiny. The heightened attention to human rights issues under President Jimmy Carter created a welcoming environment for Taiwanese activists in the United States. On International Human Rights Day in 1982 Senator Edward Kennedy held a press conference to commemorate the Kaohsiung Incident. He said, "Political repression on Taiwan blights our mutual interests and undermines ties between our two peoples. I have spoken out against serious human rights abuses in the People's Republic of China, with which we are building an important new relationship, and I believe that the American people cannot stand aloof from capricious imprisonment and persecution in Taiwan." Pressure from the United States was yet another factor complicating the KMT's efforts to stay the course on political reform.

In short, the KMT-led government faced intense pressure to reform in the early 1980s. Taiwan's economy was strong, but, paradoxically, economic success seemed only to encourage the opposition—and increase its funding. Mainlanders dominated the central government, but in business—especially the small and medium-sized manufacturing firms driving Taiwan's explosive export growth—Taiwanese ruled. As the PRC recovered from its disastrous "Cultural Revolution," the ROC's chances of recovering the mainland appeared more remote than ever; meanwhile, the ROC was losing international recognition. Squabbling between Dangwai militants and moderates continued, but the opposition pulled itself together to post impressive electoral gains. A succession of scandals early in the decade only reinforced the gloomy prognosis facing the KMT-led authoritarian regime. The early release of the Kaohsiung Incident defendants—Lin Yi-hsiung in 1984, Annette Lu in 1985, Chen Chu in 1986, Huang Hsin-chieh and others in 1987, "ringleader" Shih Ming-teh in 1990—represented a tacit admission that the case against them was unjust.

Since the days of Lei Chen, the Dangwai's ultimate goal had been to found a new political party. Both strands within the movement shared this objective. For a new generation of militants organizing in the 1980s, founding a party was another way to challenge the KMT's monopoly on power. For the moderates, it was a tool for more effective electoral combat. In 1985, Dangwai candidates joined local elections under the slogan, "New Party, New Atmosphere and Self-Determination will Save Taiwan." A year later, Kang Ning-hsiang joined militant activist Lin Cheng-chieh to found the Committee for Organizing a Party and Carrying Out Its Construction.

Dangwai activists took encouragement from signs the reform faction was gaining ground in the KMT. In early 1986, President Chiang Ching-kuo made an important speech to the KMT Central Committee. The speech suggested CCK was ready to begin lifting the remaining restrictions on full constitutional government, including martial law, the ban on new political parties, the suspension of national-level elections, and measures limiting local autonomy. The list included all of the issues Dangwai activists cared most about, although the president did not address the activists' intangible concerns, mainly equality for Taiwanese and Mainlanders and the increasingly popular idea that Taiwan should think of itself as a self-determining entity.

On September 28, 1986, Dangwai activists gathered at Taipei's Grand Hotel to finalize their candidate list for elections three months later. As a pet project of Chiang Kai-shek's wife, the Grand Hotel seems an odd choice for the opposition's meeting, but the grandeur of the setting suited the historic business they had come to conduct.

If their business was historic, it was risky, too. Only a few days earlier, the minister of justice had reminded Taiwanese that forming new parties remained illegal and punishable by law. To avoid trouble, the Dangwai activists reserved their meeting room in the Grand Hotel under the guise of a local Rotary Club—although with Dangwai celebrities like the newly released political prisoner Chen Chu in the room, no one was fooled. The participants had a full agenda, and it was late in the day when a proposal to found a political party came to the floor. The activists debated the measure—would a new party give the KMT a pretext to exclude their candidates from the December election? Would it be better to form a committee to *study* founding a new party?—but when the chair called the vote, the answer was unequivocal. Moderates and militants stood united behind the banner of the Democratic Progressive Party (DPP).

The opposition's move sparked a vigorous debate within the KMT. Conservatives believed failing to enforce the law against the new party would invite chaos. Reformers feared the regime's shaky legitimacy might not survive another crackdown. In the end, President Chiang and his pro-reform team prevailed. Following behind-the-scenes assurances from DPP moderates that the new party would stay away from the KMT's chief taboos— Communism and Taiwan independence—the regime did nothing. A week later, CCK told the *Washington Post* he intended to lift martial law as soon as a national security law was in place, a promise he delivered in July 1987.

Ending martial law enabled massive changes in Taiwan's political scene. Martial law provisions had restricted far more than dissident political activity and new political organizations. To begin with, it sharply limited the media. Prior to 1987, only thirty-one newspaper licenses existed in Taiwan. For decades, publishers had traded those licenses within a narrow circle of

KMT-linked organizations and firms. The end of martial law opened the industry to anyone with the capital and ambition to publish a newspaper. Among the first new licenses was one issued to Kang Ning-hsiang's *Capital Daily*. Like most of the papers born in that heady moment of possibility, the paper failed. But the new papers failed for financial reasons, not because their political views threatened the KMT. The government did not issue new television broadcasting licenses, so the three existing stations—all closely tied to the regime—kept their monopoly, but it did open new radio frequencies. Hokkien and Hakka-language broadcasters were the main beneficiaries.

Ironically, the DPP was not the first opposition party to gain official recognition when martial law ended. Technically, it was still illegal, while several other parties applied for and attained legal status as soon as martial law was gone. However, none of those parties had the DPP's political weight; a significant third party was not born until 1993, when the Chinese New Party split from the KMT. The DPP proved too important to ignore, and within a few months, the Democratic Progressives had achieved formal recognition. Taiwan was now officially a multiparty state.

President Chiang Ching-kuo accomplished these critical changes just in time. On January 18, 1988, barely six months after ending martial law, he died. His reformist agenda lived on, however, in his successor, Lee Teng-hui. Lee was born in 1923, a subject of the Japanese empire. It was not until he was a grown man that Lee became a Chinese citizen. He studied in Kyoto during World War II and served in the civil defense forces. A decade later, he was in the United States, studying at Iowa State University. He worked as an economist in Taiwan for several years then returned to the United States, earning a PhD in agricultural economics at Cornell University in 1968.

One element missing from Lee Teng-hui's varied background was any relationship with China or its ruling party. Still, when Lee returned to his homeland after graduate school, the KMT was an obvious affiliation for the brilliant, ambitious, globally savvy young Taiwanese. He joined the KMT in 1971 and was put in charge of agricultural policy. In 1978 he was appointed mayor of Taipei City. Three years later he became governor of Taiwan province. From there, he moved into position as CCK's vice president.

During his years as a KMT member and ROC government official, Lee stuck close to the party's official ideology, including its insistence on recovering the mainland. He made hundreds of speeches paying homage to the KMT's dream of mainland recovery. As president, he instituted the Guidelines for National Unification, a blueprint for uniting Taiwan with mainland China. It was only after he stepped down after twelve years as president of the Republic of China that Lee was free to speak his mind. And what was in his mind was surprising indeed: he soon became the world's most prominent Taiwan independence advocate.

When he assumed the presidency in 1988, those stunning revelations were far in the future. At the time, the big news was that Taiwan's leadership at last was in the hands of a Hokkien-speaking Taiwanese, not a Mainlander transplant. The fact that Lee was also a KMT-affiliated technocrat did little to dampen his compatriots' enthusiasm. Taiwanese rejoiced—even the opposition recognized that the elevation of one of their own to the top position was a big step forward. At the same time, though, Taiwanese worried that Lee might have a hard time winning support from his KMT colleagues. He would need to be confirmed as party head, and then, in 1990, he would need to win reelection in a National Assembly vote. Many observers wondered whether Lee had the political dexterity to overcome conservatives' objections and secure his position.

In the early months of Lee's presidency, observers focused their attention on the hard-core conservatives pressing him from the right. This faction had dominated ROC politics for decades; without his mentor, CCK, Lee seemed vulnerable. What resources could he muster to counterbalance the conservatives' political weight? Lee Teng-hui's response was pure genius: instead of trying to pacify the conservatives, Lee harnessed the popularity of democratization to strengthen his own position. He became a leading reform advocate; in the process, he increased popular support for the KMT and marginalized the conservatives.

In December 1989, county and city executiveships, provincial assembly seats, and supplementary positions in the Legislative Yuan were all up for election. In its campaign, the DPP hammered the KMT on the slow pace of reform. In particular, the Democratic Progressives demanded the "senior representatives" (whom opposition supporters called "old bandits") elected in 1948 yield their seats to new representatives elected from among Taiwan's population. The issue worked well for the DPP, because the KMT—despite Lee's efforts—had not been able to persuade the senior representatives to vote themselves out of a job. While the KMT won the vast majority of seats in 1989, the DPP made significant progress. Lee used the election results as evidence that the KMT must push forward with reform to remain electorally viable.

A few months after the election, Lee's strategy faced a critical test. The presidential term Lee had inherited from CCK was ending and he needed the National Assembly—overwhelmingly peopled by senior representatives—to confirm his bid for another term. The conservatives put forward a team of their own, and it took Lee and the reform faction months to persuade his opponents to withdraw. To recapture his momentum, Lee used another bold, creative move: he convened a National Affairs Conference. The idea was to gather representatives of all political stripes with scholars, business leaders, and other VIPs to build consensus on how Taiwan could realize the democracy promised in the ROC Constitution.

Some critical issues were resolved even before the conference began. Taiwan's supreme court, the Council of Grand Justices, ruled the senior representatives must step down. Then Lee announced a plan to abolish the martial-law era statute that gave the president extra-constitutional powers. Delegates to the National Affairs Conference continued the reform trend, agreeing to pull down the remaining obstacles to democratization. Among their recommendations were direct election of the provincial governor, Taipei mayor, and Kaohsiung mayor—even the president. As the architect of the conference, Lee Teng-hui earned praise for bringing the island to consensus on completing its democratic transition.

The early 1990s saw a cascade of democratic "firsts": the first election of all-new National Assembly members in 1991, the first election of an all-new Legislative Yuan in 1992, the reintroduction of directly elected Kaohsiung City and Taipei City mayors in 1994, the first direct election of the provincial governor in 1994, and, in 1996, the first popular presidential election—which made Lee Teng-hui the first person in history to be directly elected to lead an ethnic Chinese nation.

Jason Hu left teaching in 1990 to become an aide to President Lee, joining an ROC government far different from the one his father had served in the 1940s and 1950s. In a succession of positions in the "new Taiwan," including government spokesman and representative to the United States, Hu understood that his primary duty was to the people of Taiwan. As a diplomat, his job was not to rehash the Cold War, but to cultivate support for a democratic, pro-Western Taiwan.

Lee Teng-hui was a prodigious force in Taiwan's modern history. He presided over the transformation of its domestic politics while deftly managing its fast-moving relations with the mainland. He fended off unwelcome initiatives and refused to back down in the face of military intimidation. In doing so, Lee signaled to Beijing that unification in any form would require lengthy and sensitive negotiation. He made it clear that whether Beijing's plan was to absorb Taiwan into the PRC or unite with the ROC in a marriage of equals, Taiwan would hold out for its own interests. He was wildly popular, so much so that the media coined the pseudo-psychological term "Lee Teng-hui Complex" to describe Taiwan people's attachment to him.

Inevitably, the retirement of this towering figure left a yawning hole in Taiwan's political scene, so the approaching 2000 presidential election brought Taiwan voters' excitement and uncertainty to new levels. Few observers believed a Democratic Progressive candidate could win the presidency. The party's vote share in national and municipal elections hovered around 40 percent, a respectable showing, but not enough to win a presidential contest—and its 1996 presidential candidate had done only half that well. Still, the party united behind its best hope, Chen Shui-bian.

In 1994 Chen—often called by the Hokkien nickname A-Bian—had exploited a split in the KMT's vote base to win the most valuable prize in Taiwan's local politics: the Taipei City mayorship. Elected with only 44 percent of the vote, Chen set aside ideological issues to address the city's practical needs. In his four-year term, the DPP mayor managed to win over much of Taipei's heavily Mainlander population; his approval ratings climbed to over 70 percent. Chen sought a second term in 1998, but this time the KMT was ready. It nominated its most popular politician—the charismatic Ma Ying-jeou—and made sure there would be no challenger from the conservative side. Although Chen's share of the vote improved in both number and percentage, Ma won the election. DPP supporters saw the outcome as proof that Mainlanders were unwilling to support a Taiwanese—even one as successful as Chen. The 1998 setback had at least one benefit, though: it freed Chen to run for president in 2000. And incredibly, he found himself once again facing a divided KMT.

Lee Teng-hui had several would-be successors, men waiting with ill-disguised impatience for him to step down. The 2000 presidential race was their chance. Despite party leaders' heroic efforts to defuse intra-party competition, two KMT politicians insisted on running. The first was Lee's vice president and heir apparent, Lien Chan. When Lien was named the KMT's official nominee, another presidential hopeful, James Soong, announced he would run as an independent. In 1994, Soong had been elected governor of Taiwan province, which included all of the ROC's territory except Taipei City and Kaohsiung City, making him the only KMT politician other than Lee to have experience winning a large-scale election. As governor (the position was eliminated along with most provincial governing bodies in 1998), Soong forged tight alliances with local politicians across the island. He used those relationships to challenge the KMT party apparatus and its standard-bearer, Lien Chan, in the 2000 election.

THE CHEN SHUI-BIAN ERA

When the votes were counted, the 2000 election turned out to be a replay of the 1994 Taipei mayor's race. Chen picked up the usual DPP vote share, while Soong and Lien split the KMT vote. Party leaders insisted to the end that Lien would win, and refused to transfer their support to Soong. Lien and Soong both tried last-ditch "dump-save" appeals—a popular Taiwanese electoral strategy of urging voters to "dump" a failing first-choice candidate in order to "save" their second choice—but if their appeals worked at all, they merely traded votes. In the end, the KMT won its traditional vote share, but divided in such a way that neither candidate was successful. Chen won with 39 percent. Soong followed with 37 percent, and Lien took up the rear with 23 percent of the vote.

The 2000 election was truly historic: an opposition party candidate had captured the top office in the Republic of China. Chen Shui-bian had completed his journey from poverty to presidency. After decades of struggle, Taiwan's democratic activists and politicians took enormous pride and satisfaction in Chen's victory. But they were not naïve about its implications. They knew a president elected by a plurality of the vote, facing a legislature dominated by KMT politicians who had long assumed governing was their party's birthright, would face daunting challenges. As one of Chen's young aides told me a few weeks after the election, "For about the first three hours we were ecstatic. And then the truth began to set in, and I thought, 'what have we gotten into now?'"

Some observers feared the KMT might not accept defeat, but KMT activists directed their ire inward. Some blamed Soong for splitting the vote; others blamed Lee Teng-hui, whom they said had rammed through an unpopular nominee but not done enough to secure his victory. Before long, a conspiracy theory was circulating: Lee secretly preferred Chen, and chose Lien precisely because he knew he couldn't win. The rancor within the party was too great to overcome, and before long, Lee quit the KMT. Soong founded a party of his own, the People First Party (PFP). During the Chen presidency, the KMT and PFP cooperated in what they called the "Pan-Blue Camp." Soong's fortunes declined and most PFP politicians eventually were reabsorbed into the KMT.

The Blue Camp didn't try to overturn the election results, but they had no interest in helping Chen govern, either. The Blues held a large majority in the Legislative Yuan, and they used that power to block Chen's initiatives—including some that were consistent with past KMT policy. When Chen selected a respected KMT official to be his premier, the poor man was pilloried by his former colleagues for accepting the post. Chen's high-level appointees were a mix of KMT members, Democratic Progressives, and independents; for the non-KMT administrators, this was their first taste of high-level service. Chen Chu, who had headed the labor affairs department in Kaohsiung City, was tapped to head the Council of Labor Affairs, a cabinet-level post. Losing the presidential office forced many KMT bureaucrats to look for new work. In 2001, Jason Hu left the protection of the civil service and entered the political fray as a candidate for the mayorship of Taichung City, his hometown. He won the post.

PRC policy toward the Chen administration mirrored the Blue Camp's obstructionism, denying Chen any accomplishments in cross-Strait relations. During the campaign, Chen promised to push for direct transportation links between Taiwan and China. Taiwanese businesspeople were losing a fortune in time and money by flying indirectly, typically on flights that connected through Hong Kong. What should have been a few hours' flying time from Taipei to Shanghai or Beijing became an expensive, full-day ordeal. But without Beijing's cooperation, Chen could not deliver on his promise, and the PRC was not about to hand him a political victory. The diversions to Hong Kong continued, costing Taiwanese businesses millions.

With little to show for his moderation, Chen found himself under increasing pressure from hardliners in his own party. Those who had questioned the wisdom of the moderate strategy felt vindicated: obviously, they argued, neither the PRC nor the KMT was interested in real negotiation or compromise. Trying to cooperate with them was futile; if the Chen presidency was to mean anything, they said, Chen must take whatever power he possessed and use it to advance cherished DPP goals.

The showdown came in October. When the legislature appropriated funds to complete a fourth nuclear plant, Chen refused to release the money. Opposing nuclear power was a defining principle for the DPP, but KMT legislators were so furious at what they considered an abuse of executive power that they launched a petition to recall him from office. It was the first of many recall attempts that would be made during Chen Shui-bian's eight years in office.

Chen's outreach to Beijing lasted longer, but when the first two years of his presidency passed with little sign that the PRC's position might change, Chen finally tacked in a new direction. In August 2002, Chen infuriated Beijing when he described Taiwan and China as "one country on each side of the Strait." He followed the statement with a series of policies that enraged the Beijing leadership even more—including endorsing a long-simmering campaign to institute a national referendum process. Chen argued that ballot measures could be used to signal societal consensus or resolve controversial policy issues, but the truth was, he also hoped to find a way around the legislative resistance that stymied his efforts.

Beyond these practical benefits, Chen and his party saw political advantage in the referendum plan. The idea of a referendum process made conservatives nervous, not least because the first people to mention the idea were activists in exile who hoped to use a plebiscite to bring about Taiwan independence. Still, conservatives were wary of coming out too strongly against the idea for fear they would be pilloried for trying to limit Taiwan's democracy. The DPP was more comfortable fighting on ideological ground, especially when its position could be construed as standing up for Taiwan's democracy and freedom.

If referendum in general was a winning issue for the DPP, specific referendum proposals could be even more advantageous. DPP activists believed they could design no-lose propositions—a proposal supporting Taiwan's participation in international organizations, for example—that would mobilize the party's base and appeal to centrist voters. If the referendum were held on the same day as other elections, it could have a "coattails effect" that would sweep DPP candidates into office. The timing seemed perfect for Chen Shui-bian's reelection in March 2004. The only thing lacking was legislation establishing a referendum process.

The battle to pass that legislation dominated Taiwan politics in 2002 and 2003. PRC leaders were convinced the referendum process was aimed at advancing the independence cause, and the way the DPP designed its referendum-enabling law gave credence to those fears. To make it harder for the KMT to oppose, the DPP proposal made it very difficult to call for a referendum—except in one circumstance: if Taiwan were threatened militarily, it could use a so-called defensive referendum to rally the people. To the PRC, this looked like an escape clause justifying an independence vote. To Taiwanese voters, it looked entirely reasonable. The KMT fell back on its general distrust of the DPP as its argument against the referendum proposal—a weak position.

For months, the KMT used its legislative majority to block the DPP's referendum proposal, but in October 2003, Chen Shui-bian experienced an expected windfall thanks to an unlikely benefactor: the United States. For George W. Bush, support for Taiwan was an ideological reflex. Early in his presidency he made a number of gestures that suggested he would be more pro-Taiwan than any recent predecessor, including at one point saying the United States would do "whatever it takes" to help Taiwan defend itself. America's basic policy did not change, but U.S. foreign policy officials sent mixed messages and Taiwanese officials interpreted them according to their own preferences. When it came to the referendum project, American officials were troubled by Chen's lackadaisical attitude toward Beijing's objections, but they were reluctant to go on record opposing a democratic right for the Taiwanese people.

The issue took on new urgency in September 2003 when Chen announced his intention to create a new constitution for Taiwan, to be ratified by a popular referendum in 2006 and put into effect in 2008. While Chen argued that Taiwan needed a new constitution to address inefficiencies in existing political institutions, he also said the new document would make Taiwan "a normal, complete, great state." In Beijing, these were incendiary statements; Chinese leaders convinced themselves that a new constitution would mark the beginning of an independent Taiwan. Washington was not happy with the idea either, nor was it pleased that Chen announced it without first warning U.S. officials. Nonetheless, Chen was allowed to make a transit stop in the United States a month later. American officials tried to keep the trip low key, but the Chen administration and the Taiwan media trumpeted it as proof that the Bush administration supported Chen's approach. When the White House appointee responsible for the visit, Therese Shaheen, described President Bush as Chen's "secret guardian angel" the Democratic Progressives were ecstatic.

Back in Taiwan, Chen's opponents panicked. With the United States now apparently on record supporting Chen, there seemed little point in continuing to resist his agenda. Within days the legislature passed a bill enabling referendum votes in Taiwan. KMT legislators thought the restrictions built into the legislation would make it impossible for the DPP to introduce a referendum alongside the March presidential election, but Chen quickly put forth two proposals under the "defensive referendum" rubric. With the presidential election barely four months away, the KMT was outfoxed.

Chen's first term in office did not please Beijing or the KMT, but it was not the catastrophe many had predicted. Chen delivered few of his campaign promises, but many voters blamed those disappointments on obstructionist legislators and hostile Chinese officials. Democratic Progressive strategists knew it would be hard to beat a well-prepared opponent, but with the plenty-of-blame-to-go-around logic in play and the referendum energizing their grassroots supporters, they thought luck and determination might just get Chen a second term.

The KMT and PFP united behind what looked to be a very strong Blue ticket: Lien Chan as the presidential candidate with James Soong in the vice presidential spot. The ordering of the candidates was curious: Soong had won 50 percent more votes than Lien just four years earlier. But the KMT was determined not to reward Soong for his maverick action, and Soong's grassroots connections were stale. The KMT began the electoral season with a reasonable expectation: Lien and Soong had proven they could win 60 percent of the vote running separately. Running together they could easily pass 50 percent.

Or could they? Lien Chan had never been a popular politician. Lien's clan had been on Taiwan for generations, but in the early twentieth century his family moved to the mainland. In Taiwan's complex ethnic landscape, this kind of family was known as "half-mountain"—and the term is not a compliment. Although Lien claimed to be a Taiwanese, his half-mountain status counted against him. An even stronger strike against Lien was his reputation as a silver-spoon baby. Chen Shui-bian was born to a poor farming family; his success was due entirely to his brilliance and hard work. Lien was born into wealth and privilege. Chen's wife was a democratic martyr, paralyzed when a truck plowed into her during a political rally in the 1980s. Lien's wife was a former beauty queen. Finally, Lien lacked the charisma needed to campaign effectively—a quality Chen possessed in abundance.

The campaign was intense, even more rancorous than in 2000. In that year, the KMT had been confident; the Soong challenge was annoying, but a DPP victory seemed implausible. In 2004, the Blues had learned their lesson. They were not about to lose again.

But lose they did, for many reasons. One was Lien's weakness; another was the sharp decline in enthusiasm for Soong. The DPP's crowing about the "Secret Guardian Angel" remark influenced some voters. The DPP also worked hard to avoid a repeat of the 1998 Taipei mayoral election. Chen's supporters hammered away at Blue Camp obstructionism and they appealed to Hokkien-speaking Taiwanese to show solidarity with one of their own. Their core argument was simple: the KMT never accepted the verdict we, the people, delivered in 2000, so Chen deserves another chance to show what he can do.

And then, on March 19, the night before the election, the election took a bizarre twist. Chen and his running mate, vice president Annette Lu, were standing in an open jeep, driving through the streets of Tainan, waving to voters. As the parade wound down, Chen and Lu both realized they were injured and bleeding. When they looked more closely, they discovered they'd been shot, he across the abdomen (the bullet lodged in his jacket after gashing his skin), she in the knee. Taiwan's army of talk-show hosts jumped into action. On the DPP side, pundits stirred up pity for the injured president, recalling the bad old days of KMT violence against political opponents. In contrast, KMT-leaning talk show hosts were skeptical. Sisy Chen, a former DPP activist who had morphed into Chen's most strident TV critic, used her show to propose a theory: the shooting was a setup, staged by the Chen campaign to win sympathy votes.

Sisy Chen's accusations drove the DPP's supporters to a fever of outrage. That she would jump to the conclusion, before any medical, forensic, or police evidence was available, that Chen had faked the shooting confirmed everything the "Deep Greens" believed about the mass media and Chen's detractors. It seemed there was no limit to KMT pundits' hatred of Chen, and by extension, of all those who opposed the KMT's political domination.

No one knows what effect the events of March 19 had on the outcome of the election. The race was close coming into the final week, but whether Chen would have won without the "Two Bullet Incident" is unknowable. Many KMT analysts and foreign scholars are convinced the shooting boosted turnout among Chen's supporters and won him a significant number of sympathy votes. I spent March 20 visiting polling stations in a rural part of central Taiwan, and my conversations there left me convinced that the fury at Sisy Chen's accusations was even more powerful a factor than the shooting itself. Whatever the dynamics, when the votes were counted, Chen had won by a tiny margin, less than twenty-three thousand votes, or two-tenths of 1 percent.

In 2000, the Blues had turned their frustration and disappointment inward, but in 2004, they lashed out. When the Central Election Commission declared Chen the winner, Lien Chan appeared on television, his face a white, frozen rictus of fury. Instead of the concession speech viewers were expecting he said, "This election is void. I demand a recount."

For weeks, Taiwan's democracy teetered on the brink of crisis. Angry demonstrators mobbed the streets outside the presidential office building.

The president's name was painted on pavement next to the words "spit here." KMT officials attacked Chen in increasingly provocative terms. A PFP legislator told the *Financial Times*, "We need to storm the fortifications. You cannot conduct a revolution if you think about your public image. Only with open conflict will we be able to scare Chen Shui-bian." Conspiracy theories abounded, and rumors that the PRC might use the turmoil as a pretext to "intervene" in Taiwan spread. There were even whispers that the Blue Camp might *invite* the PRC to overthrow Chen. The DPP dared not celebrate Chen's victory for fear of further inflaming the demonstrators. As one campaign worker said, "When we lose, we can't cry; when we win, we can't cheer."

At the heart of the upheaval were two mysteries: How could a united Lien-Soong ticket lose to Chen? How could two people be shot and not know it?

The first question is answered above: A combination of factors convinced a tiny majority of Taiwan's voters that Chen was a better choice. The second question requires a little up-close-and-personal description of Taiwanese elections. Taiwanese political candidates do many things an American would recognize: they make speeches, they buy TV ads, they hang posters, they stand in shopping centers and shake hands with people. They also do a few less familiar things: they wear sashes like beauty pageant contestants, they sing karaoke, they burn a lot of incense in temples (sometimes they swear oaths there, too, inviting the gods to smite them on the spot if they're lying). They also "sweep the streets."

Street sweeping is mandatory for political candidates in Taiwan. The candidate assembles a parade of supporters, some walking, others riding on sound trucks (pickups outfitted with stages and loudspeakers) who scour the streets of the district singing the candidate's praises. The idea is to cover every street, so the parade doubles back again and again, east to west, north to south, until every inch of the district is covered. Voters come out to watch, and the candidate, his wife, lieutenants, and surrogates press the flesh on all sides. To make sure no one misses the show, campaign assistants let off fireworks at every corner. I've seen men teetering atop moving sound trucks with cartons of bottle rockets balanced above their heads on one hand while they light the fuses with the other. The din is spectacular, the smoke is overwhelming, and the fireworks are a menace. This is what Taiwanese enjoy most about elections: what they call *renao*, the hot and noisy.

Chen and Lu were street sweeping in Tainan City when they were shot. According to foreign TV cameramen following in a second open jeep, the air was thick with smoke from firecrackers, and bottle rockets were bouncing off cars, people, cameras—everything. One said he could smell his hair smoldering as ash and half-burned paper from the fireworks drifted into it. Chen and Lu reported that they initially assumed the shots that hit them were ordnance raining down from their supporters—as it turns out, Taiwanese political candidates get used to being hit by hot, fast-moving debris. And as for someone hearing the shots fired, there was no chance of that at all.

A third mystery of the 2004 election—who shot Chen and Lu?—has never been solved. The case was investigated repeatedly, but no one has determined to the satisfaction of all whether it was a setup, an assassination attempt, or something even stranger. KMT efforts to unearth a conspiracy continued well into Chen's second term, but the crisis over whether he would assume office settled down more quickly. Chen helped that process by agreeing to a recount, although the KMT blocked it in the legislature. He also used his second inaugural address to calm both his supporters and his opponents.

CHEN SHUI-BIAN'S SECOND TERM—AND BEYOND

Chen's second inaugural speech focused on reuniting a society fractured by conflicts over politics, language, ancestry, and collective memory. He addressed the postelection crisis head-on, acknowledging that his victory was narrow and political trust had been damaged. "The ultimate challenge of this past election lay not as much in garnering a mandate as in the post-election hurdle of how to scale the wall of antagonism, and in finding ways to reconcile the deep divide caused by distrust," said Chen. "We must not allow the narrow margin of victory to become a source of greater conflict in society."

In the speech, Chen reiterated his determination to make constitutional reform a top priority in his second term: "In our face-off with increasingly fierce and vigorous competition on the international front . . . we must bear in mind that historic and political circumstances confine us to an existing constitutional framework that now poses the most direct impediment to effective governance." Chen delivered on a number of important consti-tutional reforms during his second term. In 2005, the National Assembly ratified amendments that halved the number of legislators and changed the rules for electing them. It also transferred its own powers to others, ef-fectively voting itself out of existence. With the most popular ideas imple-mented, the constitutional reform process lost momentum. President Chen continued to advocate further change, but most Taiwanese preferred to wait for the previous wave of reforms to take effect before implementing more.

President Chen Shui-bian had a tough ride in his first term, and his second term began under a massive cloud. Although the Blues eventually dropped their efforts to invalidate the election result, they continued to resist Chen's every proposal, and without a legislative majority, the DPP was powerless to stop them. But those challenges paled in comparison to the cascading scandals that wracked his presidency from 2005 to 2008. The trouble began when construction workers brought from Thailand to build a subway in Kaohsiung City protested their working conditions. That led to an investigation of one of President Chen's close advisors, which in turn unearthed evidence the aide was involved not only in labor exploitation, but in misappropriation of public funds as well. The scandal forced two high-profile DPP politicians to resign: Kaohsiung's acting mayor, Chen Chi-mai—a rising DPP star who happened to be the disgraced aide's son—and the labor minister, Chen Chu.

From its founding, the DPP had made corruption fighting one of its top goals. Its reputation for cleanliness was one of the few advantages it enjoyed over the KMT. Public opinion polling consistently found voters favored the KMT on measures like competence and responsibility, while the DPP got high marks for its incorruptibility. The Chen scandals undermined that reputation. To reverse the trend a group of young politicians proposed a "New DPP Movement" aimed at returning their party to its anticorruption roots. They called on their comrades to reflect on how the party had gone astray and seek correction from the public. Instead of seizing this as an opportunity for political damage control, senior party leaders—including Chen—crushed the New DPP Movement.

The number of presidential associates in trouble with the law ballooned in 2006, and prosecutors turned their attention to Chen's family. In May, his son-in-law was arrested amid a swirl of rumors that Chen's wife, Wu Shu-jen, was involved in insider trading and influence peddling. In June, the Blue Camp tried another recall petition in the legislature. Although they could not meet the two-thirds vote threshold to send the recall to the voters, they kept up the political pressure. Before long, prosecutors were interviewing Chen himself. In November, they indicted Wu Shu-jen.

The scandals undermined Chen's effectiveness and eroded his popular support. A wave of disgust and disappointment was rising, even among DPP activists. The recall efforts united DPP supporters briefly, but the mounting evidence of malfeasance in the presidential office battered their morale. In July, a group of "Green Academics"—mainly veterans of pro-democracy student activism in the late 1980s and early 1990s—circulated a petition calling on Chen to resign. On the heels of that effort, Shih Ming-teh—who had spent twenty-five years in prison for his pro-democracy activism—led a sit-in outside the Taipei train station aimed at the same goal. Shih's supporters wore red, earning them the name "Red Shirt Army" and they occupied the square for weeks. They were an eclectic mix, but most were longtime Chen Shui-bian detractors. For the many Mainlanders in the group, standing elbow-to-elbow with Shih was an education. One rushed home to tell his daughter—a former student activist with strong ties to the DPP—some shocking news: back in the day, the KMT kept political dissidents like Shih Ming-teh *locked up*!

The rest of Chen's second term passed in a blur of corruption allegations, indictments, trials, and recriminations. During the 2008 presidential race, DPP candidate Frank Hsieh so despaired over the state of affairs that he cancelled his public appearances and went into seclusion for two weeks. The KMT's candidate was the popular Ma Ying-jeou. The nomination was salt on the DPP's wound, since Ma stood out among KMT politicians in having a reputation for incorruptibility. During a stint as justice minister in the 1990s, Ma had taken on political corruption so aggressively that the targets of his efforts persuaded Lee Teng-hui to fire him. Against most KMT candidates, the DPP could say, "Our guy hasn't done anything their guy hasn't done." Against Ma it could say nothing. Ma Ying-jeou won the 2008 election with 58 percent of the vote.

When Ma Ying-jeou won back the presidency for the KMT, Democratic Progressives felt crushed. The DPP had lost most of its legislative seats in December, thanks largely to new electoral rules that the party had championed but that worked against the party in practice. Their standard-bearer, Chen Shui-bian, had barely moved out of the presidential office when he was moved into another government building: a Taipei City jail. To many of Taiwan's democracy activists and advocates, those setbacks seemed insurmountable. Grief hung over the party headquarters; scores of dedicated party workers found themselves unemployed. Some observers wondered whether Taiwan had reached the end of its democratic journey and was circling back toward KMT-dominated single-party politics.

Those fears turned out to be overblown, for it wasn't long before democracy was showing its strength anew. Neither a huge public electoral mandate nor a massive KMT legislative majority could protect President Ma from democracy. From the very beginning of his term, he faced challenges from all sides—protests from the DPP, lack of disciplined support from his own party, and low approval ratings from the public. The public's expectations for Ma were high, but he took office at the height of a global recession, and the nation's problems soon cut him down to a more realistic size. Voters began treating Ma like any other president.

And that, in the end, is what democratic politics is all about: treating every president as a fallible individual whose authority to govern comes from the voters. Ma's first two years in office frustrated his supporters—even when the economy began to revive, his popularity remained low—but they can be read as evidence that Taiwan's political miracle has stabilized.

In 2009, Taiwan's legislature decided to consolidate some of the island's municipal governments, creating four new "megacities," including an enlarged Taichung and a massive new Kaohsiung. In December 2010, the two mayors whose stories began this chapter, Jason Hu and Chen Chu, were elected mayors of the new Taichung and Kaohsiung, respectively. Conversations with the mayors in early 2010 underscored the degree to which Taiwan's democracy has become routine. Chen and Hu have strong ideas about how Taiwan should develop, but ideology does not drive their day-to-day decision making; they are preoccupied with the practical problems of governance. As Mayor Chen put it,

> I'm constantly thinking about what we can produce, what industries we can have in the future. I was talking to Hsu Wen-lung [the head of the Chi Mei Corporation, one of Taiwan's leading chemical companies] recently and he asked me, "What kind of mayor do you want to be? The kind who develops industry at all costs, or the one who, fifty years from now, people will look back on and say 'She preserved and protected our community'?" He's thinking about philosophy. Given the pressures on me, I don't really have much chance to think about that, but he makes a good point. When it comes to economic development, we don't have a lot of people thinking about how to balance these goals. We need to think about what *kind* of economic development we want.

Mayor Hu speaks in similar terms about the importance of a long-term vision. Asked what he learned from leaving the bureaucratic posts for which he had been groomed to enter electoral politics he answers, "I was reborn." He describes the months following the KMT's presidential defeat in 2000 as "a time of shock for us. We needed to take off our leather shoes and put on sports shoes." Taichung City was a special challenge for the Oxford-educated Mainlander who had built his career in the diplomatic corps. The city was known for organized crime, local factionalism, inadequate infrastructure, and industrial pollution. As Hu puts it, "When I started going to Taichung there were people who said 'he's a ballet dancer; he doesn't have what it takes to be a mud wrestler.'"

"I think the experience of running for election changed me," says Hu. "I believe all politicians should go through elections first, and should serve locally first, before they move to the national level." Serving the city forced Hu to prioritize local needs; like Mayor Chen, Hu is determined to find an economic niche for his city:

> I decided a city should have a face. Paris, London, Kyoto, maybe Shanghai—all of these cities have a face. Other than these few, most cities look about the same. That face defines the character of a city. Eight years ago I decided that Taichung must have a cultural face. We can't compete with Taipei and Kaohsiung—the center of government, the port city—we needed to do something different to distinguish our city.

Turning Taichung into a cultural center was not easy. Hu learned a painful lesson about the limits of executive power when he was courting the Guggenheim Foundation to build a major art museum in the city. "I lost the Guggenheim museum after they had made the decision to come because I couldn't get it through the city council. There was a lack of local and central support. After that I got smarter." He learned to operate more effectively within the city council and to focus on projects with wide appeal—a baseball stadium (baseball is Taiwan's most popular spectator sport), a multipurpose amphitheater, public concerts. "When we started, each citizen attended an average of four cultural events a year. Last year [2009] we averaged 33 attendances per citizen."

Mayors of major cities inevitably emphasize economic development, but Hu and Chen resemble one another in less predictable ways, too. If we look only at their backgrounds—the Mainlander bureaucrat steeped in Chinese nationalist ideology, the Hokkien dissident grounded in Taiwanese identity politics—we would expect to find them on opposite sides of Taiwan's hottest political issue. In fact, though, their views about how Taiwan should interact with the People's Republic of China are surprisingly similar, although far from identical.

Mayor Hu is famous for his humor, and one of his best lines came in a 1996 interview with *New York Times* columnist (and Hu's Oxford classmate) Thomas Friedman. Speaking about missile tests Beijing was using to intimidate Taiwanese in the run-up to the first direct presidential election, Friedman referred to China as an 800-pound gorilla in Taiwan's living room. Hu replied, "Tom, it's worse than that. Not only do I have an 800-pound gorilla in my living room, that gorilla happens to think that he's my brother!"

The quip captures Hu's outlook on cross-Strait relations. Asked how he developed such a flexible view, given his long association with the KMT he replied:

If there ever was an "old KMT" that KMT taught me to be Chinese, but not to be pro-unification. Even CCK said, toward the end of his life, that he was both Chinese and Taiwanese. We don't have to dichotomize these things. China is our father; Taiwan is our mother, or the other way around. Can we deny either one of them? I don't have to disbelieve what the old KMT has taught us to be a politician close to the people. I grew up knowing I was a Taiwanese, despite having Mainlander parents. When I was small I was puzzled: The teacher, and other people, said "Speak Mandarin," but when it was time for elections, all the politicians spoke Taiwanese. So I couldn't understand: What's wrong with speaking dialect?

Hu's attitude comes through in his actions as mayor. In 2009 Taichung hosted talks between Chen Yunlin, Beijing's top Taiwan-affairs official, and Chiang Pin-kung, his Taiwanese counterpart. The talks attracted a host of protesters to the city. Says Hu, "We did not treat the protesters as the other side. The Chinese are the other side. We Taiwanese are all on the same side." He sums up the KMT's approach to cross-Strait relations this way, "We don't want to sail any closer to China, but I think we have a better course than the previous government. We still have extremes on both sides, but they are a tiny minority."

If Jason Hu resists the die-hard unificationist stereotype of a career KMT politician, Chen Chu, too, defies easy labeling. She has been a leading proponent of Taiwanese identity, but she also advocates a moderate China policy for the DPP. In May 2009 Chen Chu traveled to the mainland to talk to officials about the World Games Kaohsiung was to host two months later. Some DPP colleagues criticized her for reaching out to the mainland, but Chen defends her decision:

> China is a very important country in the World Games, and the Olympics, which they'd just finished. To make our World Games successful I needed their cooperation. They needed to buy into the idea that the World Games is about peace among nations. Sport is never free of politics, but we wanted to minimize the politics. So we went to China. We talked to them privately, to make sure the games would be peaceful. Some people here criticized us. They said we shouldn't go, that we were giving up our ideals, but this World Games was really important for Taiwan's international recognition and reputation. We couldn't afford to let it fail. So I had to go over there and tell them this was not political, but an occasion for peace.
>
> I had a big job to do pacifying the Taiwan independence people here. I told them it's important to understand the difference between your personal goals and the responsibility you have if you're organizing a global event. If the World Games had gone badly that really would have hurt Taiwan's international image, and that's something we had to avoid. The DPP needs to understand China. China has enormous influence over Taiwan's development. China is huge—it can easily eat us up. If we in the DPP have a China policy that isn't rooted in a good understanding of China, that is really dangerous. The Chinese shouldn't just talk to the KMT. Taiwan has many people who are not in the KMT, and they need to hear what we have to say, too. They may not like my opinions, but they need to hear them.

Mayor Chen's trip was an important moment in cross-Strait relations. It not only showed the DPP's willingness to engage the PRC, but it also called attention to the range of opinion within Taiwan. Unlike some KMT leaders who had visited the mainland, Chen Chu did not bend over backward to accommodate her hosts. She was not intentionally provocative, but she did not censor herself, either.

> There was a headline that said "Beijing Mayor versus Kaohsiung Mayor" when I met the mayor of Beijing. That was a good headline, because it made us equals. We felt huge pressure while we were there. We had to be so careful

with everything we said. We didn't know what they were thinking, what they would say. Every night my shoulders were so sore from the tension. But at the very least, we went to Beijing and we went to Shanghai. And while we were there the mayor of Beijing was talking about getting funding from the central government for the Olympics and I said "President Ma Ying-jeou of our central government" and that was reported, quoted. People were really happy about that. Our government was happy. They wouldn't dare to use that language themselves [that is, to refer to Ma as "president" and the ROC authorities as a "central government"], but I didn't care about making the Beijing people happy, so I just said it.

Not all Taiwanese politicians are as wise, sensible, charismatic, and effective as Chen Chu and Jason Hu. Still, the two mayors' success and popularity bode well for Taiwan's democracy. From a distance, Taiwan politics can appear polarized and dysfunctional, but when we zoom in closer, the system looks much healthier. Compared to the corrupt and authoritarian single-party government of forty years ago, Taiwan's democracy—with all its flaws—is an infinitely more humane and sustainable form of government.

SOURCES

This chapter relies heavily on formal interviews and informal conversations. I am especially grateful to Chen Chu and Jason Hu, both of whom have agreed to be interviewed many times over the past twenty years. Chen Chu was the first Taiwanese political figure I met in Taiwan, and she has been unflagging in her support for my efforts to understand and tell Taiwan's story. Jason Hu and Ma Ying-jeou have been particularly generous with their time and encouragement, as have many other politicians of all political colorations.

The chapter also draws on the extensive literature on Taiwan's democratization. Path-breaking works in this category include early articles by Edwin Winckler, "Institutionalization and Participation on Taiwan: From Hard to Soft Authoritarianism?" and Tun-jen Cheng, "Democratizing the Quasi-Leninist Regime in Taiwan," as well as Hung-mao Tien's book *The Great Transition: Political and Social Change in Taiwan.* More recent works include *The Kuomintang and the Democratization of Taiwan* (Steven J. Hood); *Democratization in China and Taiwan* (Bruce J. Dickson); *The First Chinese Democracy: Political Life in the Republic of China on Taiwan* (Linda Chao and Ramon H. Myers); *Political Change on Taiwan: A Study of Ruling Party Adaptability* (Peter Moody); *Crafting Democracy in Taiwan* (Yun-han Chu); *Taiwan's Democratization: Forces behind the New Momentum* (Joseph Jauhsieh Wu); *Taiwan: National Identity and Democratization* (Alan Wachman); *Taiwan and*

Chinese Nationalism (Christopher Hughes); *Party Politics in Taiwan* (Dafydd Fell); and my book *Politics in Taiwan: Voting for Democracy.*

The passage from General Wedemeyer is quoted in George H. Kerr's *Formosa Betrayed.* I consulted several biographies of Chen Chu and Jason Hu for this chapter; it is Chen Yu-hua who refers to Chen's family as "democratic pioneers" in her collection *Uncommon Women* (*Buyiyang de Nuren*). Gerald McBeath's article appeared in *Asian Survey* in January of 1977. Chen Shui-bian's biography is *The Son of Taiwan: The Life of Chen Shui-bian and His Dreams for Taiwan.* David J. Toman wrote the English translation.

Taiwan's presidential office building housed the Japanese colonial government in the early 1900s.

An Austronesian artisan demonstrates seated loom weaving on Taiwan's east coast.

School children participate in a morning flag-raising ceremony at an elementary school near Taipei.

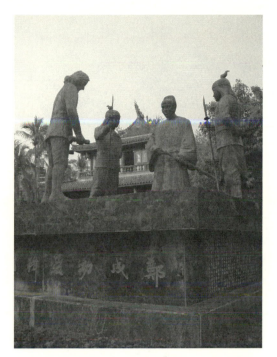

A modern statue shows Zheng Chenggong (Koxinga) receiving the Dutch surrender in the 1600s.

A traditional courtyard house shows the elegance of Taiwan's traditional architecture.

The view of Kaohsiung Harbor from the British Consulate high above the city captures the bustling maritime commerce that makes Kaohsiung one of the world's busiest ports.

The Chiang Kai-shek Memorial Hall is located in one of Taipei's few open spaces.

The Chiang Kai-shek Memorial Hall includes a 30-foot statue of the man who led the Republic of China for half a century. Above his head is the word "democracy," although most Taiwanese agree there was little democracy on the island during his reign.

Taipei's Grand Hotel is one of the city's most visible landmarks.

During his presidential campaigns, Chen Shui-bian sold merchandise that appealed to Taiwanese consumers' taste for the "cute and tiny."

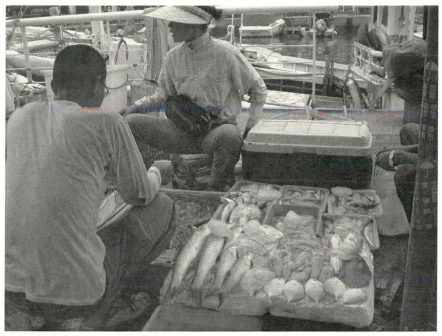

Many Taiwanese women, like this fish vendor, work in the informal sector.

The high speed rail line linking Taipei and Kaohsiung reduced the travel time between the two cities to ninety minutes.

Lighthouse near the entrance to Kaohsiung Harbor.

Worshippers at a temple in Lukang make offerings to the goddess Mazu.

Guanyin idol, Tainan.

The historic city of Lukang is a center for handcrafting ritual objects for use in Taiwan's thousands of temples.

In 2006, Taiwanese chose traditional glove puppetry as the art form that best represents their culture.

5

"America Is Boring at Night"

Driving a taxi in Taiwan is grueling, and the pay is lousy. In the city, the bright yellow sedans are everywhere—passengers rarely wait more than a minute on Taipei's main boulevards before a cab pulls up—and even in the countryside you can call a cab and one will appear out of nowhere within a few minutes. Given the intense competition, making a decent living requires long hours, smart strategy, and a lot of luck. So I was curious when a driver mentioned he'd recently returned to the island after working in the United States for a few years. Why, I asked, did you decide to come back? The answer: "America is boring at night."

It is a truism, and it is a truth. Compared to Taiwan, America is indeed, very boring at night. To most Taiwanese, American suburbs, with their single-family houses and two-car garages that are distant from shopping and restaurants, are the definition of isolation and tedium. Nighttime or daytime, Taiwanese—whether they live among the skyscrapers of Taipei, Taichung, and Kaohsiung or in rural farming villages—want to be where the action is. The American custom of retreating nightly to a private fortress for an evening of solitary TV-watching carries little appeal in a society where social interaction continues around the clock and work and leisure can be hard to separate.

A six-year-old does her homework at a table in a dingy restaurant while her parents cook outside under an awning, watching TV and chatting with neighbors. A small-town dentist excuses himself from a tea-and-fruit-fueled political debate in his tiny living room to fix a broken tooth at 10 p.m. A father walks his children to the night market for noodles at bedtime, running into a dozen friends (adults and kids) along the way. Bleary-eyed students line up at dawn to stake out seats in the central library's massive reading room while elderly ladies practice *taichi* exercises and ballroom dancing in the plaza out front. A family of five putters along the narrow dike between rice paddies on a motor scooter, big brother standing between the handlebars, Dad driving, sister wedged between her parents on the seat, and baby brother strapped to Mom's back. A dozen children sleep fully clothed wherever they drifted off the night before—tiny bodies strewn over floors, couches, a marble coffee table. These are scenes I have witnessed with my own eyes. In Taiwan, life is a twenty-four-hour-a-day enterprise, and the fuel that keeps it running is relationships.

What makes life in Taiwan so exciting are the nonstop social interactions centered on tight personal ties. Most Western descriptions of Chinese culture emphasize the importance of *guanxi*, the Chinese word for relationship. With its emphasis on mutual obligation and reciprocity, guanxi can easily shade into an unsavory you-scratch-my-back-I'll-scratch-yours form of interaction. But equating guanxi with corruption is unfair: it is much more than a simple quid pro quo. In Taiwan, most guanxi relationships are rooted in real emotion. Friends exchange gifts, they help each other when needed, but the friendship comes first. They don't call themselves friends because they exchange things; they exchange things because they are friends.

A U.S. diplomat who has served on both sides of the Taiwan Strait explained the subtle difference in "human feeling" (*renqing wei*) as it is understood in Taiwan and the mainland. "In the mainland, 'human feeling' is more like guanxi—it's very practical, and it implies some kind of exchange. In Taiwan, 'human feeling' is about relationships. It extends to friends and relatives, but it can extend further, too." In Taiwan, he says, compassion extends to strangers. From the Ciji Buddhist charities to no-kill shelters for stray animals, Taiwanese society shows its concern for those who suffer. "Even Chinese visitors to Taiwan are impressed by how civil, how polite, the people are. And everyone who's ever worked at AIT [America's de facto embassy in Taipei] wishes they could go back to Taiwan."

The density of human relationships and interactions helps explain why so many Taiwanese find American lifestyles a little dull. Another factor that keeps Taiwanese engaged in and attached to their society is the extraordinary flowering of Taiwanese culture in recent decades. Globalization and localization—trends both contradictory and complementary—have enriched Taiwanese culture enormously. The result is a unique art and literary culture that engages transnational trends and ideas, yet is recognizably Taiwanese. Taiwan's art scene has attracted international attention for artists such as Oscar-winning film director Ang Lee and the globally acclaimed Cloud Gate Dance Theater, and part of what makes it interesting and appealing is that it is so clearly rooted in a place. With their fierce determination to recover the Taiwanese essence that was driven underground during the White Terror, Taiwanese artists manage both to resist the forces of global homogenization and to avoid narrow narcissism.

Social interactions begin with the family, so let us start our tour of Taiwanese social life and culture there. In 1958, Margery and Arthur Wolf arrived in Taiwan to make an anthropological study of everyday life in a Taiwanese village, which their books call Peihotien. Margery was fascinated by the women in the village, and she eventually published two books about Peihotien's families. The books give us a baseline for measuring the rapid change in Taiwan's family structure in the decades since. On the surface, today's Taiwanese families look nothing like the ones Wolf lived among in the early 1960s, but at a deeper level, Peihotien's values and worldview are still discernable in Taiwanese family life today.

The families Margery Wolf describes in her book *Women and the Family in Rural Taiwan* were large and patriarchal. Centered on male descent lines stretching back centuries, these families revered an ideal of five generations under one roof (although few achieved it). Women "married in"; they joined their husbands' families with no lingering obligations and few opportunities even to visit their birth families. Taiwanese parents referred to married daughters as "spilled water"; something that can never be recovered. Only very rarely—when a girl had no brothers to continue her father's family line—might a family seek out a man willing (for a price) to marry into her family. When he did, he took his wife's surname, and he and his descendants owed their allegiance to her ancestors forever. Needless to say, in this value system, sons were prized above all else, and it was as the mother of a son that a woman earned status in her husband's clan.

Most studies of traditional family life in Taiwan and other culturally Chinese places focus on the dramas of the patriarchal family—sons leaving home, brothers fighting over property or "dividing the stove" (splitting the household), wives failing to produce heirs—but Margery Wolf wanted to know how women fit themselves into these structures. Based on her conversations with women in Peihotien, she learned that with their children, women built "uterine families," mother-centered families bonded by affection. Sons, she found, were responsive to their mothers even in adulthood. Daughters remained tied to their birth families; spilled water or not, they felt they owed a debt of gratitude to the households that raised them. Accepting the marriage arranged for them was one way to discharge the debt, but in very poor families, girls might risk their dignity and reputation by going out to work to support birth parents and younger siblings. In short, mother-centered bonds of affection and loyalty coexisted with the hierarchical and duty-bound patriarchal family.

One traditional element of Taiwanese family life was disappearing even before the Wolfs began their fieldwork. Before Taiwan began industrializing in the early twentieth century, many rural parents solved the problem

of finding a wife for their son by adopting a small girl into the household
when the son was still a boy. When the two came of age, they were married. Taiwanese parents liked these "simpua" marriages because they saved
the expense of a wedding and allowed the mother-in-law to train her
daughter-in-law from an early age. Taiwanese sons, however, did not like
simpua marriage: they actively resisted wedding girls who had been raised
as their sisters. As soon as they gained economic options beyond the family
farm, young men began rejecting simpua matches. By the 1970s, they were
gone—vanished like footbinding and other practices that just a few decades
earlier had seemed immutable.

Changes in family life accelerated in the high-growth decades between
1960 and 1990. A survey of married Taiwanese taken in 1986 found that
62 percent of those who married in the late 1950s had their marriages arranged by their parents. That number steadily declined, until, for couples
married in the early 1980s, only 13 percent were married to partners selected by their parents. As couples became more independent in choosing
spouses, they also embraced a more independent style of living. In 1965, 58
percent of Taiwanese households included the husband's parents; by 1986,
that number had fallen to 39 percent. There was an even sharper decline
in the share of households that included other extended family members,
such as the husband's brothers. At the same time, the preference for sons—
intense in the 1950s—has diminished. Meanwhile, the divorce rate tripled
between 1970 and 1990, and both marriage rates and birthrates have fallen
sharply. Today, Taiwan's birthrate is among the world's lowest.

Taiwanese families have been evolving away from the extended patriarchal family model the Wolfs found so prevalent in Peihotien, but family
is still very important in Taiwan. Young people may not let their parents
choose their spouses for them anymore, but parents still expect to have
veto power over a match. Young Taiwanese tend to keep their romantic
relationships quiet until they're ready to announce an engagement—in part
because they don't want their parents pushing them toward marriage until
they're sure. And the formal process of getting married begins when the two
sets of parents begin negotiating the terms of the engagement and wedding;
it is impossible to carry out a Taiwanese wedding without extensive paren-
tal involvement. The process can stretch over many months.

Traditional and modern elements collide in wedding rituals around the
world, and Taiwan is no exception. Marriage begins with an engagement,
sealed with an exchange of gifts between the families of the bride and groom.
The bride's family receives cash and gifts—half of which are returned to the
groom's family. In exchange, the couple expects generosity from the bride's
family in setting up housekeeping (the modern equivalent of a dowry). One
evolving engagement ritual is especially telling: in the past, the prospective
mother-in-law attempted to force a gold ring onto the bride's finger. The

bride was expected to put up a robust resistance; if she let her mother-in-law succeed too easily, it meant the bride would be browbeaten. Today, some brides and grooms enact a similar ritual, placing rings on one another's fingers. The partner who resists the ring longer, it is said, will have the upper hand in the marriage. The symbolism shifts the focus of marriage from the mother-in-law–daughter-in-law tie to the husband-and-wife relationship.

A second set of rituals publicizes the engagement. Among the gifts the groom's family provides at the engagement ceremony are "happy cakes." Happy cakes come in different styles and flavors, but they are instantly recognizable by their festive packaging. Individually wrapped and sealed, the cakes come in elaborate red and pink boxes. The bride's family distributes them to friends, relatives, and business associates, who are then on notice that a "pink bomb" (an invitation to a wedding feast) will soon follow. The wedding feast need not happen on the same day—or even in the same month—as the wedding ceremony. Some couples even have more than one feast, all aimed at sharing the happy event with friends, relatives, and coworkers. Guests offer gifts of cash to the banquet hosts. Most people give the cost of their meal, so the hosts generally break even on the event. Guests also can give money to the newlyweds themselves, but most do not.

Once a couple is formally engaged there is no going back. At this point, many young couples consider themselves as good as married. Sociologists have noted that Taiwan has a high rate of premarital sex compared to neighboring countries. Delving more deeply into the topic, they discovered that many couples begin having sex after they are engaged but before they are married. The percentage of Taiwanese who have sex with partners they never marry is lower.

For many Taiwanese couples, the first thing to do upon becoming engaged—even before exchanging family gifts—is to sign a contract with a photography studio. Bridal photography is a huge industry in Taiwan. Every town has at least a few shops dedicated to capturing idealized images of marital love and feminine beauty. They show the bride at her most radiant—enhanced by elaborate makeup and coiffure (even wigs), dazzling costumes, and all the tricks of the photographer's trade. The extensive makeovers brides undergo to prepare for these all-day photographic marathons (including, in many cases, shaving off the eyebrows and drawing on new ones) can make it hard to recognize them in their photos. While most images show the bride alone, there also are photos of bride and groom together in romantic poses. Photo albums contain many poses in many styles—romantic, sexy, cute, to name a few. Costumes change, along with hair and makeup, and so do backdrops. Many photo shoots are "on location" in scenic spots, especially parks, beaches, and historic buildings. Because the costumes are rented, it's no problem to climb down into a muddy lotus pond or stretch out on a grimy beach for a shot.

A typical package of bridal photographs includes at least one very large print (normally displayed in the couple's bedroom) and an ornate book of photos. Couples display their photos at their wedding banquets, and it is fashionable to give out cards (which can double as gift receipts) printed with a bridal photo—and the photography studio's contact information. The photos—de rigueur for young couples—represent a sharp departure from traditional Taiwanese weddings. Like the updated engagement ring ritual, the photos focus attention on the bride and the loving relationship between bride and groom. They celebrate modern couples' autonomy and individuality. These values are a far cry from norms in place just a few decades ago, when many couples barely knew one another on the wedding day, and the bride's future was limited to serving her in-laws and birthing sons for their clan.

For most Taiwanese, married life today lies somewhere between the fantasy world portrayed in bridal photographs and the drudgery of the not-too-distant past. Gender norms in Taiwan are more conservative than in comparable countries in Europe and North America. Men feel heavy pressure to succeed economically and provide for their families—including elderly parents. There is little opportunity or encouragement for men to relax and enjoy their families; to many Taiwanese, a successful man is one who works hard and spends his spare time carousing with his mates, not one who prefers the quiet comforts of home.

Most men (and their parents) expect wives to stay at home, especially once they have children. Even poor and working class Taiwanese share this middle-class gender ideology. At least half of married women are employed, but many view their jobs as supplementary to the husband's. Many married mothers earn money in the informal economy, but the work they do is not viewed as equivalent to a man's. As one Taiwanese sociologist put it, a man selling fish at the roadside would say he was working, while the woman selling fruit next to him would likely claim just to be doing "a little something" while the children are at school. Job discrimination is common and working hours are long, so the percentage of married women pursuing professional careers is limited, but many women work for the small family businesses described in chapter 3.

Bonnie Adrian, an anthropologist who studies Taiwan's bridal photography industry, believes the appeal of bridal photography is that it unites the bride and groom, however fleetingly, in a vision of marriage that resists the workaday reality. As she writes, "Many view the photographs as the bride's 'last time' to enjoy high status as a young, attractive, independent woman before she becomes burdened by household work and familial demands." The photos freeze a moment in time when the bride is at the pinnacle of her feminine charm, and the groom is entirely smitten. Whether or not these images bear any relationship to reality is less important than creating the image of beauty and bliss.

At any rate, once the photos are taken (and the staggering bill for them is paid), the next step is a wedding. Wedding ceremonies are private, at-home affairs. According to Adrian, most brides and grooms think of wedding rituals as "old people's business." Most have attended few, if any, wedding ceremonies—especially now that most Taiwanese have only one or two siblings. Some people—those born in the year of the tiger—are actually *forbidden* to attend other people's weddings, as they are considered bad luck. Because they are held in private and have no connection with the "wedding industry," wedding ceremonies do not follow a pattern; different families observe different customs. Still, some elements are widely shared. The wedding date is set according to complex astrological calculations that take into account the couple's birthdays as well as the state of the cosmos around the time they hope to wed. The stars often dictate timing that is quite inconvenient (say, six o'clock on a Wednesday morning), so the small attendance at wedding ceremonies is a blessing. Other common elements include bows honoring the couple's ancestors and a ritualized journey to the new home. In the past, brides were carried to their husband's homes in sedan chairs; today, most couples hire a limo decked out in ribbons and flowers.

After marriage, couples may not live with the husband's parents as frequently as in the past, but they tend to live *near* parents and other relatives. In urban areas it's not unusual for parents to buy apartments for their children to live in, which gives the older generation a measure of control. Family members interact frequently; they exchange money, help each other with childcare, and share the responsibility for caring for the elderly—most of whom live with their children. Meanwhile, most unmarried adults continue to live with their parents, both for cultural reasons—there is no stigma attached to living at home well into adulthood, and moving out may be interpreted as disloyal—and for economic reasons: housing is expensive.

These crowded living arrangements work, in part, precisely because Taiwan is not boring at night. Small, crowded apartments are the norm, but because Taiwanese spend so little time at home, the lack of space and privacy creates fewer problems than one might expect. Working hours are long—many Taiwanese work six or seven ten-hour days each week—and street life is lively. There is a dining option to fit every budget—from sidewalk carts selling fried rice and noodles for a dollar or two to five-star restaurants. After dinner, there are coffee shops, bars, parks, movies, shopping centers, fast-food restaurants, beauty salons, discos, and bookstores open into the wee hours—not to mention uniquely Taiwanese diversions like KTV (karaoke singing in private rooms), barbershops (many of which sell sexual services on their upper floors), night markets, and shrimp fishing in artificial ponds. With so much to do, "home" can be little more than a bed, a shower, and a place to leave clothes. No landline needed: the ratio of mobile phones to Taiwanese is about one-to-one.

Social life extends far beyond romance and private entertainments. Groups, clubs, and organizations are pervasive in Taiwan. From Rotary International to rotating credit co-ops, Taiwanese are busy with all sorts of extracurricular activities. One charming example is pigeon racing. From the window of any elevated train or subway line passengers can see elaborate cages on many rooftops; these are houses for racing pigeons. On race day, racers carry their birds to a release point. There, a local racing club registers the entrants, straps microchips to their skinny red legs, and takes bets. On a signal, the birds are released to find their way home. Watching the flocks of single-minded creatures tear off toward their distant dovecotes is a remarkable sight, and knowing that they will fly at full speed for up to two hundred miles is awe inspiring. Within a few hours of the release, a lead bird crosses the threshold into its cage and its microchip registers the time. Back at the release point, the times are adjusted for distance, the winners declared, and the bets settled. Successful breeding pigeons sell for huge sums; the most beloved are celebrities. Pigeons may all look the same to you and me, but to aficionados, Miss Ilan, her sleek, feathered flanks and iridescent green head captured in a popular portrait, was a unique and beautiful athlete.

The heart of social life in small-town Taiwan is the temple. Traditionally, a temple is the center of communal life, a meeting place between the natural and supernatural, and an affirmation of local residents' collective identity—which often includes a common ancestor. Most Westerners are familiar with three Chinese religions: Buddhism, Taoism, and Confucianism. Village temples are not any of these, yet they are all of them. Taiwanese folk religion is syncretic; it mixes elements of different religions, so Buddhist deities, Taoist priests, and Confucian worthies are welcome in nearly every temple (although there are some they choose not to grace with their presence). So, too, are a multitude of other supernatural forces and beings less well-known in the West.

Taiwanese folk religion imagines a world parallel to our own, inhabited by a vast range of beings and governed much like a traditional Chinese dynasty. There is a hierarchy of deities whose responsibilities differ, so that all are revered, and each is called upon in different circumstances. Some deities have centuries-old cults and millions of devotees among Chinese around the world. The Jade Emperor, sometimes called the Lord of Heaven, stands at the top of the celestial hierarchy, a vast bureaucracy of gods and protectors—endorsed in their positions by the Lord of Heaven himself—who are alternately revered, honored, served, and pestered in Taiwan's folk temples.

Some deities once were human. Lord Guan, for example, was a famous warrior of the Han Dynasty; today, he is a deity with great power to bring order and command men. Police stations in Taiwan and Hong Kong display his fierce, bearded image—as do many businesses and temples.

Guanyin began as Buddhism's male bodhisattva Avalokitesvara, but over the centuries evolved into a female figure whose devotees look to her for mercy, especially in matters of childbirth and illness. Her representation—willowy, with eyes downcast demurely in a face radiating compassion—is instantly recognizable. Wang Ye, the Plague God, represents 360 different historical figures, collectively empowered by the Lord of Heaven to defend humans against pestilence.

The goddess Mazu, whose portfolio includes protecting sailors and fishermen, commands the most popular cult in Taiwan. Her statues invariably depict the goddess wearing a rectangular mortarboard with a fringe of black beads covering her face. According to legend, Lin Mo-niang was born in the mid-tenth century on Meizhou Island, off the coast of Fujian. Blessed by the gods, the young girl performed numerous miracles in life, including saving her father and brothers from drowning. After she died, she continued to provide care and protection to sailors and fishermen, and she became a deity with the name Mazu. Taiwan has more than four hundred temples dedicated to her, and her birthday is a major religious holiday on the island. Two temples in southern Taiwan have a long-standing rivalry over which has the closest link to the "mother temple" on Meizhou, and since restrictions on travel to the mainland were lifted in the late 1980s, pilgrimages to Meizhou and other Mazu hotspots on the mainland have become an important feature of the Mazu cult.

Farther down the celestial ladder are thousands of local deities. Some have long histories, others are recent arrivals; some are revered throughout East Asia, others are recognized in only one temple. Some are represented by statues, but a name carved into a tablet, or even simply written on paper, can also house the spirit of a god. Local deities, like their superiors, generally began as humans (or, occasionally, animals) whose activities before and after their deaths brought them to the attention of local communities. Some were admired figures in life whose influence increased after death.

One well-known and exotic example of the diversity of Taiwanese gods is the central deity in the Eighteen Kings Temple in Kungliao, a small town on Taiwan's rugged northwest coast. That deity is a dog, found on the beach during the Qing Dynasty guarding the bodies of seventeen human shipwreck victims. The dog protected the bodies from scavengers until local villagers could bury them, then followed its companions into their grave.

The villagers admired the dog for so perfectly embodying the canine virtue captured in the idiom, "A righteous dog defends its master." They constructed a temple to venerate it, and before long the temple gained a reputation for miraculous events—most recently, turning back bulldozers trying to expand a nearby nuclear power plant. The temple attracted worshippers who were embarrassed to take their concerns to "proper" deities, and at the height of its popularity, taxis carrying prostitutes and gamblers jammed the road to the Eighteen Kings Temple every night. They bought charms and fortunes on the ground floor then descended a steep staircase into the dog's underground tomb where an incense burner full of lit cigarettes perfumed the air with the animal's preferred fragrance.

Taiwanese temples make room for forces both benign and malevolent. Taiwan is full of gods, and it also is full of ghosts. Ghosts are the supernatural remnants of those who died violently or tragically or without descendants to ease their way in the afterlife. All sorts of beings—humans, animals, even inanimate objects—can become ghosts or be possessed by ghosts. A cat that dies and is left to decay on the ground can become an angry cat ghost, so a Taiwanese who encounters a dead cat might fling it into a tree or bush. Twenty years ago, it was common to see heavy, gelatinous-looking plastic bags dangling from trees along rural roads—tribute to a threatening feline underworld.

Human ghosts are objects of fear, but they are treated like gods to appease them. Some can be found everywhere—"the Good Brethren" is a euphemism for humans who became ghosts because their descendants failed to provide for them. The Good Brethren cause all manner of trouble in order to extort what they need from the living; nearly every temple ritual includes some activity aimed at pacifying them. While fear dominates the relationship between Taiwanese and their human ghosts, there is an element of pity, too. In 1950, Jinmen Island (also known as Quemoy) was the site of a horrifying battle between Nationalist forces and the Communists' Red Army. In two days of fighting, more than six thousand men died. Thousands more were injured, and the battlefield was littered with corpses from both sides. In the decades since the battle, Jinmen Islanders have sought to exorcise their trauma by building temples to the soldiers who died there, both Nationalist and Communist.

Like the Good Brethren, these unknown soldiers have gained status through their deification—a transformation designed to ease their lonely, drifting souls. They are known as "Patriotic Generals," and some have been promoted to even higher ranks. Their temples are populated by statues in military dress; spirit mediums cross into the world of the dead to learn their names and carry back their requests for how they should be honored. Some Patriotic Generals have revealed they are married, and villagers have added female statues representing their wives to the temples. The Patriotic Generals temples seem to meet a psychic need for catharsis and release as well as a religious need; the loving care they receive hints at sympathy for men who died alone and far from home, as well as fear of ghostly mischief. Like all spirits and deities, the Patriotic Generals enjoy devotees' offerings of incense, flowers, food, and spirit money—the currency of the underworld.

Communication with the spirit world is an important part of temple practice. Human mediums speak for particular spirits during trances, when they provide both solicited and unsolicited information about the other world. Sometimes their messages are unwelcome—grandfather disapproves new business plans; a dead woman is demanding marriage to a living man—but most of the time their messages are eagerly sought. Spirits provide guidance on many matters, and it is important not to act against the will of an ancestor. Nonetheless, mediums themselves often resist spirit possession. Although mediums can earn both money and respect, carrying the voice of a spirit is a heavy responsibility, and the proof of possession by certain spirits—beating oneself bloody with a ritual weapon—is painful, if not during the trance then afterward, when the wounds are still raw but the ecstasy of possession is over.

Spirits also communicate through objects. It is common to see devotees in Taiwanese temples dropping *boe*, a pair of cashew-shaped wooden blocks, onto the floor in front of a deity's altar. Questions posed in prayer can be answered by boe; how they fall indicates the response—yes, no, maybe. More complicated information can be elicited through the use of a *kio-a*, or spirit chair. Worshippers hoist the kio-a onto their shoulders like a sedan chair, whereupon a spirit takes possession and jerks the bearers around the temple. Interpreters watch closely to discern the words traced by the chair's wild movements.

A Taiwanese temple procession is a world-class spectacle: a parade of silk-clad acrobats; the giant red and green puppets named "Ten-Thousand Mile Eyes" and "Ears that Hear on the Wind"; shuddering deities in elaborate sedan chairs; bloodied mediums swinging balls of nails and goose-stepping; all to the sound of high-pitched horn music punctuated with bursts of firecrackers. At the end of a procession—which might be celebrating a deity's birthday or visit to another temple—there is likely to be a show. A stage set up on the temple plaza provides a venue for the deity's favorite entertainment, usually a Taiwanese opera or puppet show. These performances, which humans also enjoy, tend to be painfully loud and extremely colorful. A little striptease during scene changes is also good fun for the gods. Taiwanese like their religion like their politics: "hot and noisy."

The hottest and noisiest ritual takes place each year in the village of Yenshui in southern Taiwan. In the mid-nineteenth century Yenshui's population was decimated by a stubborn cholera epidemic. To attract local gods' attention to their plight, townspeople set off fireworks—and the plague ended. The successful experiment became an annual ritual that attracts thousands of thrill seekers every year. Locals still carry temple gods through the mayhem in their palanquins, but the real attraction is the mayhem itself. Volunteers build truck-sized armatures covered with mesh, and insert bottle rockets until the huge structures are completely covered. On the appointed night, festivalgoers ignite these "rocket hives" one by one, setting off massive explosions. Fireworks rocket out in all directions, pelting throngs of spectators bouncing up and down like rock fans in a mosh pit. Onlookers wear heavy clothing, motorcycle helmets, and neck protectors; even so, serious injuries occur every year.

The rocket hive festival is an extreme example, but throughout Taiwan, the village temple is the point of intersection between religious life and community affairs; it is the most pervasive religious institution in Taiwan. It is hard to separate its cultural, social, and political roles from its religious identity. Other religions occupy a less ambiguous niche. These are the orthodox religions, which eschew the syncretic, little-of-this-little-of-that approach found in local temples. Of the orthodox religions, Buddhism is the most popular and the fastest growing. While Guanyin and other Buddhist deities can be found in nonorthodox temples, orthodox temples include *only* Buddhist deities—no Patriotic Generals or Plague Gods allowed.

Approximately 6 million Taiwanese identify themselves as Buddhist. Their religious practice centers on institutionalized and relatively professional temple structures, including monastic orders for men and women. Taiwan has the largest population of Buddhist nuns in the world; about three-quarters of the island's thirty thousand or so Buddhist monastics are women. Monks lead the most important sects—including the Foguangshan (Light of Buddha Mountain) and Dharma Drum communities—but nuns also play an important role. After World War II, Buddhist leaders on the island relaxed restrictions to permit women to receive full ordination, opening leadership positions—and the title "Master"—to women in the faith. Today, the most famous Buddhist organization in Taiwan (perhaps the world) is headed by its female founder, Master Zhengyan. Technically, Master Zhengyan's Buddhist Compassion Relief Ciji Foundation is a charitable organization, not a religious order, but Master Zhengyan provides religious instruction as well as secular leadership to the nuns and laypeople attached to her organization.

A faith community in which full-time religious provide both spiritual and non-spiritual leadership to their sects is a far cry from the way village temples work. Taiwanese folk religion is an egalitarian affair in which ordinary citizens staff temple committees and few religious rituals require a professional. Even most religious professionals have day jobs. The orthodox Buddhist temples operate on a very different model.

Another important difference between orthodox Buddhism and village temple practice is the Buddhists' belief in scriptural authority. Buddhists read, recite, and memorize texts. They put copies of Buddhist scriptures in hotel rooms next to the Gideons' bilingual Chinese-English Bibles. Taiwan's Buddhists listen to sermons; day or night they can tune into television shows on which famous nuns and monks explain the scriptures. None of these activities play much of a role in folk religion. Most Buddhists also observe a vegetarian diet, while the deities in folk temples are delighted to receive offerings of meat.

Another religion that asserts a strong orthodoxy is Yi Guan Dao. Rooted in earlier traditions, Yi Guan Dao gained popularity in the early twentieth century; it claims about seven hundred thousand followers in Taiwan today. The KMT suppressed the religion during the martial law era, but it continued to have a significant following as an underground movement. The government objected not to Yi Guan Dao's theology but to its potential as a vehicle for antigovernment mobilization. Yi Guan Dao is even more syncretic than Taiwanese folk religion: it accepts the divinity of Laozi, Confucius, Buddha, Jesus, and Mohammed as well as the standard pantheon of Taiwanese folk deities. The religion emphasizes charity and service and vegetarianism.

With fewer than sixty thousand Taiwanese claiming Islam as their religion, the island stands in marked contrast to the mainland, where Islam is a major religious force with between 20 million and 100 million followers. Most Taiwanese Muslims are from Mainlander families who arrived with the KMT in mid century. Today, Taiwan's mosques also serve Muslims from other countries who are visiting or living on the island.

The number of Christians in Taiwan—about nine hundred thousand—puts their population at a small but sustainable number—a little under 5 percent of islanders. Christians have played a much larger role in Taiwan's political development than their small numbers would suggest. Chiang Kai-shek was a Christian, and his wife was quite an assertive one. Their religious conviction helped win support from the United States before and after World War II, and in the three decades after the war, Christianity enjoyed a privileged position in Taiwan. Christianity was associated with elite social and educational status. Not surprisingly, its influence was especially strong among Mainlanders—the people who were closest to the center of power during Chiang's leadership. Lee Teng-hui, the island's first Taiwan-born president, also professes Christian faith.

Still, not all Christians were part of the pro-Chiang power structure. The most politically active religious group during Taiwan's democratization movement was the Presbyterian Church in Taiwan. The Presbyterians had a history of sympathizing with the Hokkien-speaking people of Taiwan. Missionaries of the church had been in Taiwan for decades under the Japanese colonial regime; the most famous of these was the Canadian medical missionary George Mackay. Mackay is a beloved figure in Taiwan—a stamp honoring him was released on the one hundredth anniversary of his death—despite (or perhaps because of) the fact that by his own account he extracted more than twenty thousand teeth during his thirty years in Taiwan.

Mackay's church played a critical role in popularizing a written form of the Hokkien language. During the colonial period, educated Taiwanese studied Japanese at school; the rich studied Chinese characters and classical Chinese grammar at home. Neither of these methods provided the Hokkien-speaking majority with a readily accessible system for reading and writing their mother tongue. Presbyterians, however, perfected a system for writing the Hokkien dialect in roman letters. That allowed them to translate the Bible and other religious material into a form intelligible to Taiwanese; it also gave them a leg up on other religious organizations, and it cemented their reputation as a religious denomination with special relevance to Hokkien-speaking Taiwanese.

After the KMT imposed martial law, the Presbyterian Church in Taiwan became a zone of relative safety for Taiwanese hoping to preserve and cultivate a unique Hokkien identity. While some missionaries remained in the country, Hokkien-speaking Taiwanese dominated the church's leadership and governance structures. Their determination to use the language in their written documents put them at odds with the KMT, which was insisting on Mandarin, but their close ties with Christian groups in the West partially protected them from the state's repressive urges. Still, the government confiscated Bibles written in romanized Hokkien and tried to stop Presbyterians from printing other romanized texts. Its top leader, Reverend Kao Chun-ming, became a political prisoner after the 1979 Kaohsiung Incident.

As Taiwan's democratization advanced, speaking the Hokkien dialect lost its subversive cachet. Soon Mainlander politicians were studying the language so they could use it in their campaign speeches. At the same time, though, more and more everyday interactions were conducted in Mandarin. This was especially true for younger Taiwanese who had been educated in Mandarin and raised with Mandarin-language mass media. Those changes created a new challenge for the Presbyterian Church, which remained steadfastly committed to romanized Hokkien. At a church conference in the early 2000s, young pastors stirred strong feelings when they asked the church's blessing to use Chinese-character Bibles—and even some spoken Mandarin—in their services. They claimed young parishioners were more comfortable reading characters than romanized Hokkien, but for many church leaders such a compromise threatened to weaken the church's Taiwanese identity.

The fight in the Presbyterian Church was largely generational. For the generation who grew up under an authoritarian government that denigrated and restricted their mother tongue, speaking Mandarin and reading a Chinese-character Bible are acts of surrender. For young Taiwanese who have lived most of their lives in a democratic Taiwan, speaking Mandarin is not a political act, but a way to communicate with all of Taiwan's residents—Hokkien, Hakka, Mainlander, and Austronesian alike. If someone's path to God is marked in Chinese characters that is alright with them.

The crisis over language and culture that has roiled the Presbyterian Church plays itself out in myriad ways in Taiwan society. The island's culture is pulled in three distinct directions: inward, outward, and "Chinaward." When the KMT arrived in Taiwan in 1945, its plan was to reintegrate the island into the Chinese nation-state, so it adopted cultural policies aimed at inculcating a particular version of Chinese culture. Although most Taiwanese defined themselves as Chinese, not Japanese, the KMT's version of "Chinese culture" bore little resemblance to their lived experience.

The more the KMT insisted on defining Chinese language as Mandarin and Chinese culture as the lifestyle and value system of China's literati, the more ordinary Taiwanese began to doubt their "Chineseness." In response, they turned inward, looking to the island as the source of its own unique culture. The struggle between these two versions of Taiwanese cultural identity played out against a background of rapid globalization. Global preferences, values, and ideas inundated the island, adding yet more flavors to the complex mix. The result is a culture that is recognizably Taiwanese, but that speaks to people in China and around the world.

Taiwan's best-known cultural figure in the West is the Oscar-winning film director Ang Lee. Lee was born in 1954 in southern Taiwan to parents who had moved to the island a decade earlier. His body of work includes films in Chinese and English, as well as multilingual films in which each character speaks the appropriate language for him or her. In the early 1990s, Lee made three films about Taiwan: *Pushing Hands*, *The Wedding Banquet*, and *Eat Drink Man Woman*. Each film addresses Taiwan's diverse cultural influences in its own way. *Pushing Hands* and *The Wedding Banquet* chronicle the difficulties facing Mainlander-Taiwanese immigrants to the United States, especially the complications of transplanting a Chinese family to American soil.

The loneliness and dislocation many Mainlanders experience is an important topic for Lee. Both *The Wedding Banquet* and *Eat Drink Man Woman* depict the close friendships and deep loyalties elderly Mainlanders forged in their years as soldiers and veterans stranded in Taiwan. *The Wedding Banquet* alludes to the political triangle linking the United States, Taiwan, and the People's Republic of China through the tangled triangular relationship among a gay Taiwanese immigrant, his American lover, and a Chinese woman of precarious immigration status. In the end, the Taiwanese and Chinese characters forge a tentative and fragile rapprochement—although true love is reserved for the Taiwanese and American couple.

Eat Drink Man Woman explores the rifts between generations, classes, and ethnic groups on Taiwan. The film traces the lives of a widowed Mainlander and the three adult daughters who share his home. The action centers on the spectacular meals the protagonist, Chef Chu, cooks for his family and friends. In one scene, Chu's middle daughter visits a construction site where she has put a deposit on an apartment. There is a Hokkien-speaking work-man at the site, and he explains that the construction is stopped due to a financial scandal. Chu's daughter struggles to understand both his words and their import; we see her dawning realization that her attempt to be-come independent has instead brought financial ruin. In one short scene, Lee reveals how gender, class, ethnicity, and generation work together to shape Taiwanese identities and expectations.

Lee's most famous films are the Chinese martial arts epic *Crouching Ti-ger, Hidden Dragon* and the film for which he won the best-picture Oscar, *Brokeback Mountain*, a contemporary Western based on a short story by the American writer Annie Proulx. He also directed film versions of iconic Anglo-American stories from Jane Austen's *Sense and Sensibility* to Marvel Comics' "Hulk." These films show the extraordinary reach of his imagina-tion and empathy, and illustrate his wide-ranging influences: Chinese, Tai-wanese, and global. The result is a richness and breadth few contemporary filmmakers can match.

Lin Hwai-min is as well-known to dance connoisseurs as Ang Lee is to film buffs. He is the founder and creative force behind the Cloud Gate Dance Theater. Cloud Gate is hugely popular in Taiwan: tickets for its shows sell out quickly, and its free performances attract thousands of view-ers. Its world tours have drawn enthusiastic reviews, including comparisons to legendary figures in modern dance.

There is nothing compromised or crowd pleasing about Cloud Gate; its works are abstract, often difficult. Lin's choreography draws on interna-tional forms and themes to express ideas that are deeply rooted in Taiwan and China. One European dance critic described his work as "a distinct and mature Chinese choreographic language"; his works borrow techniques from such quintessentially Chinese arts as Peking opera, martial arts, and brush-and-ink calligraphy. Cloud Gate's productions also evoke Taiwan. A recent work called *Listening to the River* is inspired by the Danshui River, which flows near Lin's home. The dance conveys a range of emotions, all connected to the Danshui, of which Lin says, "The river never utters a word; it merely reflects the landscape of the heart." Lin's work exemplifies the strong sense of place and engagement with Taiwan's natural and human geography that makes the island's contemporary culture at once universally appealing and unmistakably Taiwanese.

For a Mainlander like Ang Lee, Taiwanese history engenders alienation and homelessness. His art seems to transcend national boundaries; his films are multilingual and multicultural, and he himself lives in an adopted land. Lin Hwai-min, a Taiwanese from Chiayi, has made the opposite journey. Lin was born days before the 2-28 Incident; his mother hid from the chaos in the maternity hospital, but there was no hiding her son from Taiwan's struggles as he grew up. Lin's father was a local politician and KMT official who held posts in the cabinet and as an advisor to President Lee Teng-hui. Descriptions of his father conjure a classic Chinese trope, the dutiful official who longs for free time to enjoy poetry and music, but the family's identity also incorporates Japanese and Western (Christian) influences. Perhaps the most formative force in Lin Hwai-min's childhood was a British film, *The Red Shoes*. Lin claims to have seen it eleven times when he was five years old. Although at that time he could not imagine making it his profession, he fell in love with dance watching the movie.

Lin Hwai-min was not a political activist in his youth, but his early artistic works reveal a streak of rebellion. His first encounter with fame was as a writer, not a dancer. When he was twenty-four years old, he published *Cicada*, a novella that became one of Taiwan's best-selling stories. The story portrays a group of educated youths who are plagued by alienation and ennui. They debate sex, drugs, and rock and roll to a backdrop of Beatles, Joan Baez, and Bob Dylan songs. They never utter a subversive word, but their empty ambition and wasted potential constitute a powerful critique of the way KMT authoritarianism undermined freedom and prevented Taiwanese people from flourishing spiritually and intellectually. The story also shows a character struggling with his sexual identity—a risky theme for Taiwanese literature in the early 1960s.

Lin spent money he earned from his writing to pay for dance lessons, but it remained a hobby—he has said he felt too old to begin dancing seriously in his twenties. In 1969, he traveled to the United States to study writing. He picked up choreography because the Writers Workshop at the University of Iowa required students to take a minor field, but it was there he found his niche. He stayed in the United States for two years, earning a master's degree and taking classes at the Martha Graham School of Contemporary Dance and the Merce Cunningham Dance Studio.

When he returned to Taiwan, he founded Cloud Gate, named for China's oldest known dance. The company premiered in Lin's hometown of Chiayi—about as far from the center of cultural and political power as it could get. Lin's stated reason was to honor Chiayi as the location of the first Chinese settlements on the island, but the real reason, he said later, was to avoid trouble. The title of the piece was *Legacy*, and its theme was Taiwan's history. It depicted the early Chinese settlement of the island through dance, acrobatic movement, and music.

Lin likes to say Jimmy Carter made him famous, because on the day *Legacy* premiered, Carter announced his decision to normalize relations with the PRC and cut diplomatic ties with Taiwan. The revelation was a massive blow to Taiwanese, so Cloud Gate's performance of Taiwanese history had special resonance for its traumatized audience. The dance unleashed a flood of grief, fear, anger, and defiance. As Lin describes it, "The performance turned into a rally."

The Taiwanese people had taken possession of Lin Hwai-min and his art, turning them to the purposes of a people in search of its identity. Since *Legacy*, his work has been entwined with the movement for Taiwanese identity and freedom, even though Lin himself resists narrow definitions, insisting, "I never label myself as a Taiwanese choreographer; my works deal with humanity." A moment later he adds, "I am a Taiwanese artist. I live and work here. If you want a label, that is my birthright. My work grows out from this land. But of course I am a gypsy, too."

Lin professes an interest in universal themes, but Taiwanese nationalists look to his work for a political message. Many Taiwanese artists have struggled to create art that can satisfy that audience while remaining true to the artist's own vision. Even the protest singer Chen Ming-chang asked himself not only "What is Taiwanese music?" but also "What is *my* Taiwanese music?"

The pressure to create art that would speak to an audience in search of its identity without provoking the state or compromising artistic quality took a toll on Lin. In 1988 he decided he needed a break, and he disbanded Cloud Gate. For three years Lin traveled extensively, including to China. Visiting the mainland was eye-opening. He was excited to be in China, the origin of so many of his inspirations and influences, but his travels there brought home to him how different he was as a Taiwanese. A turning point came during one of Lin's stays in Taiwan, when a taxi driver urged him to resume his work, to not give up. The idea that a taxi driver would be so invested in an elite contemporary art institution touched Lin deeply, and in 1991 he restarted Cloud Gate.

As artists, Ang Lee and Lin Hwai-min expose global audiences to Taiwan's Creole culture, which combines a strong Taiwanese sense of place with Chinese and global influences. Their work is accessible to people all over the world, but it is interesting and appealing because it is not homogenized, but recognizably Taiwanese. Master Zhengyan and the group she founded, the Buddhist Compassion Relief Ciji Association, or Ciji, are bringing a similar sensibility to the world of religious philanthropy. Like its counterparts in the arts, Ciji weaves together Taiwanese, Chinese, and global values to create a uniquely Taiwanese Buddhist institution.

Compassion is a fundamental value in Buddhism, and almsgiving is a core Buddhist practice and virtue. Ciji's innovation was to create for Taiwan a model of charity that conforms to modern norms about giving. In mainstream Buddhist tradition, almsgiving is part of an individual's spiritual discipline; how alms affect the recipient is unimportant. Unlike a traditional Buddhist order, to which devotees would offer alms as a way of accumulating personal merit, Master Zhengyan and her nuns do not accept alms. They pay their expenses by selling items they produce themselves. The donations Ciji collects go directly to the association's charitable projects. Ciji personnel have responded to disasters all over the world; they were among the first aid workers to arrive after the Asian tsunami of 2006, the Sichuan earthquake of 2008, and the Haitian earthquake of 2010. This global reach underscores Ciji's universalistic conception of ethics and obligation.

In contrast to traditional Buddhist sects, Ciji is a modern philanthropic enterprise deeply interested in the quality and efficacy of its charitable acts. Ciji means-tests its recipients and collects extensive data on its programs' effectiveness. This determination to make sure its contributions go to the truly needy and make a real difference in their circumstances updates Buddhist almsgiving for an age that believes in efficiency and performance. At the same time, though, the intensity of Ciji volunteers' devotion and the enormity of their generosity rest on deep religious conviction. This combination of religious fervor and charitable pragmatism is unprecedented in the Chinese cultural world; in this sense, Ciji is something completely new.

It is probably no accident that this new phenomenon got its start in the 1960s. Ciji's development coincided with Taiwan's. The massive expansion in islanders' affluence prompted many Taiwanese to reexamine their values, to ask how they might give meaning to their newfound wealth. Ciji seems to hold special appeal for Taiwanese whose success in business leaves them wondering whether their hard-won skills might not be better used in a humanitarian enterprise. Ciji's publicity materials emphasize a salvation narrative that traces believers' transformation from money-hungry, lost souls to efficient, focused philanthropists.

It is also no accident that Ciji is a "matriarchal" sect. That the most powerful charitable organization in the Chinese-speaking world should be headed by a woman reflects the extraordinary importance of nuns in Taiwanese Buddhism. The prevalence of nuns in Taiwanese Buddhism has historical roots—in the Japanese period, groups of "vegetarian women" were an important religious force, and after 1945, Buddhist monks migrating from the mainland relied on Taiwanese nuns to help them get established on the island. But as Elise Anne DeVido writes in *The Infinite Worlds of Taiwan's Buddhist Nuns*, the nuns' dominance "is at once *a product of* the liberalization of traditional gender roles in Taiwan since the 1970s, and . . . a *force* that is creating more diverse life opportunities and choices for women in Taiwan."

Women's increased choices drive three of Taiwan's most controversial trends: falling birth rates, rising rates of "marriage refusal," and high rates of marriage migration. As recently as the 1990s, sociologists assumed that while women might delay marriage, marriage itself—sooner or later—was an obligation nearly all Taiwanese women would undertake. What we have seen in the last decade or so, however, is a sharp rise in the percentage of Taiwanese women who have never married.

One reason for falling rates of marriage is the mismatch between the traditional preference for women to "marry up"—to find a partner with higher educational and professional attainments—and the widening educational gap between women—who are pulling ahead—and men. Another reason is the realization that women do not need to make the compromises associated with marriage; increasingly, Taiwanese women believe they can prolong the period of independence and freedom by choosing careers over marriage and motherhood.

Women feel pressure to marry, but men feel it much more strongly. Not only do their parents still expect daughters-in-law and grandchildren, but also a man's independence rests on having a wife to manage the household. Few unmarried men live alone. They are far more likely to live with their parents, surrounded by reminders of their filial obligation to marry. To fill the gap between the demand for wives and the supply of women willing to marry, Taiwanese have turned to marriage migrants, whom Taiwanese call "foreign brides."

The marriage migration trend peaked in 2003, when nearly a third of marriages in Taiwan, more than fifty-five thousand, included foreign-born spouses—nearly all of them women. Two-thirds of those spouses came from the PRC; Vietnam and other Southeast Asian countries contributed the rest. Changes in government regulations and social trends slowed the flow of marriage migrants more recently, and the share of marriages involving foreign-born spouses has fallen by half since 2003. Still, about one in ten births is to a foreign-born mother.

Marriage migration is controversial. It touches on sensitive issues—national identity, gender roles, and family relationships—and exposes the magnitude of the social changes that have overtaken the island in recent decades. Above all, in a society that has spent decades debating what it means to be Taiwanese, the arrival of tens of thousands of foreign brides provokes strong feelings. Mainland-born brides are a source of special concern to Taiwanese nationalists because they seem to reinvigorate ties between Taiwan and China. Some "Deep Green" pundits have even suggested Mainland-born women will dilute Taiwan's political identity by teaching their children that Taiwan is part of the PRC.

Marriage migration is controversial, but it performs important functions in Taiwan's society. Tens of thousands of PRC women—many of them divorcees in their thirties and forties—have married elderly Taiwanese and Mainlander men. They provide companionship and care to a group whose chances of marrying locally were dim. Foreign-born women are also more willing than their Taiwanese sisters to wed men with limited education, poor financial prospects, and physical disabilities. Another contribution marriage migrants make to their adopted home is reproduction. Taiwan's birthrate is among the lowest in the world, but the influx of young wives has prevented it from falling even lower. Marriage migrants also contribute economically, both to Taiwan and to their countries of origin. In recent years, Taiwan's government has recognized these contributions by making the regulations governing marriage migrants and their integration into Taiwanese society more generous and fair.

When Marjory and Arthur Wolf conducted their anthropological fieldwork in Peihotien fifty years ago, Taiwan was a rural society steeped in tradition and ruled with an iron fist by Chinese nationalists in Taipei. It was only just beginning to embrace the forces that would shape its future: urbanization, industrialization, globalization, and "Taiwanization." Today's Taiwan reveals those forces' effects in myriad ways. From the rocket hives of Yenshui to the Ciji Buddhist Compassion Society, Taiwan's culture is a unique fusion of global and local forces, one that is integrated into the world but still recognizably Taiwanese.

SOURCES

There is no better source I've found for details about Taiwanese marriage customs than Bonnie Adrian's delightful book *Framing the Bride: Globalizing Beauty and Romance in Taiwan's Bridal Industry*. Much of the material in this chapter is drawn from this first-rate study. Statistics on the prevalence of arranged marriages come from "From Arranged Marriage toward Love Match" by Thornton, Chang, and Lin, in the book *Social Change and the Family in Taiwan*. Information on residential patterns comes from another chapter in that volume, "Co-Residence and Other Ties Linking Couples and Their Parents," by Weinstein, Sun, Chang, and Freedman. I have read many wonderful books and articles on Taiwanese religion, but my main source for this chapter is David K. Jordan's *Gods, Ghosts and Ancestors*, a truly good read.

6

"An Opportunity Full of Threats"

Cross-Strait Economic Interaction

Buried among Shanghai's futuristic office towers, just a few blocks from Xin Tian Di, China's toniest retail district, is the Little Town of Lukang restaurant, where Taiwanese expatriates pay five-star prices for night market favorites. Little Town of Lukang serves gourmet versions of Taiwanese down-home specialties—three-cups frog, salted-turnip omelet, clam-and-pork-bone soup. The most popular item on the menu—the one that keeps the place packed long after midnight on summer weekends—is shaved ice. Shaved ice with fruit, shaved ice with red beans and barley, shaved ice with condensed milk, shaved ice with pudding—shaved ice cold enough and sweet enough to bring homesick tears to the eyes of the hard-driving Taiwanese financiers and captains of industry who call Shanghai their home away from home.

Selling high-end comfort food to fellow Taiwanese in Shanghai is one of many business ventures the restaurant's Hsinchu-born owner has launched since arriving in the city in 1985. Over the years he's ridden the wave of Taiwanese investment from textile manufacturing to high-end services. He's seen whole industries come—and more than a few busted entrepreneurs go. As a boss, he's a perfectionist; he buys his waiters' clothes and haircuts because he knows if he paid them enough to cover those expenses they'd give the money to their parents instead. But after twenty years in the city, he has few local friends. Shanghaiese, he says, are too clannish to socialize with someone not fluent in their dialect. It's a lonely life, but he has no intention of returning to Taiwan. He's divorced from his wife, his children are grown and scattered, and of course, he's making money and living well in Shanghai, one of the most exciting cities on earth.

The Taiwanese customers who enjoy home-style delicacies at Little Town of Lukang reflect the two most important developments in Taiwan's twenty-first century economy. The first is a deep and growing entanglement with mainland China's economy, where Taiwanese investors occupy a critical position as employers, technology providers, and bridges to global markets. The second is a high-tech revolution that has transformed the island's industry. Together, these two trends define Taiwan's contemporary economy.

No one really knows how many Taiwanese are living in mainland China today, or how much money they have invested there, but everyone agrees the numbers are huge and growing. In 2007, Taiwanese paid 4.6 million visits to the mainland, an increase of almost 5 percent over 2006. According to Taiwan government statistics, Taiwanese invested nearly U.S.$10 billion in mainland China in 2007, with the total investment accumulated since 1987 as high as U.S.$65 billion. And even the Taiwan government admits these figures are far too low, since much of Taiwan's investment in the mainland is funneled through intermediary nations. Together, Taiwan and the two biggest intermediaries—the Cayman Islands and the British Virgin Islands—accounted for 30 percent of China's direct foreign investment in 2007. Taiwan and China also are among one another's most important trading partners. In 2006, Taiwan was China's ninth-largest export market, and its third-largest source of imports. For Taiwan, China was the number-one export market, and number-two source of imported goods.

As impressive as these numbers are, the magnitude of cross-Strait economic cooperation is even more striking when we consider that the two sides have racked up these huge travel, trade, and investment totals in barely twenty years' time. Before 1987, Taiwanese were not allowed to trade, transfer money, or even visit the mainland (although some, like the boss at Little Town of Lukang, evaded the rules). In those days, the two sides were locked in a confrontation that began with the Chinese Civil War and continued through the Cold War. They treated one another as enemy states: a Taiwanese who slipped into the mainland through Hong Kong might be accused of spying by either side—or both. Economic interactions were limited to small-scale smuggling, mostly traditional Chinese medicines. Taipei's policy was summed up in its "three nos" policy: no contact, no negotiation, no compromise.

As China opened itself to the world in the 1980s, the "bamboo curtain" began to splinter. In the past, Taipei's refusal to engage the mainland had isolated Beijing, but by the mid-1980s, Taiwan was isolating itself. Pretending the PRC did not exist, or that it was on the edge of collapse, no longer served Taiwan's political or economic interests; Taipei needed a new approach. At the same time, fast-moving domestic transformation in Taiwan was amplifying popular demands and muting hard-line voices.

In 1986, President Chiang Ching-kuo made a series of far-reaching policy changes. In October, he told *Washington Post* publisher Katherine Graham that he intended to lift martial law, and in July 1987 he carried out that promise. While new legislation kept many martial law provisions on the books, the most onerous restrictions on civil and political rights were gone. Overnight, a wave of new publications—including newspapers, which had been regulated stringently under martial law—hit the newsstands, bringing progressive ideas to a far wider audience than had ever before been possible. Simultaneously, new political parties sprang up to channel the wide range of opinions that could, for the first time, find expression in the political system.

The loudest voices calling for reform belonged to democracy activists. Despite the volume of those demands, President Chiang and Vice President (and soon-to-be successor) Lee Teng-hui were more attentive to the wishes of KMT loyalists, many of whom were deeply critical of the liberalizing trends. Both leaders recognized that reforming Taiwan and leading it into a democratic future would be possible only if conservatives could be pacified. Although the conservatives tended to be strongly anti-Communist and viscerally opposed to the mainland regime, they were sensitive to the plight of the thousands of aging Mainlanders desperate to see loved ones in China before they died. To answer that need, Chiang decided to permit humanitarian visits by Taiwanese to the mainland.

At first the visits were restricted to individuals whose families had been separated by the civil war, but once the gates were open, Taiwanese from many different backgrounds crowded through. A lifetime of China-centered education and indoctrination had made islanders intensely curious about the mainland. The opportunity to see the Great Wall and the Forbidden City, to walk Shanghai's famous Bund and visit the home temples of Mazu and other popular deities—Taiwanese had dreamed of these adventures for decades. Within two years, the number of Taiwanese visits to China skyrocketed from virtually zero to more than half a million. Most visitors were retired soldiers returning to families they had left four decades earlier, Mainlanders looking for their roots, and tourists seeking the latest thrill. But when they deplaned in Taipei at the end of their journeys, many were talking business.

Visitors to the mainland in the late 1980s and early 1990s were stunned by its poverty. Taiwanese visiting old hometowns and religious sites veered off the standard tourist itineraries, into "real China." Raised to worship "the motherland" as the home of a great civilization, they were shocked to find a nation of poorly educated peasants, drably clothed, badly housed, barely fed, and cut off from the outside world. Many came home disappointed and disgusted by what they had seen; "backward" quickly became the buzz word for China. It was common in the early 1990s to hear islanders describe the mainland as "like Taiwan was fifty years ago."

For Chinese nationalists in Taiwan, these revelations were painful. Marginal, colonized, little Taiwan somehow had surged ahead of the Chinese heartland. For Taiwanese businesspeople, though, China's backwardness was great news. By the 1980s, Taiwan's manufacturing economy was outgrowing the island. After three decades of steady growth in export-oriented manufacturing, Taiwanese wages had increased to the point where companies struggled to remain competitive. Even before the door to China opened, Taiwanese entrepreneurs were looking for a way out of the high-cost, low-profit trap. From their perspective, Taipei decided to lift the ban on mainland travel—which they took as a de facto license to invest—just in time.

The first wave of Taiwanese investors to open up shop on the mainland represented traditional manufacturing firms. In Taiwan, textiles, shoes, plastic odds-and-ends, toys, furniture, and other low-end goods were sunset industries; in China, those same industries promised a new dawn. They had the potential to launch the Chinese economy into export-oriented manufacturing guided by experienced entrepreneurs with well-established international relationships. Taiwanese had been producing goods for global brands for decades; they had both the know-how and the networks to stage manage China's global manufacturing debut.

During the 1980s, paramount leader Deng Xiaoping opened China's economy to the world, attracting investors from America, Europe, and Japan, as well as Taiwan. The Taiwanese arrived relatively late, and because Taipei and Beijing had no formal political ties, they came without the protections other countries' investors enjoyed. In the absence of normal government-to-government relations, Taiwanese entrepreneurs were forced to negotiate the China market on their own.

Most traditional manufacturing firms were small and medium-sized companies—the same nimble family-owned outfits that had powered Taiwan's economic miracle. Finding unconventional solutions was their strong suit, and they quickly figured out how to navigate the complex relationship between Taiwan and the mainland. They moved their money through Hong Kong, Singapore, and other intermediaries. Because there were no direct flights (which require government-to-government agreements) they passed through "neutral" locations en route to the mainland. Hong Kong's Kai Tak Airport became a familiar way station, filled with weary Taiwanese businesspeople dozing between flights. (A decade later, the swanky new Chek Lap Kok Airport saw the birth of a new ritual: the SIM card swap, in which planeloads of Taiwanese switched their mobile phones from Taiwan mode to mainland mode and back again in the departure lounges.)

Taiwanese investors jumped in importance in the summer of 1989, when their unofficial status suddenly became an advantage. In June, Chinese troops cracked down with bloody force on protestors in Beijing. The news of civilians gunned down by soldiers and crushed under tank treads shocked the world, leading most investor nations to impose tough economic sanctions on China. The rate of increase for direct foreign investment in China fell from 38 percent in 1988 to 6 percent in 1989 and 3 percent in 1990. But for Taiwanese, the slowdown was short-lived. With other investors temporarily out of the market, the ever-pragmatic Taiwanese doubled down. By the early 1990s, cooperation between the two sides of the Taiwan Strait had become a driving force in both sides' overall economic performance.

The business practices Taiwanese manufacturers followed when they moved to the mainland reveal much about the Chinese economy of the time. Taiwanese companies did not license Chinese firms to produce for them; they moved their own operations to China. They did not buy Chinese equipment; they dismantled factories in Taiwan and transported the machinery, in most cases through Hong Kong. They rarely purchased land for factories, preferring instead to minimize their financial exposure by leasing space. Nor did they hire local Chinese to run their factories; *Taishang* (Taiwanese entrepreneurs) moved to the mainland to supervise their operations directly. Few Taishang looked to local suppliers to provide inputs; instead, whole supply chains moved together and set up shop close together, reproducing the clustered production process they had used in Taiwan. Finally, most Taishang were slow to integrate into Chinese society. Despite the linguistic and cultural affinity between Taiwan and China, Taishang tended to huddle together for comfort—and for protection. They still do.

The most famous Taiwanese enclaves are Dongguan, a city in Guangdong that lies on the corridor from Hong Kong through Shenzhen to the provincial capital Guangzhou, and Kunshan, once a distant exurb of Shanghai, now one of the world's most important centers for high-tech manufacturing. (The first large-scale manufacturing of iPod Touch devices was in Kunshan. Three years later, Apple contracted production of its new flagship product, the iPad, to a Taiwanese-owned electronics factory in Guangzhou.) Taiwanese were attracted to Dongguan because of its proximity to Hong Kong, the leading port of entry for Taiwanese businesses in China, and because it was open to international business and investment before other parts of China.

One factor contributing to Taiwanese businesses' success in China is the proliferation of Taiwanese Businessmen's Associations (TBAs). In the absence of normal political relations between Taipei and Beijing, Taishang lack the protections ordinarily afforded to foreign investors by trade agreements, legal cooperation, and tax treaties. To compensate for this deficiency,

Taishang worked with local governments in China to organize TBAs, which act as advocates, booster clubs, and matchmakers for Taiwanese firms.

Furniture magnate Kuo Shan-hui's tenure heading Dongguan's TBA is legendary, an example of TBA leadership at its best. Kuo reached out to the Dongguan city government and built personal relationships with key local officials. He used those relationships to help other Taishang set up shop in the city, creating thousands of jobs and fattening the city's tax rolls. He also deployed Taiwanese capital strategically to cement ties between Taishang and the city, including mobilizing Taishang to underwrite prestigious projects for the Dongguan government. While Kuo was more successful than most TBA heads, his wide-ranging efforts on behalf of his constituents were typical.

Connections between Taishang and Chinese localities are at the heart of the cross-Strait economic relationship. While Taipei and Beijing were still eyeing each other warily, Taishang like Kuo Shan-hui were drawing Chinese local officials, business partners, and employees into vast webs of mutually beneficial business ties. Taiwanese paid for their opportunities in China with everything from "voluntary" contributions to local charities to "jobs" for local officials. As these relationships attest, economic engagement between Taiwan and China is a bottom-up phenomenon; neither national government can control—or even fully understand—the degree to which its economy has become dependent upon the other.

In the early 1990s, larger companies such as petrochemical firms (including Formosa Plastics), infrastructure companies, and food processors began to join the smaller-scale traditional manufacturers in China. They moved for lower wages, to be sure, but also to take advantage of China's relaxed regulations—especially when it came to environmental protection. In some cases, Taiwan was subject to import quotas, while products originating on the mainland were not. (As China's trade surpluses mounted, that logic reversed, and some Taishang, especially garment makers, found themselves outsourcing production to Vietnam, Cambodia, Sri Lanka, and elsewhere.)

The PRC government taxed imported components, but even so, Taiwanese manufacturers preferred to buy from Taiwanese suppliers, whom they believed provided better and more reliable quality and more consistent prices than home-grown Chinese companies. Taiwanese also preferred to do business with one another because their preexisting relationships allowed for flexible payment options and better terms. As one Taiwanese textile executive put it, "I use connections with other Taiwanese to get things done. Trust is a cost." Taiwanese already in the mainland wanted more upstream production to move, and rising cost pressure on Taiwanese suppliers reinforced their conviction that opening operations in China was a good idea.

For some industries, especially food processing, the promise of China's huge domestic market was the draw. Here again, cultural affinities between the two sides boosted Taiwanese manufacturers. Taiwanese firms were accustomed to manufacturing (and, just as important, marketing) inexpensive foods tailored for Chinese tastes. Taiwanese brands soon gained a reputation for quality and sophistication. All over China, restaurants cashed in on the trend.

In addition to "Little Town of Lukang," Shanghai has scores of other Taiwan-themed eateries, from stands promising Taiwan-style beef noodles to the Yunghe Soymilk King breakfast chain. Taiwanese coffee chains like Shangdao/UBC were being battered at home by up-market international brands (read "Starbucks") when they discovered Chinese customers were not too cool for the dark banquettes, set-price meals, and smoky ambiance of old-school chains. Others—notably 85 Degrees (a coffee chain named for the ideal water temperature for brewing coffee)—sell a Starbucks-style product at a China-friendly price.

Taiwan's image as a source of trendy, stylish products has paid off for all sorts of companies that sell lifestyle and image, including wedding photographers and the bakeries that provide high-end engagement cakes. In the hypercompetitive environment back home, Taiwanese entrepreneurs developed those industries to an extremely high level but eventually saturated the local market. The mainland offered a new lease on life, with hundreds of millions of Chinese looking for ways to display and celebrate their new middle-class lifestyles. Taiwanese nuptial entrepreneurs transferred their business models to the mainland fully formed, and they leveraged Taiwan's fashion-forward reputation among China's nouveau riche to inculcate the culture of romance and conspicuous consumption that had made their services a must-have in Taiwan.

A third wave of Taiwanese business migration began in 1993, when information technology (IT) and other high-technology firms began moving some labor-intensive production across the Strait. They were motivated partly by the same factors that had driven the earlier waves of outsourcing—tax incentives, lower prices for land and labor—but they also were under pressure to reduce prices. Their customers, the international IT brands, pushed Taiwanese firms to take advantage of China's low manufacturing costs.

Taiwan's high-tech revolution began in the 1980s, following patterns set in earlier stages of Taiwan's economic development. As before, the state initiated public-private collaborations that helped transform Taiwan into a global center for IT production. It encouraged foreign companies to subcontract production to the same small and medium-sized companies that had powered breakthroughs in traditional manufacturing. It also supported Taiwanese firms to develop the capacity to produce key inputs for these new industries, including semiconductors.

The most powerful agency for promoting high-tech development in Taiwan is the Industrial Technology Research Institute (ITRI). Over the years, ITRI has trained tens of thousands of researchers and scientists and spun off scores of successful companies. Among the most important of ITRI's offspring is Taiwan Semiconductor Manufacturing Company, or TSMC. Founded in 1987, TSMC is the world's largest dedicated semiconductor foundry; its clients include Intel and Qualcomm.

As with traditional manufacturing, foreign companies spurred Taiwan's entry into high-tech manufacturing when they hired local companies as contract manufacturers. Taiwanese upgraded the technical and production knowledge they had gleaned from making previous-generation products to meet the needs of foreign high-tech firms making more advanced products. For example, IBM outsourced computer monitor production to Tatung and other television manufacturers in Taiwan, while Quanta Corporation leveraged its expertise in miniaturizing calculators to become the world's largest original design manufacturer of notebook computers.

As the market for IT equipment matured, high-tech components—semiconductors, motherboards, CPUs, monitors—became commodities. With profit margins narrowing, Taiwanese suppliers came under intense pressure to lower their prices. By 1997, the pressure to lower costs had prompted a large-scale shift in manufacturing to mainland China. Five years later, Taiwanese controlled around two-thirds of the PRC's output of information technology products, and half of Taiwanese firms' IT output was produced on the mainland. Today, Taiwan-owned companies like Foxconn, Taiwan Semiconductor, Asustek, and Quanta employ hundreds of thousands of Chinese workers and have become an indispensable source of high-tech products for the world.

Most Taiwanese high-tech companies are original equipment or design manufacturers, which means they design and manufacture products that are sold under someone else's brand label (Dell, Gateway, Apple, Hewlett-Packard, etc.). Taiwan firms focus on bringing technologies acquired from their customers to market, by tweaking products, streamlining production processes, and improving product features. This is not to say Taiwanese do not innovate. In 2009 Taiwanese were granted almost eight thousand new U.S. patents (three times as many as the PRC), putting Taiwan fifth in the world. By making themselves both the most reliable and the cheapest IT hardware manufacturers, Taiwanese firms have managed to capture a huge market share in numerous industries, making 90 percent of the world's notebook computers, 98 percent of its motherboards, 78 percent of its LCD monitors, and so on, in 2007.

Branding and innovation are hallmarks of a successful twenty-first-century economy, but it took years for recognized Taiwanese brands such as Acer and Asus to appear. Still, we should not snub Taiwan firms' successes in contract manufacturing. Not just anyone can make shoes for Nike or PCs for Dell or iPhones for Apple. Those contracts are hard to get, and their relationships with global companies are among Taiwanese manufacturers' most precious assets. In China, there is a clear division of labor in which Taiwan-owned firms occupy a different—and higher-value—niche from their PRC-based counterparts. Homegrown PRC firms make most of the world's low-end footwear, but Taiwan-owned firms dominate branded shoe manufacturing in China.

Taiwanese companies manufacturing in China rarely buy inputs from Chinese-owned suppliers. Whether they are making running shoes, bicycles, or notebook computers, their supply chains are overwhelmingly Taiwanese. Global brands demand low prices, but they also require high quality and absolute reliability. Taiwanese firms have proven to the big international players—and to one another—that their operations in China can deliver both. Letting an unproven Chinese supplier into the chain puts a whole supply chain's relationship with the global brands at risk.

Taiwan's high-tech revolution and its energetic outreach to China are mutually reinforcing trends. Without the high-tech revolution, Taiwan would have missed the opportunity to build cutting-edge firms and participate in the new economy. Without the move to China, the island's IT products would have been too expensive to compete in global markets. The availability of a new, low-wage, low-regulation manufacturing base allowed Taiwan's businesses to survive and expand despite tough global competition. Firms and industries that were reaching their limits in Taiwan got a second chance in China.

Individuals, too, find the opportunities and challenges China offers revitalizing. I met with a Taiwanese businessman in Shanghai who surprised me by recognizing the brand of clothing I wore to the interview. He had spent years sourcing apparel for that U.S.-based company, but was laid off when the firm went into bankruptcy protection. He looked for work in Taiwan for two years without success. He recalled, "I was over 50, with 30 years of valuable experience in the apparel business, doing sourcing and import-export, but I couldn't get hired anywhere. Everyone thought I was too old, and too expensive, to hire." A friend offered him a job in Shanghai outsourcing clothing production to *other* countries for a China-based firm. The offer came just in time, he reported, then added, "We have a phrase for people like me: second spring."

For professionals, moving to China can be more than a survival mechanism. To his surprise, the Shanghai businessman found his horizons widening in Shanghai. "To work here requires more skills than in Taiwan," he said. "In Taiwan, the factories are mostly small. Four hundred employees is big. Here, a thousand employees is standard. That forces managers to take a global view, and it makes us manage better. You develop more as a businessman here than in Taiwan, where things are so small." A human re-sources professional from Taipei working for an Australian consulting firm in Shanghai shares his view, "In Taiwan, I couldn't get a big project, like a really big merger—a million dollar project. It won't happen in Taiwan; we don't have deals that big. This is an opportunity for me. I can learn more here. All the training programs are here. There is more chance for a promotion, and my salary is higher."

Taiwan's high-tech development followed Taiwan's traditional model in some ways—many manufacturers are small and medium-sized firms embedded in production clusters and chains, and contract manufacturing is still the norm—but it deviates from the earlier model in other respects. Some Taiwanese high-tech firms, mostly in information technology but including high-end bicycle maker Giant, have begun capturing market share under their own brands. The mainland makes it possible for them to grow large enough to achieve that goal. Perhaps the most prominent examples are Taiwan's homegrown PC brands, Acer and Asus. By 2010, Acer was second only to Hewlett-Packard in world sales of personal computers, and it led the field in Europe, where it held almost a quarter of the PC market, with Asus soaking up another 8 percent.

An even more recent wave of Taiwanese business migration to the mainland has seen retail and service firms opening operations aimed at servicing the international business community in China and taking advantage of the mainland's huge domestic market. Real estate, law, human resources, and business consulting firms are heading to China, both to serve as a bridge between Taiwanese and other foreign businesspeople and the Chinese market, and to deliver services that have only recently become available in the PRC.

Taiwan derives substantial economic benefits from its firms' participation in the PRC market, benefits that would not be available in just any low-wage country. There is a synergy between the Taiwanese and mainland economies that has accelerated both sides' growth. Taiwan was able to push up the value chain from low-tech manufacturer to producer of global IT brands in large part because China was ready for and open to Taiwanese investment at just the right moment. Without China, Taiwan would have been competing for opportunities with other, more advanced, countries. Without Taiwan, China would have lacked the technical know-how and global connections to enter high-tech markets.

These benefits are enormous, but the picture is not all rosy. Cross-Strait intertwinement carries costs and risks for Taiwan, too. To begin with, doing business on the mainland is difficult and dangerous. Countless Taishang have lost their shirts, sometimes for business reasons and sometimes because they were fleeced by unscrupulous partners, competitors, or even local officials.

Another risk Taiwan faces is "hollowing out"—the transfer of Taiwan's productive activity to the mainland. Many of Taiwan's politicians, economists, and citizens are deeply worried about hollowing out. Since the late 1980s, Taiwanese politicians have tried to moderate the pace at which firms move their operations to the mainland by capping the amount they can invest on the mainland and limiting the transfer of strategic technology, but those policies have not stopped firms from moving their operations. Being a contract manufacturer in high-tech industry has many advantages, but it provides little autonomy. The customer is the boss, and price-sensitive clients have forced many firms to move production to China when they might have preferred to remain in Taiwan.

Despite these fears, Taiwan's economy seems so far to have benefited more than it has lost, as successes in the mainland increase wealth on the island and stimulate demand for research and development and other Taiwan-based inputs. Taiwan's companies are reluctant to move the most valuable, important, and vulnerable elements of their production chain to the mainland. Research and development are risky in China, where piracy, patent infringement, and industrial espionage are rampant.

About 80 percent of China's high-tech exports are actually processing exports, products Chinese workers assembled and packaged using components produced elsewhere—mainly Taiwan. As the demand for electronic goods assembled in China grows, the demand for electronic *components* manufactured in Taiwan grows, too. Even so, many Taiwanese economists, politicians, and citizens worry that this trend will not last, and Taiwan's manufacturing economy will hollow out.

Hollowing out is an economic risk, but much of the debate over Taiwan's economic entanglement with the mainland concerns political risks. Skeptics of cross-Strait engagement worry that economic intertwinement will make Taiwan vulnerable to political pressure from Beijing. When Taiwanese acquire business interests in the mainland, they also acquire a preference for stable relations between the two sides, which could make it harder for Taipei to rebuff unwelcome overtures. Taishang often lobby for policies to ease cross-Strait business; their opponents worry their efforts are making it hard for Taipei to maintain a balanced approach. Some even fear Taiwan's economy could become so dependent on the PRC that Taiwanese might surrender to its political demands. Taiwanese have a massive amount of money tied up in the mainland; if the PRC government decides to sacrifice its own economic performance to achieve unification, that money will be at risk—and Taiwan's leaders will be under intense pressure to find a solution that protects the island's investors.

The dilemmas cross-Strait trade and investment pose are not entirely one-sided. As Chiang Pin-kung, Taiwan's chief negotiator with the PRC, told the BBC in 2009, the PRC is dependent on Taiwan, too, especially in the high-tech and innovation sectors. It is important for Taiwan to keep its competitive edge in those sectors, but as long as it holds that edge, the relationship will be one of interdependence, not a one-sided dependence in which Taiwan is always the weaker party.

Chiang is right: the two sides are interdependent, and that introduces ambiguity for Beijing as well as Taipei. Taiwanese investment has enormous benefits for China. Taishang employ millions of Chinese workers, directly and indirectly, and contribute mightily to local tax revenues. Taishang also have transferred valuable technologies to Chinese companies. But the most important benefits the PRC gains are intangible: access to modern management techniques and practices, knowledge of how international business operates, and connections to global companies and markets. Without Taishang, China would be far less advanced. Still, Taiwan's Sino-skeptics worry, after the Taishang transfer their know-how to their PRC counterparts, will China allow the Taishang to continue making money on the mainland? No one knows, but Taiwanese debate the question endlessly.

Trade and investment get most of the attention in discussions of cross-Strait interactions, but economics is not the only realm in which cooperation is expanding quickly. Currently, several thousand young Taiwanese are studying in the mainland, and Taipei's recent decision to recognize diplomas earned in the mainland is likely to increase that number. Many are graduate students hoping to learn more about the PRC and to make business contacts there. Another popular course of study is Chinese medicine.

Religious pilgrimages, too, have proliferated since 1987. Taiwan's most popular deities originated on the mainland, and devotees have embraced the opportunity to visit their gods' "home temples." Localities in China are eager to encourage and promote religious tourism, which is a lucrative industry in deity-rich areas like coastal Fujian province. Taiwanese charities, too, are active on the mainland. Volunteer relief workers from the Ciji Buddhist Foundation were on the scene within two days of the ruinous Sichuan earthquake in 2008; theirs were the first non-PRC aid teams approved to enter the quake zone.

Given the long-standing political conflict between Taiwan and the PRC, it is no surprise that observers are keenly interested in figuring out what the political implications of all this activity will be. The predominant view is that cross-Strait engagement and interdependence diminish the chances of conflict in the Taiwan Strait. Chen Shui-bian made this point in his New Year's Eve address on December 31, 2000. He said, "The integration of our economies, trade, and culture can be a starting point for gradually building faith and confidence in each other. This, in turn, can be the basis for a new framework of permanent peace and political integration." Other predictions are even bolder. Raymond R. Wu wrote in the *Straits Times* in early 2003, "With China becoming Taiwan's [Number] 1 export market at the end of last year, economic interdependence will make Taiwan's permanent separation from China increasingly improbable, thus reducing the risk of direct military conflict."

Undoubtedly, a high degree of interdependence raises the cost of conflict for both sides. But it is not a cure-all. Interdependence is not unification, so it does not satisfy Beijing's ambitions. Nor is it likely to bring about formal unification easily or inexorably; Taiwanese have enjoyed the benefits of economic interactions for more than twenty years, but unification appears no closer today than it was in 1987. In fact, the high degree of interaction in some ways reinforces islanders' feeling that they are different from mainland Chinese.

A Taiwanese student I met in Shanghai told me he was eager to visit the PRC because he imagined he would be going home. It took only a few days for him to realize that the alienation he had felt as a Mainlander in Taiwan was nothing compared to the alienation he experienced as a Taiwanese in the PRC. Another student said the happiest experience she had in China was getting a driver's license. Without the license, she needed to use her Taiwanese Compatriot ID whenever identification was required, which "outed" her as Taiwanese. With the driver's license, she finally felt she could "pass" as a local, at least in casual interactions. While some Taiwanese feel uncomfortable living as outsiders in China, others enjoy the preferential treatment Taishang receive. Said one, "We Taiwanese have money. And in China, money talks."

Feeling different does not diminish Taiwanese people's desire for cooperation, engagement, and interaction with the PRC, but it does reinforce the sense that Taiwan is and should remain politically apart. Overall, then, economic interaction is good for cross-Strait relations, because it gives people opportunities to enjoy mutually beneficial, cooperative relationships—although some relationships, both business and personal, do not work out. Interaction also alleviates the fear and animosity that feed on ignorance and isolation. But sharing mutual interests and understanding with people in the mainland has not produced a desire for political unification among Taiwanese.

Cross-Strait economic and people-to-people interactions are almost certain to continue growing. They have become a bedrock element in both countries. Still, economics is at the heart of the relationship, and if the economic calculus changes, the relationship will change. One way that might happen is if Taiwanese businesses decide they can do better elsewhere. In mid-2010, a rash of suicides by Chinese workers brought unwelcome attention to the Taiwanese electronics giant Foxconn. The company reacted by raising wages and bringing in counselors and Buddhist monks to help workers work through their feelings. But the trade group that represented Foxconn (the Taiwan Electrical and Electronics Manufacturing Association) put out a statement saying it might be time to look outside China for new manufacturing sites. Many Taiwanese companies have already moved some of their operations to other countries in South and Southeast Asia; some have even returned manufacturing to Taiwan.

Even if Taiwanese choose to stay in the mainland, they may find home-grown PRC companies edging them aside. China's economic planners are keen to acquire cutting-edge technologies for their domestic firms. They require technology transfer for many investment deals, and do little to prevent Chinese companies from using more underhanded forms of technology "transfer." The challenge for Taiwan, then, is to stay ahead of the technology curve. Taiwan cannot become complacent; to remain relevant in the global economy, it must hold its position at the cutting edge of innovation.

Efforts by the Taiwan government to limit Taiwan firms' participation in the PRC market have largely failed. In some cases, companies moved their headquarters offshore—including to China—to evade these restrictions. In other cases, they have lost market share to firms that enjoyed unlimited access to China. Still, eliminating the restraints completely is hardly a guarantee that firms will remain on the island. The solution seems to be to leverage Taiwan's comparative advantages in research and development, education, and global networking. It is also important for Taiwan to maintain and strengthen its own legal system so that the intellectual property that holds value in a knowledge-based economy will be fully protected.

Asked whether he thinks of China as an opportunity for Taiwan, or a threat, a Taiwanese man in his early twenties replied, "It's a threat full of opportunities and an opportunity full of threats." His response perfectly captured the ambivalence most Taiwanese feel toward the entanglement of Taiwan's economy with mainland China's. It is clear that deepening interdependence limits Taiwan's freedom of action and makes it more dependent on China than many Taiwanese would like. At the same time, though, economic engagement with the mainland has brought enormous wealth and opportunity to Taiwan and its people.

Continuing interest in independence and unification as potential end states for Taiwan's unsettled political status has focused the conversation about cross-Strait economic engagement on two possibilities: either the two sides will be drawn together by their economic cooperation to the point where they overcome their differences and unify, or Taiwan's determination to remain separate will cause the economic relationship to sour.

In fact, the picture is more complicated. Undoubtedly, economic trends helped take independence off the table. In the 1990s, President Lee Teng-hui instituted a "Go South" policy aimed at deflecting Taiwanese investment away from China and into Southeast Asia. Despite his efforts, Taiwanese were quick to hitch their wagons to the rising Chinese star. The combination of ever-growing cross-Strait interdependence and China's swift economic rise makes any effort to break ties with the mainland seem both foolish and futile.

But even as these economic interactions make independence less attractive, they also reinforce Taiwan's separate identity and political status. Prolonged interaction with the mainland exposes just how different the two sides have become over the past sixty years. Any illusions Taiwanese might have harbored about the "naturalness" of unification have long since been shattered.

These trends may seem contradictory, but that is true only if one accepts that unification and independence are the only options. What economic integration has done is to take *both* end-state options off the table, in favor of a broad social preference for what Taiwanese call "the status quo"—a situation in which Taiwan enjoys de facto independence while not ruling out unification in the future. For Taiwan's leaders, the task is not to resolve the problem once and for all but to manage it in a way that maximizes constructive engagement with the mainland while minimizing constraints on Taiwan's autonomy.

Taiwan's "second economic miracle" includes both the high-tech revolution and the outreach to the mainland. One of its effects has been to help the two sides of the Strait grow together, but another of its effects is to reveal the extent to which the two sides are rooted in different soil. There are real limits to how much we can expect from this "growing together" process. Ultimately, economics can take Taipei and Beijing only so far; eventually, politics must take the lead.

SOURCES

In 2006, I spent five months in Shanghai, teaching at a university and interviewing Taiwanese living and working in mainland China. This chapter draws heavily on those conversations, as well as the many discussions I've had on these topics with Taiwanese in Taiwan. The chapter also draws on research (both published and unpublished) on cross-Strait economic interactions by political-economy experts, including Tun-jen Cheng, Keng Shu, Joseph Wong, Tse-kang Leng, Gunter Schubert, Chen Ming-chi, Chen Chih-jou, Tao Yi-feng, Wang Horng-lun, and Douglas Fuller.

When it comes to cross-Strait interactions, reliable statistics are hard to come by. Government statistics show how many trips have been made between Taiwan and the mainland, but it is impossible to say with certainty how many *different* people have made the trip. Many Taiwanese travel back and forth several times each year. Conventional wisdom holds that more than a million Taiwanese reside in the PRC, but the figure is impossible to

verify. Similarly, the exact amount Taiwanese have invested in the mainland is notoriously hard to estimate, so estimates in this book—and any
other—are only that: estimates. Data on global investment in China from
1988 to 1990 is from "Foreign Direct Investment Flows to Low-Income
Countries: A Review of the Evidence," an Overseas Development Institute
briefing paper published in September 1997.

7

Making Peace with the China Inside and the China Outside

Taiwan is a wealthy country with an extraordinary record of economic self-invention and reinvention. It is an exciting country with a vigorous and sophisticated culture. But what keeps Taiwan on the front burner for diplomats and government officials—what makes it so often front-page international news—is its uniquely precarious position in the community of nations. Just calling Taiwan a "country" is enough to make some readers drop this book in disgust. The word is anathema to the PRC government and most PRC citizens. They believe Taiwan is, always has been, and ever shall be, part of China. To them, that means it is part of the PRC.

For Taiwanese, these issues are far more complicated. The island's relationship to China is an unanswered question, and its relationship to the PRC is a *different* unanswered question. The effort to answer those questions—to reach a collective decision about how Taiwan should relate to China and the PRC—has animated Taiwan politics for much of the past six decades. Coming to an internal consensus is difficult enough, but the constraints imposed by Beijing's strong preferences and rising power make the process even more arduous.

To further complicate the matter, the task of defining Taiwan's relationships with China and the PRC has become entwined in debates over Taiwan's domestic politics, including the nature and quality of its democracy and the definition of "citizenship." These are debates about identity that engage two separate, but very closely related entities: the China *inside*—encompassing both Taiwan's ancestral heritage and its recent history—and the China *outside*—the China that exists on the other side of the Taiwan Strait and is recognized today as the People's Republic.

AUTHORITARIANISM, UNIFICATION,
AND THEIR CRITICS

For decades, the KMT strove to inculcate in Taiwanese the same certainty that Taiwan is part of China that the Chinese Communist Party has propagated on the mainland. From the mid-1940s to the mid-1970s, competing claims growing out of the Chinese Civil War powered the conflict between Beijing and Taipei. Both governments believed without reservation that Taiwan was part of China. Where they disagreed was on the definition of "China." For the KMT, "China" meant the Republic of China, born on the mainland and tragically (and temporarily) exiled to Taiwan. For the CCP, "China" was the People's Republic of China. As far as the Chinese Communists were concerned, the ROC ceased to exist at the moment Mao Zedong stood on the balcony at Tiananmen and declared the founding of the PRC.

After the ROC government evacuated to Taiwan, it viewed the civil war as unfinished business, and it harnessed vast financial and military resources to its goal of recovering the mainland. It also mobilized Taiwan's people in pursuit of its goal. The young PRC was much less single-minded in pursuing unification. The Communists faced a long to-do list: rebuilding China's shattered economy, creating political institutions from scratch, unifying far-flung parts of the former Qing empire (including Tibet, which Beijing brought forcibly to heel in 1959). At the same time, they were challenged by an escalating Cold War—which exploded into hot war on the Korean Peninsula in 1950—and deteriorating ties with their primary ally, the Soviet Union. Although the Communists were unswerving in their rhetorical commitment to "liberate" Taiwan, their leader, Mao Zedong, admitted that wiping out the KMT might take time.

There was no room for Taiwanese voices in this conversation. The Mainlander-led ROC government commanded the people of Taiwan to embrace its cause wholeheartedly. It instructed Taiwanese to take pride in their island's position as the redoubt from which republican government would be restored to China. Developing and asserting a uniquely Taiwanese collective identity was unacceptable; the KMT viewed any attempt to differentiate Taiwan from China as disloyal, even treasonous. Even nonpolitical assertions of individuality met with resistance: the writer and choreographer Lin Hwai-min was once marched into a barber shop for a forced haircut when a group of policemen decided his shaggy look was subversive.

Despite the Nationalists' efforts to suppress Taiwanese identity, in the 1960s a literary movement aimed at "writing Taiwan" began to gather momentum. Authors calling themselves *xiangtu* or "Hometown" writers created characters and stories rooted in the rhythms of island life. Authors used written Chinese in unconventional ways to render the cadences and vocabulary of Hokkien speech; their stories evoked the physical poverty and cultural richness of rural Taiwan.

Hometown Literature was the first art form to invoke a uniquely Taiwanese idiom. Huang Chun-ming's story "His Son's Big Doll," captures many of the themes and feelings of the Hometown writers' movement. To support his family the young protagonist takes a job dressing as a clown and carrying a signboard. He needs the job to preserve his position as a breadwinner, but it costs him his dignity: before long, his son cannot recognize him without the ridiculous clown makeup. The story's richly described setting—the heat, the dust, the changing qualities of sunlight and street life over the course of a day—transports the reader to a moment and location that are thoroughly Taiwanese.

While the Hometown writers were crafting their genre, Mainlander writers dominated the literary mainstream. Their work informed ruling party debates over how the mainland was lost and how it would be recovered. Like their Taiwanese colleagues', the Mainlanders' works tended toward nostalgia and melancholy. One such writer, Pai Hsien-yung, mourned the fate of Mainlanders marooned in Taipei and America. In his famous story "Winter's Nights," two scholars—one living in genteel poverty in Taipei, the other drowning in loneliness in California—reminisce about their glory days as political activists in 1919. The critic Joseph S. M. Lau calls Pai's characters "the 'last aristocrats' of an *ancient regime*—the generals without soldiers, ministers without portfolios, Helens without Troy—whose paradise, once lost, can never be regained except in memory."

In 1969, Lin Hwai-min, the long-haired writer who would later win global acclaim for his Cloud Gate dance company, slipped his novella *Cicada* into the space between these competing "hometown" literatures. His story suggested a third hometown: one that was recognizably Taiwanese, but also modern and urban. *Cicada* follows a group of disaffected youths frittering away their time in cafés and bars. Lin's characters are not the sanctified peasants, martyred soldiers, and abandoned maidens who populate the other hometowns, but frustrated young people searching for meaning and identity, not as inheritors of some grand collective destiny, but as individuals. *Cicada's* central character struggles to understand his tender feelings toward his roommate, who, as a homosexual, has chosen his private desires over the obligations imposed by the Confucian family.

Cicada was a huge hit. Readers relished its depiction of authoritarian Taiwan as stifling and stultifying, offering up nothing but clichés: wasted youth and empty pleasure. Hometown Literature enthusiasts were surprised by its popularity. Joseph Lau grudgingly included *Cicada* in an anthology of stories by young Taiwanese writers he published in 1976, observing that because Lin did not use the conventions of the Hometown Literature and he "shows no particular interest in the fate of small men from small areas" his work barely qualified as Taiwanese literature, but that the story was too popular to omit from the collection.

The critic's bemusement is revealing: the effort to recover a shared identity for all Taiwanese often has pushed aside attempts to validate and celebrate individual identities. In *Cicada*, Lin ignores the Hometown writers' collectivist ethic. His concern is the individual; he despairs of finding meaning in a nation that answers its youth's longing for freedom by offering different brands of cigarettes. Lin's fiction was fiercely critical of authoritarianism, but he was more interested in exposing the ways Confucian authoritarianism stigmatizes the liberated mind, the autonomous intellectual, the "deviant" artist than in attacking the KMT. Says one character, "'Thinking! You're always thinking! Your trouble is you think too much! Who wants you to think? All you're supposed to do is study and study.'"

In the authoritarian, militarized Taiwan of the 1950s and 1960s, the purpose of study was to serve the nation, and serving the nation meant saving the motherland. This kind of study did not require independent thought, and at a time when few Taiwanese dared even to ask for freedom, debating what kind of freedom—individual or collective—they should seek was moot. Lin Hwai-min's story struck a chord with readers—although it would be decades before Taiwanese would be allowed to face head-on the questions he was raising.

The White Terror period coincided with the high point of the Cold War, when leaders in the democratic nations assumed that "Red China," as the PRC was called, was plotting with its Soviet ally to spread Communism throughout the world. To secure the borders of the "free world," leading democratic states supported unsavory regimes so long as they were anti-Communist. Taipei benefited from this logic; through the 1950s, the world's major non-Communist nations continued to recognize the ROC—which many called "Free China"—as China's sole legitimate government. Even after losing the mainland in 1949, Chiang Kai-shek's government retained the Chinese seat in the United Nations and its status as a permanent member of the UN Security Council.

By the late 1960s, this state of affairs was becoming insupportable. Even the upheaval of the Cultural Revolution, which gave some on Taiwan hope that the Communist regime might collapse, was not enough to bring down the PRC government. The KMT kept up its brave front and continued to insist that mainland recovery was its goal, but even within the ROC military, confidence that the ROC would overthrow the PRC by force dwindled. A further complication came as the Cold War evolved. Relations between Beijing and Moscow deteriorated badly, and by the late 1960s, the two nations' armed forces were engaged in a twitchy standoff on their long border.

The changes in China's domestic politics and international position led governments around the world to conclude that ignoring and isolating the PRC was unrealistic and dangerous. In 1970 and 1971, thirteen countries switched their diplomatic strategies to recognize the PRC as the sole government of China; in 1971, President Richard Nixon sent National Security Advisor Henry Kissinger on a secret mission to Beijing. By 1975, Taiwan was down to only thirty diplomatic partners. For the Taiwan government, losing diplomatic recognition was problematic, but abandoning the claim to represent all of China was unthinkable. When states raised the option of dual recognition, including in the United Nations, Taipei dismissed their offers. The domestic political cost of admitting that the ROC was *not* the true Chinese government was too high for the KMT to accept. After all, since the 1920s, the imperative of national unification had been the foundation of KMT single-party authoritarianism, and, without it, there would be no reason to deny Taiwan's people full self-government. And the KMT-led regime was not prepared for that.

In October 1971, the United Nations General Assembly passed a resolution declaring the PRC China's sole legal government and UN representative. The resolution also promised to "expel forthwith the representatives of Chiang Kai-shek from the place which they unlawfully occupy at the United Nations." Less than a year later, U.S. President Richard Nixon went to China to begin the process of normalizing relations between Washington and Beijing. The significance of these events, discussed in detail in chapter 8, was unmistakable: The KMT's claim to represent China internationally had disintegrated. Its collapse created an ideological vacancy within Taiwan. If recovering the mainland was the *raison d'être* for single-party authoritarianism, a global rejection of that project meant the ROC state would need to find a new basis for its legitimacy. As the 1970s progressed, voices from across the political spectrum offered different views of how the state should reconstruct itself. Many of these—including some from within the KMT itself—converged on a common vision: Taiwan's future should be democratic.

For the regime, political reform offered a way to rebuild its flagging legitimacy. For decades, the ROC had emphasized "China," but the ROC lost that case when the world declared its verdict favoring Beijing. Democracy offered a new basis on which to constitute the Republic of China, this time putting the emphasis on "Republic." As Chiang Ching-kuo prepared to take over from his aging father, he gradually revealed his plan for a measured, controlled unwinding of the authoritarian system.

Taiwan's democratization had many advocates, but their motives differed, and they often did not recognize their common purpose. For CCK, easing restrictions on civil liberties and amplifying the voices of native Taiwanese in existing political institutions, especially the KMT, were ways of preserving the ROC in the face of flagging international support. For activists outside the regime, those were only the first, tentative steps on a journey toward full democracy. Pressure for change also came from a third group: political activists for whom democracy carried ethnic overtones.

In their view, democratization could not be separated from the elimination of the Mainlander minority's political and social privileges. For them, the ideological vacuum created by the failure of mainland recovery created space for a new vision of the ROC as the government of, by, and for the Taiwanese people. In their view, Taiwanese were more than just a minority within the whole Chinese citizenry; they were the majority in the areas the ROC government controlled, and as such, they deserved full political representation. They drew encouragement from the Hometown Literature movement, which helped support their political claims by defining a cultural identity for Taiwanese.

Outside Taiwan, a more radical response to the ROC's failing legitimacy was taking shape. For decades, Taiwanese had been leaving the island. Many were Mainlanders who saw no future there, and chose instead to settle in the United States, Canada, Australia, and beyond. But many others were Taiwanese—mainly Hokkien speakers—who chafed under the KMT's authoritarian control. In the 1950s and 1960s, educated Taiwanese who attended graduate schools in the West discovered a measure of freedom they had never experienced at home. In the West they could speak their mother tongue without embarrassment—and in the libraries of Oxford, Harvard, Cal Tech, and other universities they could read a version of the ROC's recent history very different from the one taught in Taiwan.

Overseas, critics of the Kuomintang government's performance on the mainland were plentiful. A few Westerners even condemned the ROC's behavior in Taiwan. The most prominent of these was the American diplomat George Kerr, who published *Formosa Betrayed* in 1965. Kerr was in Taiwan when Kuomintang troops arrived in 1945, and he witnessed the 1947 uprising and its bloody aftermath. His book gave many Taiwanese living overseas their first uncensored glimpse of the 2-28 Incident. On Taiwan, the events of 1947 were too sensitive to discuss—whole chapters were erased from family histories because victims dared not tell their own children and grandchildren what they had suffered.

Taiwanese authors, too, assailed the KMT in overseas publications. The exiled scholar and democracy activist Peng Ming-min published *A Taste of Freedom* in 1972. The book detailed Peng's persecution in Taiwan and his flight to the West. A Taiwan historian living in Japan and writing under the name Shih Ming published alternative histories of Taiwan, revealing facts about the island few young Taiwanese knew. In 1974, George Kerr published a second book, which detailed Taiwan's early efforts to attain home rule and self-determination.

Many Taiwanese students who encountered the truth about their own history for the first time while living far from home were drawn into political movements aimed at rescuing their homeland. Some devoted themselves to democratizing the ROC, while others believed Taiwan could never be free so long as it was under a state calling itself "Republic of China." The latter group embraced the idea of a Taiwan fully independent of Chinese control, influence, or identity. They took inspiration from early gestures toward a Taiwanese state, including a brief episode in 1895 and talk of Taiwan independence during the colonial period.

The most important touchstone for the burgeoning Taiwan Independence Movement (TIM) was the 2-28 Incident, which TIM activists argued had demonstrated the Taiwanese people's longing for liberation—a longing crushed by force and smothered by repression. TIM's ranks grew as more and more disaffected Taiwanese left their homeland for exile abroad. The KMT saw TIM as a threat to its survival, and cracked down ruthlessly at the first sign that independence activism might be spreading to the island. It even sent agents abroad to infiltrate Taiwanese organizations and spy on Taiwanese living overseas.

Taiwan independence is a tricky, contested concept, so it's worth pausing here to define it more precisely. The ROC name, symbols, and constitution link Taiwan to China (although not to the People's Republic of China). Even though Taiwan's government no longer claims jurisdiction over the mainland, its constitution still defines the island as part of a Chinese political entity. Most observers agree that abandoning that definition—adopting a name, symbols, and constitution that define Taiwan as separate from the mainland—would reconstitute Taiwan as fully independent, no longer part of the historical entity known as "China."

The PRC government's position is complex, but it centers on just this understanding of independence. In its rhetoric, Beijing insists Taiwan already is part of the PRC, because it is part of China, and since 1949, China has meant PRC. Its official policy spells out its position:

> The Chinese Government advocates that the final purpose of cross-Straits negotiations is to achieve peaceful reunification; and that to achieve this purpose, talks should be held based on the principle of one China. However, the proposals for "Taiwan independence," "two Chinas" and "two states," aiming for separation instead of reunification, violate the One-China Principle, and are naturally unacceptable to the Chinese Government.

The PRC rejects the claim that two Chinas—PRC and ROC—exist today, but it tolerates the ROC in practice because under the ROC framework, Taiwan maintains its connection to China. If Taiwan were to sever that link by changing its name and national symbols, Beijing almost certainly would react forcefully to reverse Taipei's action. But even here there is a catch:

normally, international recognition is necessary for a state to exist, so if no other governments recognized the newly independent Taiwanese state, it *still* might not be independent under international law. From Beijing's point of view, however, that technicality would not matter much. Its focus is keeping Taiwan connected to China to preserve the possibility of unification someday. How Taiwan defines the China to which it is connected is less important to Beijing than maintaining the connection.

The relationship between Taiwan and China today is like a failing marriage: the couple is separated, but not divorced. Taiwan independence would constitute a divorce—Taiwan would begin using its "maiden name." Once a divorce is final, reconciliation is unlikely, so even though remaining separated is hardly Beijing's preference, it prefers separation to divorce. For Taiwan, the trick is to maintain as much freedom of action as it can without finalizing the divorce; the PRC's goal is to end the separation.

Within Taiwan, politicians and citizens continue to debate the meaning of independence. Hardcore independence activists believe the only way for Taiwan to become the master of its own destiny is to finalize the divorce, to drop the pretense of being Chinese, and face the consequences of declaring independence. A more popular take on the matter is one first espoused by political-prisoner-turned-DPP-chairman Shih Ming-teh in 1993. Shih observed that Taiwan, doing business as the ROC, had no need to declare independence, since the Republic of China was an independent state already—and had been since 1912. Independence, in his view, could be discovered rather than declared. His basic position—that the independence already enjoyed by the Republic of China was good enough—has become the mainstream preference of Taiwanese—although a substantial fraction of them would be happy to finalize the divorce if it could be done peacefully.

PULLING DOWN THE WALL
DIVIDING THE TAIWAN STRAIT

The façade of KMT power appeared strong into the 1980s. It wasn't until 1984 that the American scholar Edwin Winckler, a keen observer of Taiwanese politics and society, ventured his hypothesis that the decade had seen a shift from "hard to soft authoritarianism." In hindsight it is evident that behind that façade things were changing fast. A new generation of KMT leaders was beginning to recognize the need to allow greater rights and liberties to Taiwan's population, especially the Hokkien and Hakka speaking majority. A Taiwanese cultural renaissance was gathering speed, powered by the Hometown literary movement. Taiwanese democracy activists were winning allies among politicians and human rights advocates overseas.

And not least, the local politicians the KMT had recruited into the party to help manage and pacify Hokkien-speaking communities were gaining confidence and becoming ambitious for higher offices and greater authority.

Meanwhile, conditions on the other side of the Strait were changing, too. Mao's death in 1976 broke the stalemate between political factions that had blocked political and economic progress since the beginning of the Cultural Revolution a decade earlier. Deng Xiaoping and his faction were eager to launch reforms to revitalize China's economy and stabilize its politics. Domestic reform and opening dovetailed with Deng's foreign policy of rapprochement with the West, especially the United States. Nixon-era negotiations had left Chinese leaders confident that Washington's support for Taiwan would cease when the United States and China normalized their relationship, and as normalization talks progressed, Beijing's rhetoric toward the Taiwan issue changed to reflect that confidence. Where past leaders had spoken of their determination to "liberate" Taiwan—to bring it under Communist rule, by force if necessary—in 1979 Deng promised "peaceful unification" in which Taiwan would enjoy a "high degree of autonomy" under the "one country, two systems" framework. Deng's changing rhetoric reflected a tacit convergence with the KMT's position. Whereas a few years earlier Taipei had insisted on recovering the mainland, and Beijing on liberating Taiwan, "peaceful unification" implied a mutually acceptable solution. But just when the two governments were making their first tentative moves toward common ground, skepticism about unification was rising among ordinary Taiwanese. Martial law controls prevented those feelings from being publicly expressed or accurately measured, but it soon became clear that the Taiwanese public did not share its government's enthusiasm for unification—peaceful or otherwise.

In 1987, the logjam that had held Taiwan's domestic politics and its relations with the mainland in suspension for forty years finally broke. In July, President Chiang Ching-kuo announced the end of martial law, restoring civil rights to ROC citizens and opening the door for full-scale democratization. In October, the government lifted its ban on travel to the mainland. The rationale for the decision was humanitarian. Thousands of elderly Mainlanders, mostly retired servicemen, were in danger of dying without seeing the families they had left behind four decades earlier. Family visits were the only trips permitted in the first wave of travel, but a second wave followed quickly, and it included sharp-eyed entrepreneurs.

Lifting the travel ban transformed Taiwan people's perceptions of the PRC. For four decades, the mainland had been "The Enemy," a fearsome, threatening presence just across the turbulent waters of the Strait. The ROC government used innumerable devices to reinforce citizens' fear of the "Communist Bandits," everything from civilian air-raid drills to beaches studded with antitank devices to annual National Day parades bristling with powerful weapons. Now, suddenly, mainland China was a real place, populated by real people. The first Taiwanese visitors returned with stories of a China far too mired in poverty and backwardness to threaten Taiwan. A poignant scene captured in the documentary *Tug of War: The Story of Taiwan* shows a well-dressed, middle-aged Taiwanese man arriving in China and weeping at the sight of the elderly relative awaiting him. The scrawny, ragged Chinese man with his long-stemmed tobacco pipe looks as if he has stepped out of a 1930s-era photograph.

Within a few months of the opening, Taiwanese began pouring into China. Many were tourists eager to see the places they had learned about in Taiwan's Sino-centric schools, but the visitors included many businesspeople. Entrepreneurs who visited China in the late 1980s quickly recognized the mainland's potential as an investment target. China's low wages and flexible regulations offered a perfect environment in which to revitalize Taiwan's sunset industries. As Taiwan's economy blossomed in the 1970s and 1980s, rising wages had squeezed profits in traditional manufacturing sectors such as textiles, shoes, toys, and low-end electronics. Moving those industries to the mainland promised them a new lease on life. As China's economy became even more prosperous, other industries—including high-tech manufacturers—made the move.

While Taiwanese citizens were exploring the mainland for its social, cultural, and economic possibilities, the ROC government was considering options for dialogue with Beijing. Chiang Ching-kuo died in 1988, leaving his vice president, Lee Teng-hui, in charge. Lee inherited Chiang's approach toward the mainland, including pursuing talks with the CCP while holding up unification as his ultimate goal, but he was even more open to cross-Strait economic cooperation than was his predecessor, and the process accelerated quickly. After the Tiananmen Incident in 1989 most countries suspended economic ties with the PRC to protest the Chinese Army's crackdown on the demonstrators, but Taiwanese investors continued to pour in.

In 1991 Lee called an end to the "Period of National Mobilization for the Suppression of Communist Rebellion," a designation that kept Taiwan on a war footing. In doing so, he gave tacit recognition to the PRC government's jurisdiction on the mainland and unilaterally declared an end to the Chinese Civil War. The thaw also included round after round of secret talks between the two sides' envoys. To institutionalize the negotiations they formed two nominally unofficial organizations, Taipei's "Straits Exchange Foundation" (SEF) and Beijing's "Association for Relations across the Taiwan Strait" (ARATS). Representatives from SEF and ARATS began meeting regularly to resolve technical problems and to construct a modus vivendi for further negotiations.

The high point for cross-Strait political cooperation during Lee's presidency came in the early 1990s, when the two sides held talks in Singapore and Hong Kong. The lead negotiators were well-respected senior figures in their respective countries. Taiwan's spokesman was Koo Chen-fu, a prominent Taiwanese businessman; Beijing sent the Shanghaiese politician Wang Daohan to represent ARATS. The two men worked out important agreements on technical matters, from mail delivery to returning hijacked aircraft. They also worked out a framework that allowed them to skirt the fundamental question of "What is China?"

Under what has come to be called the '92 Consensus, both sides agreed there was only one China and that both sought unification, but they left unstated the precise definition of "one China." Instead, each side expressed its understanding of "one China" orally. Taiwanese interpret the '92 Consensus as "one China, each side with its respective interpretation"—an agreement to disagree. The PRC understands it somewhat differently, but the two sides have continued to use the '92 Consensus as a basis for negotiations.

DEBATING THE FUTURE IN
A DEMOCRATIC TAIWAN

Even as Taiwanese investors flooded into the mainland and the ROC government ramped up its diplomatic outreach to Beijing, a growing number of Taiwanese were voicing skepticism—even opposition—regarding unification. Lifting martial law touched off a free-speech explosion, and once Taiwanese were allowed to speak they had plenty to say. The most popular topics were local history, culture, and identity. Hokkien, Hakka, and Austronesian people were tired of being second-class citizens in the ROC, and they used their newfound freedom to advocate for first-class citizenship in a country that recognized its fundamental nature as a Taiwanese polity. The more Taiwanese learned about mainland China, from its poverty to its repressiveness, the less they believed Taiwan had to gain from unification.

The cascade of democratic reforms that followed the end of martial law fostered these feelings. In 1991, the KMT stopped enforcing the "black list"—a long-standing ban on political opponents returning from exile. Among the exiles who entered Taiwan in 1991 were members of a leading TIM group, the World United Formosans for Independence (WUFI). WUFI activists had spent decades refining their viewpoint abroad, and they were eager to carry the torch back to the homeland. Their presence awakened an even more robust debate over Taiwan's future. That same year, a group of Taiwanese students was prosecuted after visiting Taiwan independence guru Shih Ming in Japan. Only a few years earlier, arrest on those charges would have been a disaster for the youths, but in 1991, the whole event seemed anachronistic and perfunctory, and the students were soon released. To add to the excitement, Taiwan held its first comprehensive National Assembly election in December.

As democratization accelerated in the 1990s, debates over Taiwan's identity and future reached new heights. The question of Taiwan's political relationship to China—whether to seek independence or unification—was only one topic of debate. Even more Taiwanese were drawn into discussions about Taiwan's identity, about how Taiwanese people ought to understand and define their place in the world. Those conversations are detailed in chapter 2.

WUFI and other hardcore independence groups did not find Taiwan as welcoming as they might have expected. It's no surprise that the KMT and its political allies fought hard to limit the appeal of independence ideas, but many in the opposition were wary of independence, too. One reason Taiwan independence struggled to win popular support was that its ideology was an awkward fit with democratization. For the hardcore independence camp, achieving independence was more important than achieving it through a democratic process.

Pro-independence hardliners developed the notion of Taiwanese nationalism—the idea that Taiwan constituted a nation worthy of its own, fully sovereign state—to support their case. Taiwanese nationalists rejected historical discourses that situated Taiwan within China's traditional sphere of influence. Instead, they claimed Taiwan was a unique ethno-cultural entity—a community of shared history, blood, and culture—in which Austronesian, European, Chinese, and Japanese elements blended to form a unique nation.

As we saw in chapter 2, Taiwanese nationalism assumed a homogeneity that Taiwan does not possess; in doing so, it alienated Taiwan's minority groups. Too often, affirmative nationalism and pride degenerated into what Taiwanese call "Hokkien chauvinism"—a tendency of the Hokkien-speaking majority to assume that its history, blood, and culture define Taiwan. Although the discourse was directed against Mainlanders, Hakkas and Austronesians resisted it, too, because it echoed the Hokkien exclusivity and ethnocentrism they had suffered under for centuries. The KMT had played its own form of ethnic politics, discriminating against other groups to keep Mainlanders in the top positions. But that history did not excuse some Hokkien politicians' tendency to demonize Mainlanders and blame the whole group for the KMT's sins.

By the early 1990s, Taiwan's political parties had staked out strong positions on many issues, so the first-ever direct presidential election, held in 1996, presented Taiwanese voters with a clear choice. At one end of the spectrum stood two strongly pro-unification candidates, both of whom were lifelong KMT members. At the other end stood the DPP candidate, P'eng Ming-min, whose book *A Taste of Freedom* had awakened political consciousness in so many Taiwanese studying abroad. Even though the DPP had adopted a pro-independence platform plank in 1991, many Democratic Progressives believed independence was a losing issue for their party. Shih Ming-teh's "ROC independence" idea allowed the party to skirt the issue, but candidate P'eng dismissed Shih and other DPP moderates and campaigned on a hard pro-independence line. His campaign logo was a whale, representing his vision of Taiwan as an emancipated sea creature, a marine nation totally detached from the Asian continent. The campaign sidestepped the inconvenient fact that an island cannot swim.

The fourth candidate in the 1996 presidential race was the incumbent, Lee Teng-hui. Lee's position was more subtle than the other candidates.' Although he had led the effort to achieve rapprochement with the mainland earlier in the decade, Lee faced opposition from his KMT co-partisans precisely because his commitment to the unificationist cause seemed to be wavering. Lee had sponsored the Koo-Wang negotiations, but as the talks progressed, he began to worry the process might not protect Taiwan's interests. He wanted to reduce the tension in the Strait, but he was in no hurry to discuss political topics that could lead to unification. His own National Unification Guidelines stipulated that unification would occur only when both sides were equally democratic and equally prosperous. Lee Teng-hui's team was hoping to engage the mainland in a win-win relationship that would reduce tension in the Strait and buy the PRC time to evolve into a more suitable partner for unification, but Beijing wanted a unification deal soon. As the talks unfolded, Lee saw little evidence of political or economic convergence, yet his Beijing counterparts seemed eager to move the talks toward unification.

Lee recognized that a weak, isolated Taiwan could not resist China's pressure, so he launched a new foreign policy strategy he called pragmatic diplomacy. The idea was to win international support by setting aside the old Chiang-era insistence on formal recognition and building unofficial relationships with other countries. After two decades of relative quiet on the international front, Taiwan began reaching out to governmental and nongovernmental actors around the world. The most important target was the United States. In 1995, Lee's overtures to Washington bore fruit: he was granted permission to travel to the United States and give a speech at Cornell University.

Chinese leaders saw the move as a betrayal both by the United States, which had promised to keep relations with Taiwan unofficial, and by Lee Teng-hui. Lee visited Cornell in June; in July, Beijing acted on its outrage. Chinese leaders mobilized the People's Liberation Army (PLA) for a series of military exercises, including missile and live ammunition tests near Taiwanese territory, amphibious landing practice, and naval maneuvers. As the March 1996 presidential election approached, the PLA continued to carry out tests and exercises aimed at intimidating Taiwanese. In January, the Chinese premier Li Peng said Beijing "cannot promise to give up the use of force" to unify the country, and in the first two months of 1996, one hundred thousand PLA troops were gathered in Fujian, the province opposite Taiwan. In March the PLA announced more missile and live-fire tests, this time close enough to Taiwan's shores to disrupt shipping in the island's two major ports. For the first time since the 1950s, the Taiwan Strait seemed on the verge of armed conflict.

Beijing accompanied its military exercises with increasingly heated verbal attacks on "separatists" in Taiwan, a category Chinese said included Lee Teng-hui. One Chinese official warned Taiwan's people to "rein in" separatists, whom he said had reached "the brink of the precipice." Premier Li Peng said the military exercises were a warning to "foreign forces" scheming to realize Taiwan independence. As election day neared, the warnings became even more pointed, more hysterical. The defense minister told a group of Chinese officials "We have more troops stationed in Fujian because we are facing a grim situation, in which Lee Teng-hui and his gang are vainly attempting to split China." A major editorial in China's official newspaper accused Lee of promoting independence, and promised to stop at nothing to thwart him. The editorial injected an ominous note: "We mean what we say."

If Beijing's goal was to defeat Lee at the ballot box, its strategy failed. If anything, its fury increased Lee's attractiveness. To Taiwanese, Lee was not at all extreme, and he was not someone they associated with the independence cause. P'eng Ming-min, on the other hand, was a bona fide independence activist, and many voters saw him as an extremist. But Lee Teng-hui had a long record of promoting unification. He had initiated Taiwan-China communication and even stood behind the Koo-Wang talks. In Taiwanese ears, Beijing's accusations sounded ridiculous. In the end, Lee walked away with 54 percent of the vote in the four-way race. P'eng's 21 percent vote share was significantly lower than the DPP's share in other recent elections.

China's military intimidation in 1995 and 1996 did not defeat Lee Teng-hui or convince Taiwanese that they should hurry up and unify with the mainland, but it was not a useless gesture. From 1987 to 1995, Beijing-Taipei relations saw unprecedented amity. After decades of civil war, the two sides were negotiating. For the first time in a century, Taiwanese were traveling to the mainland regularly, setting up businesses and investing huge sums. At home, Taiwanese were focused on exercising their newly won democratic rights: there were five national elections between 1989 and 1996!

Beijing's military intimidation arrived in Taiwan's freewheeling atmosphere like a SWAT team at a fraternity party. It showed Taiwanese that the newfound friendship between the two sides was shallow and fragile, and it forced them to face a painful reality: the PRC was serious about unification.

The independence movement did not disappear after 1996, but the debate changed in a fundamental way. Before 1996, independence was a largely domestic matter: do we Taiwanese want to be independent, or do we aspire to unify with the mainland? The obstacle to independence was the KMT, the China inside; removing that obstacle would free Taiwan's people to make their own decision. After 1996, it was clear that to achieve formal independence, Taiwanese would have to defeat not only the KMT but also the Chinese Communist Party—and the People's Liberation Army. Since 1996, the independence debate has centered on the China *outside*—the PRC. The central question has become, "Given the PRC's potentially violent determination to stop us from becoming independent, what should we do? Should we try to find a way around China's opposition, or should we give up on formal independence, at least for now?"

Lee Teng-hui used his landslide victory in 1996 to address the tensions tearing at Taiwan's society. Seeing the need to unite the island's people behind a shared vision that would preserve their newfound freedom, democratic system, and economic prosperity, Lee introduced the concept of the "New Taiwanese." According to Lee, everyone living on Taiwan, regardless of when they or their ancestors had arrived, was part of a single "community of shared fate." It was their job to work together to protect Taiwan and all it represented. In effect, the New Taiwanese concept "naturalized" Mainlanders and offered them full membership in Taiwan's society. Lee's insistence that "we're all Taiwanese" reinforced the shift of Taiwanese resentment from the China inside to the China outside.

At the same time, Lee tried (with little success) to slow the flow of Taiwanese business to the mainland, urging businesses to explore Southeast Asian markets instead. He also ramped up pragmatic diplomacy. He co-opted the DPP's long-standing idea of seeking United Nations membership for Taiwan, and spent vast resources selling foreign audiences on the idea that Taiwan deserved to be in the world body. During a 1999 interview with the German radio network Deutsche Welle, Lee described the relationship between the ROC and the PRC as "a special state-to-state relationship." The remark infuriated Chinese officials, who said it proved Lee was a splittist. The vitriol aimed at Lee reached stratospheric heights; one PLA major general called Lee an "abnormal 'test-tube baby' bred by international anti-China forces in their political lab." In fact, Lee's statement said nothing about Taiwan independence, but it did assert the existence of an ROC state. During his presidency Lee never advocated policies that were incompatible with eventual unification—and in fact continually asserted his support for unification—but he insisted that unification must be a marriage of equals, a merger of sovereign states, not the absorption of a smaller entity by a larger one.

For Beijing, acknowledging ROC sovereignty was impossible. The PRC had staked its right to represent China internationally on the idea that the

Republic disappeared in 1949. It claims, "Since the KMT ruling clique re-treated to Taiwan, although its regime has continued to use the designations 'Republic of China' and 'government of the Republic of China,' it has long since completely forfeited its right to exercise state sovereignty on behalf of China and, in reality, has always remained only a local authority in Chinese territory." In insisting on a position at odds with the lived reality on Taiwan, Beijing painted itself into a corner: as much as PRC leaders hated to admit it, the ROC stood between Taiwan and independence. Nonetheless, rather than acknowledging that reality and engaging the ROC on equal terms, PRC lead-ers demonized Lee Teng-hui, a move that alienated and confused Taiwanese, for whom the existence of the ROC state was an unassailable fact.

Lee Teng-hui's efforts to unite Taiwanese behind a shared vision of an ROC that would be friendly with the PRC while retaining its own sover-eignty did not entirely succeed. On one side, pro-unification conservatives shared Beijing's perception that Lee was a closet independentista. On the other, a powerful enthusiasm for Taiwanese identity swept the island, un-dercutting Lee's efforts to persuade islanders to accept the ROC *as* Taiwan. Even Taiwanese who did not support formal independence wanted to participate in the Taiwanese cultural renaissance. For all of its limitations, Taiwanese nationalism was an important and positive stage in Taiwan's self-discovery. Before Taiwanese could achieve the kind of individual libera-tion the characters in Lin Hwai-min's *Cicada* were seeking, they needed to liberate themselves from the Chinese nationalist orthodoxy that cut them off from their history, denigrated their culture, and justified an undemo-cratic political system.

The ethnomusicologist Nancy Guy has traced the progress of Taiwanese self-discovery through popular music. Early on, the political opposition adopted melancholy old Hokkien ballads as its anthems. Their titles—"A Flower in the Rainy Night," "Longing for the Spring Breeze," "Mending Broken Nets"—capture the sadness, nostalgia, and longing of a political movement struggling to emerge from the dark night of White Terror. They soon had a new harvest of songs to choose from, however, performed by folk singers whose preoccupations dovetailed with those of the Hometown writers. Luo Dayou's wildly popular "Little Town of Lukang" captured the singer's homesickness for the preindustrial Taiwan of his—and many others'—childhood. In the 1980s and 1990s, as restrictions on speech fell away, Taiwanese musicians branched out stylistically and politically. Hok-kien songs—old and new, political and apolitical, from saccharine pop to hard-edged rap—became mainstream.

In 1989 a group of musicians calling themselves the "Blacklist Work-shop" released the album *Songs of Madness*. One cut, titled "Democracy Bumpkin," tours the listener through the decade's political outrages, from overzealous riot police to delusional unificationists. Five years later, the artist known as Pig-head Skin (Zhutoupi) released "Long Live Punk'N'Funk," taking the Republic of China to task for everything that is wrong with Taiwan, and ending with a tiny twist of pronunciation that changes "long live the ROC" to "totally smash the ROC." These songs reflect the focus on building Taiwan in opposition to the "China inside"—they label the ROC, KMT, and Mainlanders as enemies of Taiwan's culture as well as its freedom. The fact that they could become hits reflects the opposition movement's success in expanding the limits of permissible expression and capturing the popular mood.

The 1990s was a transformative decade in Taiwan, and not only in popular music. Change was accelerating on every front—in politics, economics, society, and culture. The 1996 presidential election swept away the last restrictions on Taiwanese people's right to elect their leaders, completing Taiwan's democratic transition. Conversations about Taiwan's identity and future that had been suppressed for decades were now out in the open and hotly pursued: Taiwanese were actively debating the full range of options, from unification to independence. Anything seemed possible. To top it off, Taiwan would begin the new millennium with a presidential election—and Lee Teng-hui, the man who led Taiwan across the bridge from single-party authoritarianism to multiparty democracy, would not be a candidate.

THE CHEN SHUI-BIAN ERA, PART I

The 2000 election underscored the changes in Taiwan since the previous contest. In 1996, voters had clear choices regarding Taiwan's future. P'eng was a Taiwanese nationalist who sought formal independence as a way of purging the China inside. Two other candidates were Chinese nationalists who defined Taiwan as part of a Chinese nation that should include Taiwan and the mainland. Lee Teng-hui defined the ROC in political, not ethnic, terms, and while he believed in putting Taiwan first, his pragmatism led him to prefer a policy that eschewed both independence *and* unification. In 2000, all three candidates adopted versions of Lee Teng-hui's approach. Even though the DPP technically still endorsed independence in its party platform, Chen Shui-bian downplayed it in his campaign. He did so not because his party had lost its desire for independence, but because the instant he took office, it became clear that the KMT was *not* the only obstacle standing between Taiwan and independence. There was another barrier—one far more potent and powerful—that would have to be overcome: the PRC. Rather than challenge Beijing, Chen and his party feinted to the side, putting forward a 1999 resolution on Taiwan's future as the party's guide to action. The resolution put the DPP on record as supporting, for the time being at least, a de facto independent Taiwan under the ROC label.

When it came to economic engagement with the PRC, Chen was the most enthusiastic of the candidates. His stump speeches made a strong case for stepping up economic ties with the mainland. If Chen's DPP predecessor had made a virtue of his own radicalism, Chen did precisely the opposite, emphasizing at every opportunity his pragmatism and reasonableness. Chen's opponents, too, shied away from ideological claims. All three candidates sang a different tune when they were with their core supporters, but in their public presentations, each tried to "out-moderate" the others.

Before the election many Taiwanese feared Beijing would react violently to a DPP victory. If the PRC government had disliked the "closet independentista" Lee Teng-hui, it loathed the on-the-record-splittists of the DPP even more. There was real concern as the election approached that Beijing might act preemptively to make sure Chen would not have a chance to act on his party's pro-independence platform. In the end, though, Beijing took a different tack, announcing its intention to "listen to what he says and watch what he does."

The first year of Chen's term offered an opportunity to reset the relationship between the two sides. Chen was eager to show Taiwan's voters that electing him would not endanger the island's interests, and he hoped to intensify Taiwan's economic relationship with the mainland. His inaugural address made it clear that he was prepared to set aside ideology to stabilize and even improve cross-Strait ties. The speech included five nos: no declaration of independence, no revision of the name "Republic of China," no attempt to insert Lee Teng-hui's "special state-to-state relationship" idea into the constitution, no abandonment of the National Unification Guidelines, and no referendum on the question of independence or unification. At the end of the year Chen went even further when he said, "The integration of our economies, trade, and culture can be a starting point for gradually building faith and confidence in each other. This, in turn, can be the basis for a new framework of permanent peace and political integration. Eventually, there will be unlimited possibilities for benefiting the people on both sides of the Taiwan Strait in the 21st century."

The Five Nos and other gestures were meant to persuade Chinese leaders that Chen Shui-bian was not the unrepentant independentista they believed him to be, but his friendly words fell on deaf ears. PRC leaders listened and watched, but nothing they heard or saw convinced them Chen meant what he said. Instead of welcoming his comments, Chinese leaders insisted he was masking his splittist agenda behind pretty words, and they refused to engage him. They set acceptance of their "One China Principle"—or at least the 1992 Consensus—as a precondition for engagement. But the DPP had long rejected both.

Chen's Five Nos disappointed many of his core supporters, people who had hoped his election would usher in a more assertive posture on cross-

Strait issues. To Chen, the gestures he made early on were meaningful concessions and expressions of goodwill—and the political price he paid for them was proof of his sincerity. For Beijing, however, Chen's moves did not go nearly far enough. From its perspective, even Chen Shui-bian's most magnanimous statements fell far short of Lee Teng-hui's position. Although the Chinese leadership had long accused President Lee Teng-hui of insincerity in the pursuit of unification, at least he had paid lip service to that goal. Chen Shui-bian was unwilling to do even that much. President Chen hoped PRC leaders would reward him for moving his position toward theirs, but from their perspective, even Chen's new-and-improved cross-Strait policy left Taiwan farther from an accommodation with the PRC than ever.

The political scientist Robert Putnam developed a concept for studying international bargaining called the "win-set." In negotiations between countries, each side's win-set is the range of outcomes that government would be willing to accept, and for which it could win approval domestically. If countries' win-sets overlap, they can reach an agreement. If there is no common ground, the negotiations will fail. Win-set analysis is a useful framework for thinking about Taiwan and China's efforts to move their relationship beyond the prickly status quo.

Beijing's win-set centers on unification; the spread is provided by the different forms unification might take. At one extreme, the PRC government would be thrilled to be able to annex Taiwan to the PRC through a peaceful process—to bring it under the PRC government just like any other province. The other end of Beijing's win-set is harder to discern; the evidence suggests it is somewhat flexible. The most generous offer Beijing has made to Taiwan was Jiang Zemin's Eight Points (enumerated in 1995), which offered Taiwan complete autonomy in domestic political affairs, including the right to retain its military forces and unofficial relationships with foreign countries, within a unified China.

It is unclear whether "China" must mean the People's Republic of China. Most of the PRC's policy statements suggest it must, but PRC officials occasionally have hinted that unification could look more like a merger than a hostile takeover. The most famous statement to this effect came from Vice-Premier Qian Qichen in 2000, when he said on a few occasions that "the mainland and Taiwan are both part of one China," pointedly omitting any reference to the PRC as the sole Chinese state. Beijing's 1990s-era cross-Strait negotiator Wang Daohan expressed this idea more explicitly in 1997 when he told a Taiwanese interlocutor, "the so-called 'One China' concept does not refer to either the ROC or the PRC." Statements like this are encouraging, but it is unclear whether they are acceptable to enough Chinese officials and citizens to be included in the PRC win-set.

For Taiwan, configuring win-sets is more complicated. Different political parties, even different individuals, have different win-sets. Despite their differences, though, virtually all Taiwanese include maintaining the status quo—defined as continued government by a democratic state entirely separate from the one headquartered in Beijing—as one of the options they can tolerate. The KMT's win-set incorporates some forms of unification—not absorption or annexation into the PRC, but a unification negotiated between the two sides acting as equals to craft a new Chinese state that would preserve Taiwan's democratic system. Such an outcome resembles the scenario Wang and Qian suggested.

Taiwanese citizens might well come to accept such an outcome. After all, Taiwan has never been recognized as an independent state; its sense of nationhood is only aspirational. Most Taiwanese recognize their Chinese heritage, even as they reject China's contemporary political claims. A unification arrangement that acknowledged the cultural and historical connections between the two sides but preserved Taiwan's political autonomy might win widespread approval—if Taiwanese could be persuaded that China would not renege on the deal. But it would have to overcome the passionate resistance of a vocal minority, the Taiwanese nationalists.

For the DPP, one end of the win-set is formal independence. Independence is still a goal in the party platform and many DPP supporters hope to achieve it someday, although they recognize the chances are slim. The other end is less well-defined. It includes substantial economic and social integration, but not a merging of political systems. Whether the DPP could accept a symbolic unification deal that satisfied China's demand for a single Chinese flag but fully preserved Taiwan's political independence is hard to say. When I posed that question to a DPP activist friend recently his response was instructive. He sighed and frowned and said, "I understand how that might help our situation, and it might even be okay, but it is just very hard for us to accept."

Viewed this way, it is easy to see why Chinese officials were so disheartened by Chen's presidency. They saw no common ground between their preferences and his; as far as they were concerned, there was no hope of meaningful progress so long as he was in office. Chen's conciliatory gestures did not come close to Beijing's win-set, but they extended well beyond his own party's comfort zone. As the months stretched on without reciprocal gestures from the PRC, Chen's party comrades reined him in. In effect, Taiwan's win-set was shrinking.

While the China outside was cold-shouldering Chen, the China inside seemed to be doing much the same thing. The Pan-Blue Camp's unbending opposition pushed Chen into a corner and heightened his supporters' feeling of embattlement. Increasingly, Democratic Progressive strategists looked for ways to go around the institutions the Blues controlled so they could push through their agenda. The idea of using referendums—bypassing the legislature in favor of direct popular votes—was one such measure.

The DPP also tried to use constitutional reform to improve its position. Over the course of his first term, Chen became increasingly devoted to writing a new constitution. The existing constitution was flawed from having been amended haphazardly over the previous decade, but the proposal for a new constitution was driven largely by the Democratic Progressives' desire to create institutions that would give them more traction. In gatherings of the faithful, Chen and other DPP leaders hinted that a new constitution would be more than just a technical change—it would (as the PRC government feared) represent the birth of a new nation.

Chen's second term began amidst the worst political turbulence Taiwan had seen since 1947. The election-eve shooting of Chen and his running mate added the threat of violence to the mix. Chen used his inaugural address to calm the nation's fears and bridge its divisions. He addressed the postelection upheaval with a bluntness rarely seen in politics, admitting that his victory was narrow, and political trust was damaged. President Chen also used the occasion to speak to his people about the long-term factors that were weakening their society, especially their divergent heritages and histories. He chastised those in his own camp who had indulged in anti-Mainlander agitation. He observed that all Taiwanese had been victimized by authoritarianism; the White Terror and other political abuses were acts of a few leaders, not "historical representations of subjugation by ethnic groups." Therefore, he argued, "no single ethnic group alone should undeservingly bear the burden of history." Hokkien Taiwanese must not hold "Mainlanders" as a group responsible for the tragic events that occurred under the authoritarian regime, even if that regime was disproportionately peopled by members of the Mainlander minority. In fact, the president said, Mainlanders suffered, too, under the old regime.

President Chen's speech echoed President Lee Teng-hui's rhetoric from the early 1990s, claiming a common destiny for all residents of the Republic of China. Exactly what that destiny might be he did not say. Instead, Chen described what it was that unified Taiwanese despite their differences: "the deep conviction held by the people of Taiwan to strive for democracy, to love peace, to pursue their dreams free from threat, and to embrace progress."

While the bulk of the speech was aimed at uniting Taiwan's internal divisions, Chen also addressed the China outside when he said, "We can understand why the government on the other side of the Strait, in light of historical complexities and ethnic sentiments, cannot relinquish the insistence on the 'One China Principle.'" That statement showed Chen's realism, and his respect for the PRC's aspirations. He reinforced the message when he said, "We can seek to establish relations in any form whatsoever. We would not exclude any possibility, so long as there is the consent of the 23 million people of Taiwan."

THE CHEN SHUI-BIAN ERA, PART II

It seems the story should end here, with Taiwan society united under a president bent on binding its wounds, with cross-Strait relations embarking on a new, amicable journey. But a single speech, however eloquent and heartfelt, does not guarantee a happy ending. Chen's speech did not alter his reputation in Beijing, nor did it shake the Blues' conviction that he had stolen the election. The partisan rancor persisted, and, as Chen's presidency unraveled under the avalanche of scandal that began in 2005, it worsened. The Blues smelled weakness, while DPP stalwarts interpreted calls for Chen's resignation as a Mainlander-led campaign to "put the Hokkiens in their place." In response, the government doubled down on its strategy of promoting Taiwan identity and nationalism.

Defining a policy that would embody the DPP's ideology and aspirations within the confines of economic realism was not easy. The party had long since retreated from its once-robust pro-independence position, and it had accepted the inevitability of economic intertwinement with the mainland. As the DPP hunkered down defensively, its position on economic relations with the mainland evolved even further. In the 1990s, the DPP adopted the pro-engagement slogan "Go West Boldly!" During Chen's first term, the party moderated its position to emphasize the importance of managing the relationship. That policy was captured neatly in a slogan: "Active Opening, Effective Management." In the second term, the slogan changed again, to "Effective Opening, Active Management." The new arrangement of adjectives shifted the focus from opening up to controlling the process.

Their changing economic slogans reflected the Democratic Progressives' central dilemma: they recognized that economic integration could not be reversed and that barring an extreme event, attaining formal independence was impossible, but they were still quite Sino-phobic. They worried that living under KMT leadership—including educational and cultural institutions that deliberately inculcated Chinese nationalism and identity—was sapping Taiwanese people's will to resist unification. As interactions between the two sides became routine, they feared, Taiwanese would forget that they were different and would let their short-term interest in making money or living a more luxurious lifestyle blind them to the long-term dangers of getting too close to the PRC.

By the middle of Chen's presidency, most DPP politicians were resigned that there was little they could do to influence the situation on the mainland. Their best hope, some averred, was to wait for the PRC system to collapse. Another possibility was that globalization and internationalization might make national boundaries obsolete, opening the possibility that in the future, economic and cultural influence—arenas in which Taiwan is strong—would matter more than political sovereignty and military might.

In the meantime, if they couldn't change the situation on the mainland, DPP strategists reasoned, they needed to change Taiwan internally by guiding public opinion in a more Taiwan-centric direction.

To implement this approach the Chen administration redoubled its efforts to propagate Taiwanese identity and encourage Taiwanese consciousness so as to fortify islanders against Beijing's enticements as well as its coercive measures. The idea was to strengthen Taiwan's determination to resist unification and lay the groundwork for independence should an opportunity arise. The campaign was not so much a new initiative as it was the intensification of long-standing DPP efforts—with the added power of the president's bully pulpit. President Chen proclaimed this new direction in his 2006 New Year's address when he said, "Taiwan consciousness breaks the shackles of historical bondage and political dogma, and is founded upon the 23 million people of Taiwan's own self-recognition, devotion to the land and understanding of their shared destiny."

This new emphasis included a variety of strategies. Many were aimed at affirming Taiwanese identity, but others sought to downplay Chinese elements in Taiwan, both institutional and cultural. Under the KMT, many of Taiwan's high-profile institutions included "China" in their names. Many—from the Bank of China to the national flag-carrier China Airlines to the state-owned oil monopoly China Petroleum—were transferred from the mainland at mid century; others were founded in Taiwan. In both cases, the DPP went after them with a vengeance, changing names wherever it could.

The president also stepped up efforts to reform Taiwan's educational system by reducing the attention given to mainland history, geography, and literature and devoting more resources to the study of Taiwan, including Hokkien, Hakka, and Austronesian languages. He elevated the status of officials and institutions responsible for Hakka and Austronesian affairs. Cultural bureaus were encouraged to support Taiwanese folk arts and practices and downplay Chinese "high culture." In 2006, Taiwan chose traditional glove puppet theater as a symbol to represent the island internationally.

These efforts met resistance from the usual suspects—and from some unexpected quarters. That the PRC government (and many KMT politicians) decried the policy, which they labeled "desinification," was no surprise. What *was* surprising was the resistance from many islanders—and not only Mainlanders. Many parents opposed devoting class time to "soft" subjects like Hokkien. In their view, the intense competition Taiwanese youth faced from China and other Asian nations demanded precisely the opposite: more resources invested in the "hard" subjects that would secure their economic future. For students, the new textbooks posed a different dilemma: figuring out how the mix of old and new material would be covered on the all-important high school and university entrance examinations.

In late 2005 I met with several groups of Taiwanese students, many of whom expressed ambivalence about the changes. Asked what political issues were important to her, one student replied, "Educational policy is most important, for example, the textbook reform. I was in school when they started the textbook reforms, and it turned out to be a real mess. They kept changing everything, and no one knew what they should really learn. No one could tell what direction things would go in the future." Her classmate added, "also the examination system. Because the curriculum is changing all the time, no one knows what the content will be on the exams. We study for each test, but they all end up being different, and we are really overworked and confused."

Did that mean they resented Taiwanization of their textbooks, I asked. The reply: "Not resented, exactly, but people in my classes didn't find the Taiwan history part very useful. Even after we studied all that Taiwan history, a lot of us didn't really feel like we knew very much about Taiwan. The new text books were supposed to increase our economic competitiveness, but instead they just made things harder, and more confused." "People still like putting Taiwan back in the curriculum. But some people are mad at the government." Why? "The reason is that they didn't do a good job. It's okay to do educational reform, but you need to do a thorough job. If you try one thing, and then you run into problems so you try something else, then you change things again, this is really troublesome."

The students' frustration with the government's erratic policy style (which was not entirely the Chen administration's fault, what with the legislature and local governments constantly seeking to undo its reforms) helps explain their lukewarm reaction to policies aimed at building up their Taiwanese consciousness. So, too, does another factor: the perception that by putting Taiwan identity at the center of its political platform, the DPP was politicizing something that need not—and for many islanders, ought not—be politicized. For example, most young Taiwanese can understand Hokkien, but they are more comfortable speaking Mandarin, and they reject the idea—popular among older DPP activists—that speaking Mandarin means they don't care about Taiwan. They find the DPP's tendency to use extravagant displays of Taiwan consciousness as proof of their love for Taiwan off-putting, even offensive.

The DPP's overemphasis on the identity issue may even have provoked a backlash. Not yet two decades into its democratic transition, Taiwan was seeing a rise in political cynicism—fueled largely by the corruption scandals tarnishing both major parties. By defining Taiwan consciousness as a DPP trait and using it against political adversaries, the DPP invited that cynicism into the discourse about Taiwan consciousness. Speaking of her politically active sister, one student said, "Her ass makes up her mind."

The DPP's efforts to build Taiwanese consciousness also faltered because they confused "pro-Taiwan" with "anti-China." For many Taiwanese—young and not-so-young—mainland China is no longer the enemy it was during the decades when Taiwan followed its "three nos" policy of no contact, no compromise, and no negotiation. A young journalist, Yeh Kuo-hua, captured the outlook of a growing number of Taiwanese when he wrote in *The Journalist* magazine in 2004, "China is a reality; it is right next to us. When it comes to Taiwan's future development—whether it's politics, economics, society, and culture, even international relations—the so-called 'China factor' is something we cannot ignore." Before 1987 it made sense for Taiwanese to think of the PRC as a distant, vaguely threatening presence. But today, China offers threats *and* opportunities. To measure a person's commitment to Taiwan by her eagerness to reject the mainland makes little sense.

The DPP's campaign to mobilize Taiwanese consciousness for political gain fell short for yet another reason: it was too late. Taiwanese consciousness was already mainstream by 2005, so efforts to inculcate it seemed propagandistic. The pop music impresario Landy Chang pointed out this change in a 2002 interview when he explained to Gavin Phipps of the *Taipei Times* why the craze for politically themed, Taiwan-centric music had evaporated: "With the DPP in power and martial law lifted, there is little call for Taiwanese-ness." Of course, the change was not absolute. In 2007, the extreme metal band Chthonic, whose front man, Freddie Lim, is an independence activist in full zombie makeup, toured the United States. Their shows attracted crowds of aging Taiwanese-Americans willing to risk hearing loss (and no doubt considerable befuddlement) to support their treasured cause.

The Chen administration's campaign to emphasize Taiwan consciousness aimed to minimize the influence of the China *inside* as a way of countering the rising influence of the China *outside*. Its first goal was met; by the beginning of Chen's second term, Taiwanese consciousness had become mainstream. On the second count, however, the DPP's efforts fell short: the PRC's importance in Taiwan's economy and society continued to grow.

The balance among these trends was revealed in May 2005, when the KMT's senior leader and party chair, Lien Chan, traveled to China. It was a risky move, but Lien had little to lose. His two successive presidential defeats had put an end to his political ambitions; everyone agreed the party's future belonged to Taipei City mayor Ma Ying-jeou. That left Lien free to play the senior statesman role, taking on a project that—if it succeeded—could pay a big dividend to his party.

Not surprisingly, Lien's visit was a hit in the PRC. While most Taiwanese describe Lien as stiff and distant, Chinese found him funny and relaxed.

He gave a speech at Beijing University that was heavy on history and light on controversy, but he met the expectations of his home audience when he called for democratization in the PRC. On cross-Strait relations he called for maintaining the status quo; he did not utter the word "unification." He met with PRC President Hu Jintao, and the joint communiqué the two signed included an offer from the PRC to help Taiwan gain representation in international organizations (as a non-state participant, of course). The statement also called for talks based on the 1992 Consensus—an encouraging development, given Beijing's insistence throughout the Chen years that Taiwan accept its One China Principle before talks could resume.

The welcome Lien—who was emphatically *not* Chen Shui-bian—received in the mainland was expected, but it was unclear how the visit would go over in Taiwan. Pundits wondered whether he would bring home meaningful accomplishments, and many Taiwanese feared he would fall into a "divide and conquer" trap laid for him in Beijing. In the end, however, Taiwan's public concluded the visit was good for Taiwan. The warm response Lien received in China helped soften the attitudes of Taiwanese accustomed to seeing Beijing treat their leaders disrespectfully. Even the DPP and the presidential office restrained their criticism, fearing that a strong rebuke to Lien would backfire. Shortly after Lien's trip, James Soong made a similar visit.

The Lien and Soong visits marked the beginning of a warming trend in cross-Strait relations. The timing seemed odd; it began just after China's National People's Congress passed legislation authorizing the use of force to stop Taiwan from moving toward independence. China's "Anti-Secession Law" (a name many Taiwanese mocked, as Taiwan could hardly secede from the PRC, having never been part of it) at first appeared to be an aggressive gesture, but its primary purpose seems to have been to quiet hardliners in Beijing so that talks could go forward. Talks, that is, with leaders of the Pan-Blue Camp, not with President Chen, his government, or his party. When Lien and Soong visited China in 2005, observers wondered whether they were opening a door that President Chen would soon walk through. But before such a possibility had time to ripen, Chen's presidency was in crisis, mired in scandal and under attack from all sides.

As Chen's presidency drew to its excruciating close, both of the candidates hoping to succeed him—the KMT's Ma Ying-jeou and the DPP's Frank Hsieh—adopted moderate positions on the cross-Strait issue. Ma's mainland policy centered on his promise to improve economic and political relations with the PRC while preserving Taiwan's fundamental interests—including its status as an independent and sovereign state called the "Republic of China."

Despite their shared positions on fundamental issues, the public viewed the candidates very differently. Hsieh spent much of his time distancing himself from Chen and the DPP's strong pro-independence reputation, while Ma was challenged to convince voters he was not a traditional KMT unificationist true-believer. And although they shared the view that Taiwan should cultivate better relations with the mainland, the candidates disagreed on exactly how to put that goal into practice. Ma's position was aggressively pro-engagement, while Hsieh supported a more cautious approach. For example, the Hsieh campaign called Ma's "cross-Strait Common Market" idea a "one China market," and claimed it would flood Taiwan with low-wage, socially inferior mainland Chinese workers and dubious Chinese capital. In the last week of the campaign, the Hsieh campaign ran a newspaper ad showing three men urinating in public; the text read "With a One China market, our public parks will turn into public toilets."

Anti-China sentiments like that one contradicted the moderate image candidate Hsieh sought to convey in his stump speech. The speech urged voters to have confidence in Taiwan, which Hsieh called "the most politically free, socially open, culturally pluralistic and creatively lively of the ethnic Chinese states," and he cautioned them not to put economic performance ahead of political liberalization, as Singapore had done. Taiwan's leaders, he said, needed to be "tenacious and caring, to strive for peace while making no provocation so that Taiwan can achieve its ideals without economic losses or social instability," seeking "coexistence and reconciliation" with the mainland—not independence or unification.

Ma's pro-engagement position extended to political issues. He believed Taiwan would benefit from reopening political talks, and he was prepared to revive the 1992 Consensus if that would get the negotiations moving. The DPP saw that as one of many signs the KMT candidate was more committed to making nice with China than to protecting Taiwan's interests. Hsieh's campaign rallies rang with accusations that Ma and the KMT were preparing to "sell out Taiwan" to the PRC. To make their case, however, DPP speakers needed to ignore or dismiss the many public statements in which Ma warned Beijing to keep its expectations low.

Ma's campaign message regarding unification centered on two themes. First, he flatly stated that unification would not be a topic for dialogue during his term of office. This unequivocal statement, reiterated regularly throughout the campaign, put Beijing on notice that moving too quickly to press Taiwan on unification would backfire. It also reassured Taiwanese voters that electing Ma would not result in precipitous changes in Taiwan's status. Ma's second campaign theme was his "three nos" formula: no unification, no independence, no armed conflict. That statement addressed the deepest fears of the PRC and the Taiwan electorate alike.

Lest Beijing miss the point, Ma added a stinging coda at the very end of the campaign. On March 18, with violence raging in Tibet, Ma issued a statement that landed on every one of Beijing sore spots: "The Republic of

China is a sovereign independent democratic state. The future of Taiwan should be decided by Taiwan's 23 million people, and no intervention by the PRC is to be tolerated." Of PRC Premier Wen Jiabao's recent assertion that mainland Chinese people should have a role in determining Taiwan's status, Ma said it was "not only rude, irrational, arrogant, and absurd, but also self-righteous." Beijing's crackdown in Tibet he called "a savage and stupid act." Overall, Ma's campaign message to Taiwan's voters prepared the island for aggressive moves toward closer economic relations and better political relations across the Strait, but his message to Beijing was equally blunt: don't expect me to deliver Taiwan on a silver platter if I win.

Ma's position regarding the Republic of China is important. It is not merely strategic—preserving the ROC is an important part of the KMT's historical mission and legacy—but it does have strategic value. To the extent to which KMT politicians truly value the ROC, their position is problematic for the DPP and other "green" political forces because it locks Taiwan into a Chinese identity, and that can make unification seem inevitable. As a stratagem, though, insisting on the survival of the Republic of China is useful because it neutralizes an important element of Beijing's antagonism. It is easy for China to oppose "Taiwan," but it is not so easy for the Chinese Communist Party to rationalize its opposition to the Republic of *China*.

After his inauguration in May 2008, Ma moved quickly to implement the economic agreements Beijing had concluded with Lien Chan in 2005. Economic talks between the two sides culminated in 2010 when they signed the Economic Cooperation Framework Agreement (ECFA), a broad-ranging pact to reduce trade restrictions and promote cross-Strait economic ties. ECFA is a good example of how Ma's approach meshes with Beijing's strategy—despite their divergent goals. For Ma, expanding trade helps Taiwan's economy grow without binding its hands politically. Ideally, strong cross-Strait economic and people-to-people ties will reduce the PRC's appetite for conflict and expand its win-set so that eventually the two sides can arrive at a form of unification that both can accept. Maintaining good relations in the short run is critical to achieving that long-term goal.

Beijing's strategy is to prevent Taiwan from moving farther toward formal independence while allowing the forces of economic integration and political amity to pull Taiwan more deeply into the PRC's orbit. Beijing would prefer to achieve unification peacefully, and to make economic ties more appealing it is willing to sacrifice its own economic interests. Most observers agree that while ECFA will bring economic advantages to both sides, Taiwan will benefit more. But for Sino-skeptical Taiwanese, that suggests ECFA is a Trojan horse designed to make Taiwan vulnerable to Beijing's blandishments—and coercion.

The long-term effects of deepening cross-Strait economic ties on the two sides' political relationship are impossible to predict, and the short-term benefits Taiwan has gained by linking its economy to the PRC's are evident. That makes it risky for DPP politicians to take too hard a line against ECFA and other agreements, however nervous they may be about the future. Opposing ECFA is problematic, too, because there is little evidence that the economic links forged so far have had the political effects Beijing anticipates. Support for unification among Taiwanese is extremely low—and it shows no signs of growing. Taiwanese take a dim view of the PRC government; almost half believe it is hostile to their government, and a plurality believes it is hostile to their people. If the PRC has a strategy of "buying" support for unification, there is little sign that approach is working.

The Taiwanese political scientist Chu Yun-han sums up public opinion this way: "While the prospect of peaceful reconciliation has turned more promising, a negotiated peace between the two sides is still far off. . . . Democratization has reinforced the Taiwanese quest to retain charge of the island's own future, making the threshold for constructing a winning coalition for reunification extremely high." The 2008 presidential election campaign supported Chu's analysis: given two candidates who agreed that neither unification nor independence was a good near-term option, Taiwan's voters chose the one whose claim to moderation seemed more credible. Those events reveal something important: Despite the deep disagreements over strategy and tactics that remain, Taiwanese have reached consensus on two critical points. They feel themselves to be citizens of a sovereign, independent state (the name of which they're still debating), and they believe they alone have the right to change that status.

This consensus came into being so gradually and organically that many islanders do not recognize it as a consensus—it seems simply the natural state of things. But compared to the 1990s, when advocates of formal independence and proponents of full unification did not even recognize one another as fellow citizens, it is a profound transformation. After decades spent debating how to reconcile Taiwan with the China *inside*, islanders have turned their attention to the China *outside*, and the growing threats and opportunities it proffers.

In early 2010 I sat down with Mayor Chen Chu in her Kaohsiung City office and asked her whether, after more than three decades as a political activist, she thought of herself as an idealist or a pragmatist. Her answer revealed the maturity of Taiwan's best political thinking:

> Must there be a conflict between idealism and pragmatism? My ideals are things I can realize, and I'm very much a pragmatist, too. Pragmatism is not the same thing as compromise, or giving up. It is the way I achieve my ideals. . . . What is the definition of ideals? I differentiate between "ideals" and "dreams."

I'm an idealist, but not a dreamer. An ideal needs to be something attainable. When I was head of the Council of Labor Affairs I often ran into this kind of thinking. People from the labor movement would criticize me. They said, "You're abandoning your ideals." I told them, if you are at zero, and you want to get to 100, if you can get to 100, great. But if I can get you to 80, why would I agree to stay at zero, just so I could say I didn't give up my ideals? Eighty is a lot closer to 100 than zero is. You need to tell me, what, concretely, do you mean when you say I'm giving up my ideals?

"What about Taiwan independence," I asked. "Is that an ideal or a dream?" She replied,

Taiwanese people must have the power to decide their own fate, their own future. We can't get too fixated on one idea about what we want. What I want now, as mayor, is for Taiwanese to have power to decide their own future direction, to participate in the decision-making process. They need to have the right to speak. For that to happen, Taiwan needs to have strength, power. It is power that will make other countries care about Taiwan. If you have no power, no one will care what happens to you.

Independence, in sum, has cycled back around to where it began: to a demand for self-determination for the people living on Taiwan. In the early days of the opposition movement, self-determination meant the right of people born on Taiwan to decide their own fate, not have it dictated to them by the China *inside*—the KMT. Today, self-determination means the right of the people living on Taiwan to choose when and how they will engage the China *outside*—the People's Republic of China. But those choices are not easy, because the revolution in Taiwan's sense of itself has coincided with a precipitous increase in China's power—a trend that could threaten Taiwan's newfound equilibrium.

SOURCES

This chapter's overview of the ongoing tension between Taipei and Beijing is informed by a vast scholarly literature. Among the most influential scholars in this field are Richard Bush, Nancy Bernkopf Tucker, Alan Wachman, Robert Sutter, T. Y. Wang, John Garver, Robert Ross, Chien-min Chao, Edward Friedman, Taylor Fravel, Philip Saunders, Steven Goldstein, Alexander Huang, Steve Tsang, Christopher Hughes, Stephen Krasner, Alan Romberg, Yu-shan Wu, Lowell Dittmer, and Michael Swaine. The comments by Chinese leaders on the 1995 Taiwan Strait crisis are quoted in Robert Ross, "The 1995–1996 Taiwan Strait Confrontation: Coercion, Credibility, and Use of Force"; and Alan Wachman, *Why Taiwan: Geostrategic Rationales for China's Territorial Integrity*. The statements by Qian Qichen and Wang Daohan hinting at a relaxed interpretation of "one China" statements are discussed at length in Suisheng Zhao's "Strategic Dilemma of Bejing's Taiwan Policy," in *The "One China" Dilemma*, edited by Peter C. Y. Chow. Yun-han Chu's analysis of public opinion on cross-Strait relations comes from his chapter in *Power and Security in Northeast Asia: Shifting Strategies*, edited by Byung-Kook Kim and Anthony Jones.

Joseph S. M. Lau edited the volume *Chinese Stories from Taiwan: 1960–1970*, providing an English translation of several of the most famous examples of Hometown Literature. His comments about "Winter Nights" and "Cicada" are found in editor's notes introducing each story. Passages from the stories are Lau's translations from that volume. Regrettably, Nancy Guy's fascinating paper on Taiwanese popular music is as yet unpublished.

8

The International Birdcage

In 2007 Taiwanese young people discovered the online game Click Click Click. Each time a player clicked a button on the Web site www.clickclick-click.com, the site credited that click to the player's home country. At a preset day and time, the country with the largest number of clicks was declared the winner. In the game's first four rounds, Taiwan inched up from eighty-fourth to fifty-eighth place. Then, suddenly, Click Click Click took Taiwan by storm. Young Taiwanese clicked away feverishly, using every form of social networking from word-of-mouth to text messaging and viral video to spread the word. They created robot programs that clicked automatically around the clock. In the seventh round, Taiwan's "netizens" logged 1.3 billion clicks in seven days—fifty-five clicks for every person on the island—to win first place.

Winning the game no doubt gratified the young people who spent hours programming robots and exhorting their schoolmates to log on and click, but it's hard not to wonder: why would so many people go to so much trouble to win such a meaningless contest?

Click Click Click was a fad, and fads are by nature irrational. But the prodigious labor Taiwan's young Web users invested in this seemingly senseless exercise calls for a deeper explanation. One possibility: Taiwanese netizens' determination to make Taiwan visible on the Click Click Click Web site was a cry for affirmation from a nation starved for international recognition.

Throughout its history, Taiwan has been at the periphery of great powers. It was an outpost of the Qing Dynasty, a colony of the Japanese empire and a remnant of the Republic of China. At the height of the Cold War it was treated as something more, but even then Taiwan was honored as a means to an end—the restoration of "Free China"—not as an end in itself. In the 1970s, as more and more countries accepted the People's Republic of China as the "real China," Taiwan sank into isolation. As the first decade of the twenty-first century drew to a close, only twenty-three nations recognized the Republic of China as a state. To the rest of the world, Taiwan was an oddity: a self-governing territory without sovereignty, neither legally independent nor ruled by any other state.

To Taiwanese, of course, the Republic of China is entirely real—and fully independent. Even those who would prefer to call their nation "Taiwan" would agree that for the moment, at least, the ROC exists. After all, the ROC issues their passports. When a landslide buries a highway or a typhoon wipes out a mountain village, ROC rescue personnel and repair teams respond. Taiwanese get their health care through the ROC National Health Insurance program. President Chen Shui-bian (and thousands of others) were arrested by ROC police, judged in ROC courts, and confined in ROC prisons. Taiwan's citizens vote in ROC elections—sometimes several times in a calendar year.

Yet the ROC flag and anthem are recognized in only a handful of countries, mostly small or tiny. When Taiwan's athletes enter an Olympic stadium they carry a flag designed specifically for that occasion, and their team placard identifies not their country, but their ethnicity and capital: "Chinese Taipei." They have no representation in the United Nations, although about 150 countries with smaller populations do, and they comply with many international conventions and agreements they are forbidden to join. Even Taiwan's most important friend, the United States, treats it as a nonentity. When Harvard University invited President Ma Ying-jeou to deliver an address in 2010, he did so through a telecast because the island's top leaders can set foot in the United States only on an approved stopover en route to another destination.

Taiwan's shaky status helps explain its young netizens' determination to show the world—or at least everyone else on Click Click Click—that their country was real, real enough to rack up a billion clicks in seven days. It also helps explain many aspects of Taiwan's foreign policy. Taiwan's leaders believe international recognition is crucial to their country's survival as a self-governing state. Their options are limited—like a bird in a cage, Taiwan cannot fly far—but Taiwanese are determined to do everything they can to avoid extinction. And, like the caged bird, one thing Taiwan can do is to sing.

The goal of this chapter is to explore Taiwan's international position by looking at several questions. How did Taiwan come to be caged? Why is it so important to the PRC to keep it in a cage, to limit its international role and relationships? How does Taiwan sustain itself as an international player in the absence of official recognition and support? What about the

United States? How does it view Taiwan? What role does it play in keeping Taiwan afloat?

BUILDING THE BIRDCAGE

The "international birdcage" metaphor captures Taiwan's diplomatic predicament. So long as it does not claim national status, Taiwan is able to manage its own affairs and have substantive relations with most countries in the world. Its economic ties are largely unaffected by its political isolation—although in an age of proliferating free-trade agreements, that may change—but its ability to defend its political interests is minimal. It has fought hard to retain a handful of diplomatic partnerships, but it has paid a high price for limited success. It also sacrifices much to participate in a handful of international organizations. Building the birdcage took decades, and it has become a very effective constraint on Taiwan's freedom of action in the international community.

Taiwan's fate had been determined by others for centuries, so islanders raised little objection when the international community engineered its incorporation into the Republic of China at the end of World War II. At the Cairo Conference in 1943, Franklin D. Roosevelt, Winston Churchill, and Josef Stalin agreed to reward the ROC's participation in the Allied effort against Japan by turning Taiwan over to China. Other Japanese colonies—most notably Korea—would become independent, but not Taiwan. At the time, some Taiwanese expressed regret at this arrangement, but most islanders took it in stride, at least until the 2-28 Incident in 1947. By then it was too late.

After the Chinese Communist Party drove the ROC government into exile in 1949, many nations continued to recognize the ROC as the legal government of Taiwan and mainland China. Taipei even retained the Chinese seat at the United Nations. Most Western governments accepted the KMT's logic that the PRC was illegitimate (having seized power by overthrowing a democratically elected government), hostile, and not long for this world. That position was not sustainable, though, as it soon became clear the PRC was not collapsing. Ignoring the world's largest nation—no matter how odious its ideology—was not a realistic policy, and governments and international organizations began shifting their recognition to Beijing.

For a long time, the ROC's authoritarian leaders refused to accept the diminution of their territory; they rejected any suggestion that the world might acknowledge two Chinas, or one China and one Taiwan. They demanded other governments choose between the ROC and the PRC—even after it was clear this policy was isolating Taiwan. Eventually, Taiwan was so marginalized internationally that a two-state solution might have been acceptable to its leaders, but by then it was too late: Beijing had acquired veto power over Taiwan's international relationships. Now it was Beijing's turn to rule out dual recognition. But why?

WHY TAIWAN MATTERS TO THE PEOPLE'S REPUBLIC OF CHINA

Beijing's stance on Taiwan is unequivocal and uncompromising. A White Paper published in 2000 spelled out the fundamentals of its policy:

> Taiwan is an inalienable part of China. All the facts and laws about Taiwan prove that Taiwan is an inalienable part of Chinese territory. On October 1, 1949, the Central People's Government of the PRC was proclaimed, replacing the government of the Republic of China to become the only legal government of the whole of China and its sole legal representative in the international arena, thereby bringing the historical status of the Republic of China to an end. [T]he government of the PRC naturally should fully enjoy and exercise China's sovereignty, including its sovereignty over Taiwan.

Any government that hopes to have normal diplomatic relations with the PRC must not challenge this position. Beijing shuns governments that refuse to break official ties with the Taiwanese government. Scholars have written whole books asking why the PRC takes such a hard line on this issue; what follows is a summary of the most important explanations.

The Mandate of History

According to the PRC government, history both justifies its claim to Taiwan and compels it to assert that claim. Because Taiwan was part of China in the past, it is part of China today, and because it is part of China it *should be* governed by the PRC. These claims are not identical. One is factual, the other is aspirational, and that difference underscores a central feature of China's position: history has handed the PRC government a mandate—both in the sense of a license and of a command—to bring Taiwan under mainland control. The PRC Constitution makes this clear: "Taiwan is part of the sacred territory of the People's Republic of China. It is the inviolable duty of all Chinese people, including our compatriots in Taiwan, to accomplish the great task of reunifying the motherland."

A PRC document published in 1993, "The Taiwan Question and the Reunification of China," summarizes the historical narrative that places Taiwan within the Chinese "motherland":

> China has a long history of 5,000 years. The Chinese people have lived and multiplied on this land where all ethnic groups have mixed together, in the

course of which they have developed a powerful cohesiveness, and the values of cherishing and safeguarding unity. Over the long course of history, the Chinese nation has witnessed changes of dynasties, transfers of governments, local separatist regimes, and foreign invasions, especially the untold invasions and dismemberment by foreign powers in modern history. However, unity has always been the main trend in the development of Chinese history. After every separation, the country was invariably reunified, only to be followed in its wake by rapid political, economic, cultural, scientific and technological development. Our compatriots in Taiwan have a glorious tradition of patriotism, and have performed brilliant exploits in the struggles against foreign invasions of Taiwan. Since the founding of the PRC, the Chinese people have particularly valued their hard-earned national independence, firmly upheld state sovereignty and territorial integrity and struggled unswervingly for reunification of the motherland. The 5,000-year history and culture have been implanted deeply in the minds of the Chinese people, sprouting the strong national consciousness of the need for national unification.

This fervently held narrative is not uncontroversial. Historians outside the PRC, including many in Taiwan, dispute many of its assertions. In their view, Taiwan was incorporated into China's territory relatively late, giving the two places at most a few hundred years of shared history, not the five thousand years official PRC accounts imply. In her work on Chinese travel writing, historian Emma Teng observes that as late as the Ming Dynasty (1368 to 1644), China was understood to be "bounded by natural geographic features." One of those features was the Taiwan Strait, and that put Taiwan outside China's borders. Ming leaders also recognized European states' jurisdiction over the island for several decades, as Tonio Andrade details in his book, *How Taiwan Became Chinese*.

Teng's sources reveal a strong disdain for the island among officials of the early Qing Dynasty (1644–1911) as well. One wrote, "Taiwan is merely a ball of mud beyond the seas, unworthy of development by China. It is full of naked and tattooed savages, who are not worth defending. It is a daily waste of imperial money for no benefit." The territories Beijing today claims as its inheritance reflect a more recent historical moment: the height of the Qing empire. But at that time the Qing—a dynasty established by Manchu tribes from outside the Great Wall—did not think of itself as a Chinese nation-state.

PRC historians have answers for the skeptics, including documents they say demonstrate Taiwan's incorporation into China from earliest times. The back-and-forth among scholars is more than academic. Activists on both sides of the Strait use the historical record as they see it to make the case for their preferred political outcome. Many pro-independence Taiwanese believe it is important to "prove" that Taiwan was only briefly incorporated into the Chinese state. Supporters of unification, in contrast, muster evidence that Taiwan has been part of China since ancient times. Despite their disagreement over historical facts and interpretations, these groups share the belief that the past should determine the future—which is itself a debatable claim.

To Chinese in the mainland, the fact that Taiwan was Chinese territory in the past is reason enough to include it in China today. But for most Taiwanese, that idea is unpersuasive. They view political identity as malleable and believe that the preferences and desires of living people should matter. In view of these trends, the British scholar Christopher Hughes described Taiwan as "post-nationalist" in his book *Taiwan and Chinese Nationalism*. An essay in *The Journalist* magazine published in 2004 captured this point of view. The writer Lee Tuo-tzu used the metaphor of a refrigerator to describe his feelings about the mainland. He compared his parents' large, well-stocked refrigerator to the small, mostly empty cooler in his apartment:

> If Taiwan is the little cooler, China is the big refrigerator. The items in the big refrigerator are abundant, but I'm not so willing to take things out of it, because they're no longer my things. What's more, I don't need a big refrigerator. And I'm certainly not going to tell people that the little cooler in my room is actually a big refrigerator, or that the little cooler isn't anything much, because the refrigerator in my old house was so big, and had so much stuff in it. I know my parents think of their home as *our* home, but after I'd been living independently for several years, that house inevitably became, over time, my parents' house.

The contrast between the mainland view of history as destiny and the Taiwanese belief that national boundaries should evolve to accommodate people's preferences and reflect the consent of the governed reveals an enormous ideological gulf between the two sides. As the PRC document quoted above puts it,

> The Taiwan separatists' attempt to change Taiwan's status as a part of China by referendum on the pretext that "sovereignty belongs to the people" is futile. . . . The sovereignty over Taiwan belongs to all the Chinese people including Taiwan compatriots, and not to some of the people in Taiwan. . . . The only future for Taiwan is reunification with the China mainland, and certainly not separation. Any attempt to separate Taiwan from China through so-called referendum would only lead the Taiwan people to disaster.

Restoring China's Rightful Status

A second reason for the PRC's intense determination to incorporate Taiwan also has its roots in history, but emphasizes different historical events. This line of argument holds that Taiwan's separation from the mainland is a legacy of China's weakest age, the period in the late nineteenth and early twentieth centuries when parts of China were invaded and colonized. In this view, the "main melody" in Chinese history is national unity and glory. Restoring those traits requires eliminating the last, aberrant vestige of China's late-Qing weakness: Taiwan's separation from the mainland. "The Taiwan Question and the Reunification of China" incorporates this reasoning:

> The modern history of China was a record of subjection to aggression, dismemberment and humiliation by foreign powers. It was also a chronicle of the Chinese people's valiant struggles for national independence and in defense of their state sovereignty, territorial integrity and national dignity. The origin and evolution of the Taiwan Question are closely linked with that period of history. For various reasons Taiwan is still separated from the mainland. Unless and until this state of affairs is brought to an end, the trauma on the Chinese nation will not be healed and the Chinese people's struggle for national reunification and territorial integrity will continue.

This discourse, in which China is constructed as a splendid civilization brought low by foreign bullying, focuses on nineteenth-century efforts to "carve up China." Most of the participants in those efforts were European states, although Japan and the United States were implicated, too. In this narrative, China's weakness was an aberration, a temporary setback in a long and glorious history. China's national greatness entitles it, as the political scientist Alan Wachman puts it in his book *Why Taiwan: Geostrategic Rationales for China's Territorial Integrity*, to "respect and a degree of deference," especially where its self-defined core interests are at stake. In this context, Taiwan's continued separation from the mainland stands as the last remnant of China's self-proclaimed "century of humiliation," a deficiency that must be overcome if China is to see its rightful glory restored.

One puzzling element in China's logic is the disproportionate attention it gives Taiwan compared to other territorial claims. In the nineteenth century, China lost massive swathes of territory to foreign conquest, yet none of its other claims has provoked a similar level of passion. The PRC enjoys good relations with Mongolia, an independent state carved out of Qing-held territories. It has ceded land to Russia far exceeding Taiwan's total area with barely a fuss. As Wachman writes, "Beijing has invested far more political capital in pursuit of its claims to Taiwan than it has in most of the territorial disputes it settled with neighbors. . . . One would find few to contest the proposition that the PRC has insistently injected into its relations with other states its uncompromising view of China's sovereignty over Taiwan while the PRC's outstanding contests about other territories rarely feature as prominently." The PRC's own behavior suggests that not all historical claims are created equal, which begs the question yet again: why Taiwan?

Breaking the Island Cordon: Taiwan as a Resource
for "Strategic Denial"

In his book *Why Taiwan*, Wachman argues for a geopolitical answer to the question of why Taiwan matters to the PRC. He claims it is not so much *what* Taiwan is, but *where* it is that makes it important to Beijing. He does not discount the ideological and political motives that dominate PRC statements regarding Taiwan, but he advises analysts to bear in mind a more hard-edged line of reasoning. PRC diplomats rarely express China's interests in Taiwan in geostrategic terms, but there are many in China— especially the PRC military—who do. In Wachman's view, these voices contribute significantly to China's domestic debate, and the heart of their argument is this:

> As long as it remains outside the PRC's sphere of influence—or, worse still, within the U.S. sphere—Taiwan is seen as the westward edge of an insular cordon that flows through Japan to the Philippines, putting the PRC's maritime ambitions at risk. As part of the PRC's domain, though, Taiwan becomes the easternmost edge of an oceanic arena in which the PRC can exercise "sea control" in coastal waters and with which it can puncture the belt of strategically located islands that the United States, as the maritime hegemon, is perceived to be using to check the expansion of PRC power.

Taiwan's geostrategic value to China rests on strategic denial—what Wachman calls the "Shi Lang Doctrine." Shi Lang was the admiral who persuaded the Qing court to seize Taiwan from Zheng Chenggong's Ming loyalists back in the 1600s. Shi Lang told the court that despite the expense, Taiwan needed to be incorporated into the empire to prevent it from becoming a haven for troublemakers, putting him firmly in the camp that advocates holding Taiwan to keep it out of enemy hands—that is, for strategic denial.

Wachman's book shows how Chinese governments' resolve to hold Taiwan has waxed and waned in response to external threats. Neither the Qing nor the KMT nor the CCP cared much about the island, its resources, or its people, except when it seemed the island might become a military staging ground for their adversaries. More than a decade after Japan invaded the Chinese heartland, Chiang Kai-shek and his government still did not regard Taiwan as part of China. The tune changed slightly with the publication of Chiang's tome *China's Destiny* in 1942. In it, Chiang identified Taiwan as a buffer region useful for "safeguarding the nation's existence." Taiwan, in short, was a means to a strategic end—the defense of the Chinese homeland—but it was not part of the homeland.

As for the CCP, it too showed little interest in Taiwan until the 1940s. In 1936 Mao Zedong told the journalist Edgar Snow that his party would extend its "enthusiastic help" to Korea's struggle for independence from Japan and that "the same thing applies for Taiwan"—a comment Snow published in his widely read *Red Star over China*. It was only after Taiwan became a KMT refuge under American protection that the Chinese Communists found their passion for the island. Resentment of U.S. interference in a matter Beijing considers its internal affair reinforces the sense that the West's wrongs against China have never been redressed. In "The Taiwan Question and the Reunification of China" Beijing asserts, "It is clear . . . that the U.S. Government is responsible for holding up the settlement of the Taiwan Question. . . . One cannot fail to note that there are people in the U.S. who still do not want to see a reunified China. They have cooked up various pretexts and exerted influence to obstruct the settlement of the Taiwan question."

A sense of injured national dignity is important to Beijing, but geostrategy plays a role, too: In China's view, the U.S. ability to influence Taiwan and its relations with China threatens China's security and limits its capacity to expand its power. Thus, the PRC's "strategic denial" logic has a very specific target: the United States. In a variation on the Shi Lang Doctrine, Beijing worries that if it does not control Taiwan, the island will become a stronghold of hostile (read: American) forces. Ideology matters, too, of course. In an era in which China lacks the power to challenge the U.S. military, it is especially important to keep the pressure on the one area China views as critically important. Wang Jisi, a Chinese specialist on U.S.-China relations, describes Chinese thinking this way:

> Without any doubt, the single most important issue that arouses Chinese indignation about the 'hegemonic behavior' of the United States has been its policy toward Taiwan. Few, if any, Chinese on the mainland doubt that Taiwan is a Chinese territory and that people in Taiwan belong to the same Chinese nation as mainlanders. Therefore, the U.S. rejection of China's territorial claim of Taiwan and its continued arms sales to the island as part of the plans to thwart Chinese efforts to reunify it are regarded as showing hostility to the Chinese nation.

By Popular Demand: Taiwan and China's Domestic Politics

Wang's reference to the widespread opinion of Chinese people brings us to yet another reason frequently offered for why the PRC government has devoted itself so assiduously to unification. China is not a democracy; its leaders are not compelled to follow public opinion as a matter of political survival. Still, it is not immune to political conflict and competition, and the status of Taiwan has become an important issue in its domestic politics. Analysts in the United States sometimes argue over whether the zeal for unification bubbles up from ordinary people or is inculcated and nurtured by elites. Practically speaking, the outcome of that debate matters little. Whether "natural" or "manufactured," ardor for unification has taken root among Chinese citizens—especially a population of nationalistic youth who are quick to criticize their own government when they think its stance toward the island is too permissive.

By emphasizing unification so strongly and making the "rectification" of this "vestige of humiliation" a primary goal of national development, PRC leaders have turned the Taiwan issue into a yardstick by which their own performance is measured. No leader can afford to appear irresolute in protecting what the CCP defines as a core interest of the Chinese nation. Chinese Communist leaders are not subject to popular election, but they compete fiercely for promotions and power. "Soft on Taiwan" is the kind of reputation that can halt an ambitious leader's rise, while talking tough rarely carries a cost. More than once, the fear of making one-sided concessions has caused the PRC to miss opportunities to improve relations with Taipei.

Taiwan as Precedent-Setter

Yet another reason for Beijing's anxiety about "losing" Taiwan is that some PRC citizens look to Taiwan for clues to their own futures. Taiwan is not the only territory claimed by the PRC where dreams of independence linger. Tibet, Xinjiang (a predominantly Muslim region in northwestern China), and even Inner Mongolia all resemble Taiwan in that they were incorporated into the Chinese state relatively late. Unlike most Taiwanese, those areas' original occupants are ethnically distinct from the Chinese majority, making China's claims over them even more attenuated. If Taiwan were to become independent, Beijing might find itself facing independence movements in other territories as well.

Taiwan also has precedent-setting potential when it comes to China's own political development. Chinese Communist leaders believe the form of government employed in the PRC—which the Chinese Constitution defines as a people's democratic dictatorship—is the best system for China. Western-style democracy, they aver, is a poor fit with China's traditional culture. That position was fortified when the Singaporean statesman Lee Kwan-yew and other leaders in the region put forth the "Asian Values" thesis in the mid-1990s. According to Lee, Asian values, which are rooted in Confucianism, differ from Western values. Competitive democracy, in particular, he says, does not work in Confucian cultural contexts.

Since Taiwan became democratic, however, it has become much more difficult to claim that Chinese people are "unsuited" or "unready" for democracy—unless one is prepared to say that Taiwanese are not Chinese, which is the *last* thing the CCP can accept. Taiwan's vibrant democracy is a daily challenge to the PRC's claim that competitive democracy cannot work in a Confucian society. As Dan Blumenthal and Randall Schriver put it in a 2008 report for the American Enterprise Institute, "Taiwan's successful democratic transition demonstrates that Chinese culture is not inimical to democracy—a powerful answer to those who claim that free institutions and popularly elected governments are the sole preserve of the West."

Taiwanese sometimes identify the difference in political systems as a reason to postpone unification. President Ma, for example, has insisted that Taiwan will not contemplate unifying with a nondemocratic PRC. Beijing rejects this line of argument out of hand. According to the White Paper on the One-China Principle:

> In recent years the Taiwan authorities have repeatedly declared that "democratization on the China mainland is the key to the reunification of China" and that "the real essence of the cross-Straits issue is a contest between systems." This is an excuse for postponing and resisting reunification, as well as a scheme to deceive compatriots in Taiwan and world opinion. . . . It is totally unreasonable and undemocratic for the Taiwan authorities to seek to obstruct reunification on the pretext of the "controversy about democracy and system" and to force the more than 1.2 billion people living on the Chinese mainland to practice the political and economic systems in Taiwan.

KEEPING TAIWAN IN THE BIRDCAGE

The various motivations underlying China's Taiwan policy reinforce one another in ways that make Beijing fiercely resolved on its view. Nonetheless, it has not always had the capacity to compel others to comply with its preferences. Since the 1980s, China's power has increased, and with it has come an increasing ability to enforce its interpretation of the Taiwan issue. At the same time, "winning" the Taiwan issue has become even more important to China's international reputation. It is one thing for a developing country to tolerate or even downplay a violation of its sovereignty. It is another matter for a rising global power to endure such an insult. As the PRC has moved from the first category to the second, its determination to "solve the Taiwan problem" has strengthened—both for reasons of domestic legitimacy and for reasons of international pride.

Today, Beijing defines Taiwan as a "core interest" of the PRC, a matter on which the Chinese government cannot lose. It asserts it will pay any price to avoid the outcome it deems unacceptable: the permanent separation of Taiwan from China. That said, it is difficult to determine what—short of a declaration of independence by Taipei—would constitute "losing." One of the perpetual challenges for Taiwan is to discern the limits of Beijing's tolerance, and to protect its interests as fully as it can without exceeding those limits.

Back in the 1990s, when Taiwanese politicians held out formal independence as an option to pursue, the "red lines" were clearer. Political changes within Taiwan have muddied those lines. Today, few Taiwanese favor pursuing formal independence as long as Beijing objects; they are content to maintain their status as a de facto independent state called the Republic of China. This shift in Taiwanese thinking has left Beijing—which still desires unification—in an awkward position. If Beijing pushes too hard, it will be accused of trying to change the status quo through coercion. But if it does not push at all, it will seem to be acquiescing in a situation that falls far short of its preferences. It is hard for Beijing to persuade other governments to help it squeeze Taipei when "all Taiwan wants" is to continue a state of affairs the PRC has tolerated for decades.

One way Beijing manages this dilemma is by policing the international community's relationships with Taiwan. It cannot compel Taipei to comply with its preferences, but it can pressure other countries to deny Taiwan recognition. Isolating Taipei internationally allows Beijing to minimize the damage from Taiwan's continuing resistance. Of course it would prefer Taiwan not strengthen its internal rhetoric of separation, but as long as Beijing controls Taiwan's international status it can nullify any pro-independence moves. The real danger for Beijing is that other nations might acknowledge Taiwan as a state; so as long as other states do not contest China's claim to the island, that claim is safe, even if Beijing does not actually control Taiwan.

At the level of official relations, Beijing's efforts to isolate Taiwan have succeeded. Taiwan is excluded from international organizations almost entirely. It has no voice in the United Nations—not even the observer status granted to Palestine and the Vatican. It secured membership in the World Trade Organization as the "Separate Customs Territory of Taiwan, Penghu, Kinmen and Matsu." It competes in the Olympics as "Chinese Taipei." While Taiwan has figured out ways to work around its exclusion in most cases, being barred from international groups has consequences, both symbolic and real.

Taiwan's exclusion from the World Health Organization provides examples of both. During the 2006 bird flu scare, the WHO published a map showing Taiwan as infected even though the island had not seen a single bird flu case in birds or humans. The map reflected not the medical reality but the WHO's political decision to define Taiwan as Chinese territory—and mainland China *did* have bird flu cases. The map fracas was largely symbolic (although Taiwan complained it might cause travelers to avoid the island), but Taiwan's limited access to the WHO had practical consequences, too. It meant Taiwan was not fully integrated into global disease reporting, surveillance, and treatment networks, which could put its citizens at risk in a pandemic.

Taiwan's international isolation also applies to bilateral relationships. The last two large countries to break ties with Taiwan were South Africa and South Korea—fellow members of a "club" of international pariah states united by their unsavory authoritarian regimes and fierce anti-Communism. In contrast to Taiwan, democratization erased those countries' pariah status. As of 2010, only twenty-three small countries maintained formal diplomatic ties with the Republic of China: Belize, Burkina Faso, the Dominican Republic, El Salvador, Gambia, Guatemala, Haiti, Honduras, Kiribati, the Marshall Islands, Nauru, Nicaragua, Panama, Paraguay, Pulau, Sao Tome and Principe, the Solomon Islands, St. Kitts and Nevis, St. Lucia, St. Vincent and the Grenadines, Swaziland, Tuvalu, and Vatican City.

To hang on to those partners Taipei has expended untold resources, including billions in foreign assistance, from food aid to medical care to agricultural extension services. Not all the money is well spent. During the height of the diplomatic competition between Taipei and Beijing, both sides spent huge sums to cultivate friendly politicians—sometimes with little benefit to those leaders' nations. In private, Taiwan's diplomats sometimes deplored the outrageous demands foreign leaders and their staffs made during visits to Taiwan—demands Taiwan's government held its nose and met, so much did it fear the loss of even one diplomatic partner. After Ma Ying-jeou took office the pressure lifted somewhat, apparently because the two sides instituted a tacit "diplomatic truce"—meaning they each stopped trying to woo away the other's diplomatic partners.

If we count unofficial relations among Taiwan's international ties, the picture is brighter. In 1972, Japan established diplomatic ties with the People's Republic of China. At the same time, it created an innovative set of institutions and practices that allowed it to continue its substantive interactions with Taipei. These accommodations established a model many others have followed. When embassies withdraw, they leave behind "representative offices" operated as quasi-independent organizations. Using public funds laundered through nominally independent organizations and diplomats "furloughed" from government service, representative offices conduct all the functions associated with embassies and consulates except receiving official visits and communications from the host government. They issue visas, sponsor trade delegations, promote investment, and conduct public diplomacy, all in the name of some institute or foundation. Working through these quasi-official representative offices, as well as its huge and lively private sector, Taiwan has succeeded in maintaining robust trade, investment, and people-to-people ties with nearly every country in the world. Altogether, about fifty countries have representative offices in Taiwan, and Taiwan has them in almost sixty states. If we count these unofficial offices, Taiwan actually has *more* foreign representation than many other states have.

TAIWAN AND THE UNITED STATES

Taiwan's most important "officially unofficial" relationship is with the United States of America. When the United States severed its diplomatic ties with the ROC in 1979, the two countries still had a mutual defense treaty and the United States had defended Taiwan, sometimes reluctantly, since the end of World War II. Nonetheless, Washington was willing to cut off relations with Taipei and abandon its treaty obligations in order to secure diplomatic ties with Beijing. At the time, it was not at all certain that an independent Republic of China would survive the break.

In July 1971, the White House announced that President Nixon's national security advisor, Henry Kissinger, had visited China, and Nixon himself would soon follow. Nixon's decision to open a dialogue with China reflected his strategic calculation that, given the chance, Beijing would side with the United States against the USSR. Although he had often made political hay by asserting his strong commitment to Taiwan, Nixon was actually far more interested in squeezing the Soviets. He also expected Beijing to help him extricate the United States from the increasingly unpopular war in Vietnam. Officials in Taiwan recognized Nixon's visit as a signal that the United States and China were preparing to normalize their relationship. Nixon would not go to China without the promise of a diplomatic breakthrough, and the Chinese would not allow such a breakthrough unless the United States made a major concession on Taiwan's status. The question was, just how much was Nixon willing to give?

In October 1971 the other shoe fell. The PRC rallied its allies in the United Nations to endorse its campaign to be seated as the government of China. Taiwan was out. Then, when Nixon returned from China in February 1972, Taipei learned just how much the Sino-American rapprochement would cost the ROC. The price of normalized relations was Nixon's signature on the Shanghai Communiqué. In the communiqué, the Chinese stated their position that Taiwan is part of China and the PRC is China's sole legal government. The Chinese statement went on, "The liberation of Taiwan is China's internal affair in which no other country has the right to interfere."

The United States asserted a different view. According to the Shanghai Communiqué:

> The United States acknowledges that all Chinese on either side of the Taiwan Strait maintain there is but one China and that Taiwan is a part of China.

The United States Government does not challenge that position. It reaffirms its interest in a peaceful settlement of the Taiwan question by the Chinese themselves. With this prospect in mind, it affirms the ultimate objective of the withdrawal of all U.S. forces and military installations from Taiwan. In the meantime, it will progressively reduce its forces and military installations on Taiwan as the tension in the area diminishes.

Washington's position was subtle. It did not endorse any particular view of Taiwan's relationship with China; instead, it simply nodded to the position held by "all Chinese on either side." The word "Chinese" was chosen deliberately, as some U.S. policy makers argued many *people* in Taiwan (specifically, many Hokkien-speaking Taiwanese) did not agree with that position. In effect, the United States stated it would not challenge the position held by *governments* in Beijing and Taipei at that time. The Shanghai Communiqué also committed the United States to withdraw its military forces from Taiwan, a promise that required Washington to abrogate its mutual defense treaty with the ROC, but it conditioned the decline in U.S. military assistance on reduced tension in the Taiwan Strait. These nuances provided Taiwan with some protection, but they could not obscure one central fact: the United States had started down a path that ultimately would lead it to de-recognize the Republic of China on Taiwan in favor of the PRC.

Closing the normalization deal took longer than expected. Nixon fell into disgrace soon after signing the Shanghai Communiqué and he resigned in 1974, leaving the U.S. presidency in the hands of a caretaker, Gerald Ford. Ford's successor, Jimmy Carter, was eager to complete the normalization, but by the time he took office, the Chinese side was in disarray. Mao died in 1976, and he, too, left a caretaker in charge. It was not until Deng Xiaoping solidified his position as China's top leader in 1978 that normalization talks resumed. The two sides announced their normalization deal in December 1978; it became effective on January 1, 1979.

The six years between the Shanghai Communiqué and the normalization announcement were critical for Taiwan. The Taipei government was surprisingly passive; the impending loss of U.S. support seems to have been more than the aging Chiang Kai-shek and his advisors could absorb. But outside the state apparatus, responses to the changes were robust. Within Taiwan, advocates of political reform redoubled their efforts. In the United States, a Taiwanese diplomat quietly assembled a group of Taiwanese-American scholars to draft legislation the U.S. Congress could use to protect Taiwan's interests after normalization and organized a lobbying campaign to get that legislation enacted. The key ideas in their proposal eventually were incorporated into the Taiwan Relations Act (TRA); Congress passed the law in 1979, establishing a framework for continued relations between Washington and Taipei in the wake of normalization.

Like the final fairy's blessing in the "Sleeping Beauty" tale, Congress' action could not reverse the "curse" of de-recognition, but passing the TRA did soften its effects. It mandated that the U.S. government treat Taiwanese nongovernmental entities the same as those of recognized states. It established a de facto U.S. embassy to manage relations, the American Institute in Taiwan (AIT), and invited Taiwan to set up a similar institution in Washington, which today is called the Taiwan Economic and Cultural Representative Office (TECRO).

Perhaps the most consequential clause in the TRA was the requirement that the United States provide Taiwan with defensive weapons to fend off PRC attempts to coerce Taiwan into unification. The TRA stipulates that it is U.S. policy "to consider any effort to determine the future of Taiwan by other than peaceful means, including by boycotts or embargoes, a threat to the peace and security of the Western Pacific area and of grave concern to the United States." The law does not commit the United States to defend Taiwan, but it says the United States must "maintain the capacity . . . to resist any resort to force or other forms of coercion that would jeopardize the security, or the social or economic system, of the people on Taiwan." Finally, the TRA mandates that Congress play a role in shaping Taiwan policy; Taiwan's fate cannot be decided by the executive branch alone.

The TRA put the brakes on Taiwan's slide toward international irrelevance, but it did not change the bottom line: the ROC had lost the battle to represent China internationally. From then on, Taiwan would struggle to survive as an autonomous political entity in a world that no longer recognized its sovereignty—a world increasingly inclined to bend to Beijing's will.

Taiwan owes its survival as an autonomous entity in international relations to three critical developments. First, the island's successful economic development and upgrading have made it a key economic player, globally and within the PRC, and its economic contributions have enabled a degree of international engagement and protection that mitigate its political isolation. Second, economic development, international setbacks, and political reform converged in a virtuous cycle that produced, by the mid-1990s, a democratic Taiwan. The third development—one that owes much to the other two—is Taiwan's close relationship with the United States. Washington's continued engagement with Taipei provides direct benefits, and it also is a powerful signal to other nations that Taiwan is not on the verge of eclipse. That reassurance encourages others to engage Taiwan, too.

The major elements of U.S. policy toward Taiwan have changed little since 1979. Diplomats refer to the first element as America's "one China policy," but don't be fooled by the phrase's resemblance to Beijing's "One China Principle," as the meaning is very different. The policy is rooted in the Shanghai Communiqué and the 1979 normalization agreement with Beijing, which states, "The United States of America recognizes the Government of the People's Republic of China as the sole legal Government of China. . . . The Government of the United States of America acknowledges the Chinese position that there is but one China and Taiwan is part of China." Once again, the United States avoided a clear endorsement of the PRC's claim over Taiwan, although it has weighed in against Taiwan independence, as in a Reagan-era communiqué asserting the United States "has no intention of infringing on Chinese sovereignty and territorial integrity, or interfering in China's internal affairs, or pursuing a policy of 'two Chinas' or 'one China, one Taiwan.'"

"One China" statements constitute one element of America's Taiwan policy. Another, equally important, component is the U.S. interest in "peaceful resolution." President Nixon asserted this goal when he met Chinese Premier Zhou Enlai in 1972. Nixon's talking points from the trip included, "We will support any peaceful resolution of the Taiwan issue that can be worked out." Congress elaborated on this point—and codified it into law—in the Taiwan Relations Act, which states that it is the policy of the United States "to declare that peace and stability in the area are in the political, security, and economic interests of the United States, and are matters of international concern."

American statements about "peaceful resolution" have subtle implications. U.S. officials take pains to avoid endorsing any particular "resolution." U.S. government documents rarely mention "unification" and "independence," in part because Washington does not want to limit the forms "resolution" might take to those two options only. During the Lee Teng-hui and Chen Shui-bian administrations, when it seemed *Taiwan's* actions might destabilize the Strait, the United States restated its "peaceful resolution" principle in a slightly different form, as opposition to "unilateral changes to the status quo." The phrase implied that either side's efforts to change the situation on its own would conflict with the U.S. interest in peaceful—and by extension bilateral—resolution.

At other times, U.S. statements about "peaceful resolution" have emphasized Washington's determination to protect Taiwan's interests. In 2000, President Bill Clinton added a new dimension to U.S. policy when he said, "We'll continue to reject the use of force as a means to resolve the Taiwan question. We'll also continue to make absolutely clear that the issues between Beijing and Taiwan must be resolved peacefully and with the assent of the people of Taiwan." The addition of the phrase "with the assent of the people" was a nod toward Taiwan's democratization. No longer would the United States offer carte blanche to the two governments to settle the issue over the heads of their respective peoples; in a democratic Taiwan, such an important decision would require democratic ratification.

It should be clear by now that America's Taiwan policy is subtle and complex, and that is no accident. Students of U.S.-Taiwan-China relations characterize this approach as "strategic ambiguity." The policy is ambiguous in the sense that neither Taipei nor Beijing can be entirely certain how the United States will respond to actions they might take: while nothing in U.S. law or policy requires it to come to Taiwan's defense, most politicians in the United States, Taiwan, and mainland China assume that under some circumstances, the United States would use military force to help Taiwan avoid forcible unification. Still, the United States has never stated the precise circumstances under which it would defend Taiwan, and U.S. leaders have hinted there *are* circumstances—including moves toward formal independence—under which America might *not* come to Taiwan's rescue. The policy is strategic because it constrains the other two players (by forcing them to make decisions with limited information) while giving the United States maximum flexibility to pursue its interests in light of changing circumstances.

Strategic ambiguity has its critics. Some, like Ted Galen Carpenter, the author of *America's Coming War with China: A Collision Course over Taiwan*, argue the policy encourages Taiwan to take U.S. support for granted and risk its own interests and those of the United States in a reckless drive for independence. Others believe it could mislead the PRC into thinking it could safely attack Taiwan. In 1996, members of Congress introduced a resolution calling on the government to promise to defend Taiwan in the event of an attack by the PRC. Nonetheless, despite regular calls for greater clarity, strategic ambiguity remains U.S. policy, primarily because policy makers have yet to develop a better option. As Emerson Niou and Brett Benson conclude in an unpublished study of strategic ambiguity, "To achieve both of its deterrence goals simultaneously, the US cannot be explicit about the conditions under which it will defend Taiwan. Ambiguity . . . introduces just enough uncertainty to dissuade the disputants from taking the risk of testing U.S. commitment."

A third critical element in U.S. policy—one that is rooted in both legal and strategic reasoning—is the sale of defensive weapons to Taiwan. Legally, the United States is bound by the Taiwan Relations Act to provide Taiwan with defensive weapons and maintain its own capacity to protect Taiwan so long as a threat exists. In 1982, the Reagan administration signed a communiqué with Beijing promising that the United States "does not seek to carry out a long-term policy of arms sales to Taiwan, that its arms sales to Taiwan will not exceed, either in qualitative or in quantitative terms, the level of those supplied in recent years since the establishment of diplomatic relations between the United States and China, and that it intends to reduce gradually its sales of arms to Taiwan, leading over a period of time to a final resolution." Beijing reads the 1982 communiqué as a promise to cut off arms sales, and many in Congress and elsewhere view it as a betrayal of Taiwan and a violation of the TRA. To Reagan, at least according to a memo he prepared for Congressional Republicans, it was an attempt to reinforce the "peaceful resolution" element of U.S. policy. Reagan also sent Taipei a message called the "six assurances." It promised continued adherence to the TRA and affirmed America's long-standing Taiwan policy.

Whatever President Reagan intended, the offer to roll back arms sales has never materialized, to Beijing's great disappointment. China's strong opposition to the sales, which appears to be intensifying, has prompted some in the United States to question whether the TRA still serves U.S. interests. In November 2009 retired Admiral Bill Owens published an essay in the *Financial Times* in which he said the TRA did "more harm than good" and that selling arms to Taiwan was "not in our best interest." In mid-2010 Senator Dianne Feinstein, the chair of the Senate Intelligence Committee and a leading Congressional voice on China policy, questioned Secretary of Defense Robert Gates about what developments might allow the United States to end arms sales, which she called a "substantial irritant" in U.S.-China relations. Owens and Feinstein were calling attention to a fundamental question: Given the importance to the United States of good relations with China, and given Beijing's fervent opposition to arms sales, at what point should we conclude that the benefits of continuing to sell arms do not justify the costs?

Washington's rationale for selling arms despite Chinese leaders' strong objections has both military and political elements. On the military side, strong Taiwanese defenses help deter Beijing from using force against Taiwan. In response to Senator Feinstein's question, Secretary Gates cited the PRC's rapid and unrelenting military buildup opposite Taiwan—including nearly two thousand ballistic and cruise missiles targeting the island—as evidence that the need for arms sales had not diminished. The fact that the PRC has never renounced the use of armed force against Taiwan—and in fact passed legislation in 2005 authorizing force in certain situations—reinforces the view that Taiwan faces a very real threat. Aggression and violence anywhere in the world disrupts peace and stability and the United States has a stated interest in protecting Taiwan from coercion—two good reasons for helping Taiwan deter the PRC from using force.

Another military argument for continuing arms sales circles back to strategic ambiguity. Strategic ambiguity rests on the possibility that the United States might intervene in a cross-Strait conflict. In view of that prospect, deterring a conflict becomes an even higher priority. Moreover, successful U.S. intervention depends on Taiwan's ability to participate effectively in its own defense. As retired Rear Admiral Eric McVadon wrote in a response to Admiral Owens' comments published in the *Nelson Report*, "Taiwan cannot defend itself against today's China and PLA without U.S. intervention. The Chinese will attempt to deter or delay a U.S. response with military, technical, and political means. Taiwan needs weapon systems that will help it hold on until the Americans can achieve effective intervention. Beijing must recognize that factor, or it will be emboldened or tempted to use military force in some arising crisis, perceived or real, concerning Taiwan's future direction."

On the political front, the U.S. government is convinced that a strong, well-defended Taiwan offers the best chance for peaceful resolution of the Taiwan Strait issue. I asked Randall Schriver, a former deputy assistant secretary of state for East Asia and leading voice on U.S. Taiwan policy, how a stronger defense increases Taiwan's bargaining power. He replied,

> It's hard to measure the direct action-reaction pattern—it's not a case where we make a package available, and they go negotiate. The relationship between arms sales and bargaining power is really a theory and a concept. But in what other instance involving negotiation is the weaker party better off? Where can you point to a successful negotiation in which there was a great disparity in power, where the weaker party was able to get fair terms? Historically, what you find is where there is equal power—or at least credible deterrent power—you get better outcomes.

In short, a confident Taiwan has a better chance of striking acceptable deals with the PRC. President Ma Ying-jeou made this point in a December 2009 interview with the *Wall Street Journal*: "The relaxed tensions [across the Strait] depend very much on the continued supply of arms from the United States to Taiwan. Certainly Taiwan will not feel comfortable to go to a negotiating table without sufficient defense buildup in order to protect the safety of the island."

What's more, negotiating from strength makes it far more likely that Taipei will be able to "sell" the results of a negotiation to its own people. If Taiwan were weak, beleaguered, and desperate, its government might strike a deal that its citizens would perceive as an unacceptable surrender. An agreement imposed against the will of Taiwan's people would be unjust, and it would cause a massive—potentially violent—backlash. That would make implementing the agreement extremely difficult, with potentially dire results. To conclude a successful agreement, Taiwan's leaders must be able to convince their people the deal is in their interests. A deal accepted under military threat cannot meet that standard; nor could it protect other nations from abrupt and destabilizing changes in the regional power balance.

The arguments for the policy the United States has followed since 1979 are strong, but they rest on one potentially controversial assumption: Taiwan matters to the United States. In the next chapter, we look at the arguments for and against that claim.

SOURCES

Studies of Taiwan's role in Chinese history include Emma Jinhua Teng's *Taiwan's Imagined Geography: Chinese Colonial Travel Writing and Pictures, 1683–1895* and Tonio Andrade's *How Taiwan Became Chinese: Dutch, Spanish, and Han Colonization in the Seventeenth Century*. Leo Ching (*Becoming Japanese*) and Melissa Brown (*Is Taiwan Chinese?*) also write in interesting ways about the origins of Taiwan identity and its historical relationship to China and Japan. The PRC document "The Taiwan Question and the Reunification of China" includes a *précis* of the evidence for Taiwan's connection to China. It begins: "Taiwan has belonged to China since ancient times. It was known as Yizhou or Liuqiu in antiquities. Many historical records and annals documented the development of Taiwan by the Chinese people in earlier periods. References to this effect were to be found, among others, in Seaboard Geographic Gazetteer compiled more than 1,700 years ago by Shen Ying of the State of Wu during the period of the Three Kingdoms. This was the world's earliest written account of Taiwan." For a definition and discussion of postnationalism, see Christopher Hughes, *Taiwan and Chinese Nationalism: National Identity and Status in International Society*. Lee Tuo-tzu spins his metaphor of Taiwan growing into independent adulthood in "My Littler Cooler and Their Big Fridge," an article appearing (in Chinese) in the magazine *The Journalist* in 2004. Alan Wachman details the case for Taiwan's importance in China's geostrategy in *Why Taiwan: Geostrategic Rationales for China's Territorial Integrity*. Dan Blumenthal and Randall Schriver's argument that Taiwan's democracy is important to the United States can be found in their essay, "Strengthening Freedom in Asia: A 21st-Century Agenda for the U.S.-Taiwan Partnership."

My discussion of the Nixon administration's overtures to China in the early 1970s and their long-term consequences for U.S.-China relations owe much to Nancy Bernkopf Tucker's superb history of those years, *Strait Talk*. As it turned out, Nixon was prepared to give quite a lot. According to recently released documents, Kissinger assured the Chinese negotiator Zhou Enlai that the Taiwan issue would be resolved "in accord with your expectations." According to Tucker, the PRC believed subsequent measures the United States took to defend Taiwan's interests represented a betrayal of the tacit agreements made with Nixon and Kissinger, and this has complicated Sino-American relations ever since. Emerson Niou and Brett Benson defend strategic ambiguity in an unpublished paper from 2001, "Comprehending Strategic Ambiguity: US Security Commitment to Taiwan." Full texts of all the PRC documents quoted here can be found on various PRC government websites.

9

Why Taiwan Matters to America and the World

As countries go, Taiwan is on the small side. Its square mileage puts it 138th in the world, smaller than Switzerland but bigger than Belgium. Its population puts it in a neighborhood with Malaysia, Ghana, and Syria—about 50th in the world. When it comes to economics and politics, though, Taiwan carries disproportionate weight. The island's steady ascent up the manufacturing ladder from textiles and toys to high-tech equipment and IT services positions it at the global economy's cutting edge. Its refusal to accept the constraints Beijing seeks to impose on it has made it a consistent focus of international attention—and sometimes conflict. Taiwan's economic success and political tenacity both have their roots in the island's vibrant, ambitious society, with its tight social networks and inexhaustible appetite for work and interaction.

Taiwan commands the world's attention because its people have crafted a nation too important to ignore on an island the pundit Thomas Friedman described to David Letterman as a "barren rock in a typhoon-laden sea." Friedman went on to point out that Taiwan—which he called "one of my favorite countries"—owned the fourth largest financial reserves in the world. Still, the People's Republic of China also is too important to ignore, and its significance is growing even faster than Taiwan's. Meanwhile, the PRC is determined to draw Taiwan into its orbit, not just socially and economically, but politically as well.

No one knows exactly what political unification would entail, but Beijing has made it clear that engineering a merger is its unshakeable goal—and it will not look favorably on nations that help Taiwan resist its embrace. These trends create real challenges for nations that value Taiwan's contributions but also hope to maintain good relations with China.

Increasingly—and understandably—citizens in those nations are asking: Why should we sacrifice good relations with the world's fastest-rising economic, political, and military power to help Taiwan remain autonomous? What do we gain by challenging Beijing on a matter it has defined as one of its core interests? Do the benefits we get from helping Taiwan resist Beijing's pressure justify the costs to our ties with China? In short, why does Taiwan matter *to us*?

During the Cold War these questions were easier to answer. Taiwan was important to the United States and its allies because it was a frontline state in the fight against Communist expansion. But with the end of the Cold War and the rise of a globally engaged China, some citizens have begun to question whether the complex, delicately balanced Taiwan policies described in chapter 8 still serve U.S. interests. Commentators like Ted Galen Carpenter argue that Taiwan's value to the United States is too low to justify the irritation it causes in U.S.-China relations. In their view, U.S. support for Taiwan allows Taipei to postpone hard decisions about its future and undermines America's relationship with the PRC.

Since the end of the Cold War, the rationale for supporting Taiwan's efforts to determine its own future has changed, but it has not disappeared. Some of the reasons Taiwan matters to the United States and other nations are very practical. On the economic front, multinational corporations rely on Taiwanese suppliers to make thousands of products for sale under their brands and to provide critical equipment and services. Disrupting those suppliers' operations is extremely costly to the world economy, as we discovered in 1999 when a power transmission tower on a remote mountain in central Taiwan toppled, blacking out the island's high-tech industry for a day. The interruption nearly doubled the world price of memory chips and the supply of TFT-LCD flat screens took six months to return to normal. A man-made disaster—especially one linked to military tensions or armed conflict—would be far more disruptive.

Another practical factor influencing politicians and policy makers is Taiwanese people's active advocacy of their interests to foreign governments and peoples. The Taiwan government uses its "officially unofficial" representatives to pursue both traditional government-to-government diplomacy and public diplomacy aimed at securing popular support for Taiwan in democratic countries. At the same time, Taiwanese living in the United States, Canada, and Europe are adept at mobilizing to promote what they see as Taiwan's interests. Their influence is most visible in the United States, where the Formosan Association for Public Affairs (FAPA), Taiwanese-American Associations, the Formosa Foundation, and others have had considerable success in securing support for Taiwan, especially in Congress. FAPA, in particular, adroitly deploys its members—and their campaign donations—to influence elected representatives to take an active interest in Taiwan-related issues.

Economic interests and political advocacy help keep the Taiwan issue on the front burner in the United States and other countries, but they alone are not enough to justify defying China's preferences on this critical issue. Taiwan's economic value is only tangentially related to its ability to determine its own fate politically, and China's white-hot economic growth means its importance is fast outstripping Taiwan's. In Washington, the vaunted pro-ROC "China lobby" of the Chiang Kai-shek era is overshadowed by a PRC-backed "China lobby" today. At the same time, democratization has encouraged the proliferation of views and opinions among Taiwanese, undermining its once-monolithic diplomatic effort. Today, the positions taken by overseas Taiwanese communities and those promoted by Taipei's professional diplomats conflict at least as often as they overlap.

To understand more deeply why Taiwan matters we must consider not only what it does, but what it is. Making sure Taiwan has a voice in deciding its own future is important to the United States and other democratic countries because democracy in Taiwan is an indicator and inspiration for democracy everywhere.

For Americans who remember World War II and the early years of the Cold War, affinity with Taiwan—and suspicion of the PRC—comes naturally. Admiral Eric McVadon captured this sentiment when he said, "Americans of my generation feel close to Taiwan, have affection for its people, and cannot bring themselves to succumb to the reasoning that we would be better off by abandoning support for Taiwan. Taiwan is like a blood brother; it need not do any more to warrant loyalty. The PRC is, in contrast, a stranger. Its qualities run hot and cold. Its origin and upbringing create uncertainties; trust has to be developed. And these feelings, in both cases, are reciprocal." He continued, "I have gone to great lengths to listen to and understand the Chinese position on Taiwan. It is one thing to understand and even to accept the realities of their obsessive views. It is easy to feel close to Taiwan—even with its inordinate share of crackpots; it is very hard to feel close to the PRC, with its inordinate share of people who believe that the party of Mao Zedong, the Great Leap Forward and the Cultural Revolution has all the answers—including the future of Taiwan."

Few young Americans share the affinity with Taiwan that developed during the Cold War, but they, too, should take encouragement from Taiwan's development. Taiwan's democratic transition proves that democratization is possible—and need not require outside intervention or bloodshed. "Taiwan has grown into a society that represents most of our important values that we try to promote elsewhere in the world," says an American diplomat with experience in Taiwan and China. "Look at all we've done to promote these values in Iraq and Afghanistan—Taiwan achieved everything we want, all on its own." "It sounds syrupy," says another former U.S. official, "but Taiwan can offer hope to other countries—the fact that it can stay vibrant in spite of all its limitations is inspiring."

Colonel Albert Willner, a former defense liaison at the American Institute in Taiwan and close observer of Taiwan's military, views Taiwan's economic and political success in the face of international isolation as especially noteworthy:

> Taiwan is unique in a lot of ways. Its status makes it unique, and so does its history. It's something of a Petrie dish: If Taiwan—which is cut off from so many of the usual tools and opportunities that other countries have—can succeed at moving from White Terror to democracy, that has a lot of lessons for others. The Taiwanese are a unique people in that their history imbued them with a sense of survival and the ability to rise to a level where they could do things on their own. And they *had* to do things on their own because they had none of the usual tools. It says something about their leadership and about the people that they adapted in spite of this. You have to ask: What other people would have fared so well in the kind of isolation Taiwan faced?

"Taiwan worked! It became a market economy and a democracy," says Admiral McVadon. The combination makes Taiwan an important counter to claims that authoritarian governments provide better economic outcomes for their people. As Michael Fonte, the Democratic Progressive Party's liaison in Washington puts it,

> Taiwan has been able to make a transition from an authoritarian state to a real democracy. It's got its faults but so does everybody else. People are really engaged in the political process at a time when some authoritarian governments think they alone have the answer to economic policies and other things. Taiwan stands as an example of how you can have a vibrant democracy and a vibrant economy at the same time. You can protect human rights, promote democracy and have a good economy—all at the same time.

In fact, Fonte argues, Taiwan's experience shows that democracy works better than authoritarianism because it offers a more-just mechanism for resolving social problems. "Democracy," he says, "allows a country to address the inequalities that come with development."

Democratization has made Taiwan a better place to live, too. Fonte's first contact with Taiwan came in the dark days of the authoritarian period when he served as a Catholic missionary on the island. In the four decades since he watched as democracy transformed Taiwan and its people.

> It was always a wonderful, warm place when you were with your friends, but once you got out in to the world, you were always worried, looking around. Spies were everywhere, or everyone thought they were. When I lived in Taiwan

with my teachers in 1967 what bothered me most was the overarching fear and what that did to people. It made them timid, unable to speak their minds in public, even in a classroom. And now I go back to Taiwan and those same people—my teachers—are engaged, able to live a full life. And when I look at people who are the age I was then, they're just living a normal, free life. The psychological change is what's important. That's the big change I feel now, the fluidity and freedom.

As Admiral McVadon put it, "All one has to do is observe the relative roles of civil society on each side of the Strait to know why Taiwan matters to me and everyone who looks to making this a better world, with no fear of that knock on the dissident's door in the night."

If societies aspiring to install or consolidate democratic political systems look to Taiwan for inspiration, they also look to the United States and its allies for signs that they will support young democracies. Nancy Bernkopf Tucker, the leading historian of U.S.-Taiwan relations, points out, "The United States bears some responsibility for Taiwan's democracy, not least because it made those changes with encouragement and pressure from us." An American diplomat concurs,

> If we are seen as reducing our commitment to Taiwan it will have an impact on our position around the world. It would seem we don't believe in our own values. Taiwan *is* a means to an end for the US, at least in the sense that it helps us maintain our values and credibility around the world. Our presidents describe Taiwan as a beacon of democracy in their congratulatory statements but when we get down to business that conviction is not carried out with the gusto it deserves.

Richard Bush, who served as America's top Taiwan policy maker under Presidents Clinton and George W. Bush and is a leading observer of the U.S.-PRC-Taiwan triangular relationship, takes this point even further. He notes that past American decisions constrain Taiwan's options and opportunities to this day, and that obligates the United States to pay particular attention to Taiwan and its interests.

Taiwan is critical to U.S. credibility in another way, too: how Washington handles the security aspects of its Taiwan policy is an important indicator of its capacity and willingness to honor other commitments around the world. Says Admiral McVadon, "American credibility as an alliance partner and as a bulwark of peace and stability in the region and around the world would be sorely diminished were we to abandon the TRA, cease support of Taipei, and lead Beijing to conclude that it can attack Taiwan and not be repulsed." In the future, some American allies might choose to draw closer to China, but they should not be driven to that position by fear.

America's Taiwan policy substantiates its commitment both to its core values of democracy and freedom and to the global security architecture it helped to build in the 1940s and 1950s. After World War II, the United States and its allies created institutions to promote peace and stability around the world. Some, led by the United Nations, were political organizations open to all countries, while others—such as the North Atlantic Treaty Organization—were military alliances that provided collective security to member states. Others, like the European Common Market (later the European Union) and the General Agreement on Trade and Tariffs (precursor to the World Trade Organization) promoted a liberal economic order based on free markets and open trade. The military alliances stabilized the international system while the economic and political organizations nurtured shared interests among nations. This system, in which the United States has served as chief enforcer and guarantor, secured for the developed world, at least, more than six decades of peace, stability, and prosperity.

This U.S.-led world order is far from perfect. Developing countries suffered terribly from proxy wars and economic isolation during the Cold War, and in the post–Cold War period, new threats—from climate change to HIV/AIDS to transnational terrorism—have appeared. Although the bipolar competition between two superpowers has disappeared, the need for global cooperation to address economic and security challenges has not. Nations around the world continue to look to the United States to provide leadership in mobilizing that cooperation and addressing those threats.

If Washington appears to be backing down or backing away from its commitment to its alliances and the institutions in which it has invested so much, other governments will take that as a sign that they may not be able to rely on those institutions to ensure their safety in the future. That will force governments to become more competitive and individualistic. According to Colonel Willner, America's friends already are alert for signs of a decline in U.S. power: "There is a growing sense in the world that the US is a fair-weather friend, it won't be there for the long run. This causes people in many countries to maneuver ahead of time, to get into position in anticipation of the day the U.S. pulls back. If the U.S. makes decisions regarding Taiwan that reinforce this perception, it will have profound implications for our other relationships."

A good example of this dynamic is Japan, a nation whose military expansionism in the early twentieth century left the region deeply scarred. Since World War II, the size and mission of Japan's armed forces have been sharply limited, and pacifism has replaced bellicosity as the predominant popular mood. But those changes were possible only because an alliance with the United States guaranteed Japan's security. Without faith in that alliance, Japanese leaders would be compelled to consider expanding their armed forces. That, in turn, would raise the specter of a resurgent Japanese militarism, which might well spark an arms race in the region.

Even though the United States has no formal alliance with Taiwan—indeed, it doesn't even recognize Taiwan as a state—the island retains an important symbolic role in this system of alliances, institutions, and relationships. If the United States were to indicate by word or deed that it was no longer committed to making sure Taiwan is not coerced into decisions its people oppose, that would indicate weakness in U.S. capability or resolve—or both. Other nations would be forced to consider whether their interests, too, might be at risk.

The arguments made so far—that Taiwan matters because it stands as proof of the feasibility of democracy and the credibility of American alliances—have been around for many years. As China has become increasingly powerful, another argument is gaining currency. According to its logic, Taiwan matters because, as the former AIT head Stephen Young likes to say, Taiwan is the canary in the coal mine for China's rise. In other words, how China behaves toward Taiwan is an important indicator of how it will perform its role as a lead actor on the world stage. As Randall Schriver put it, "Beijing's ambitions go beyond Taiwan, but right now, it's the Taiwan issue that drives their military modernization, so it's very important to us. Taiwan is a prism through which we can understand China's evolution, and gain insights into it." By extension, how the United States and its allies treat Taiwan is an important indicator of what other countries can expect from *them* as the PRC's influence expands.

Asked why Taiwan matters, Richard Bush replied,

> On the importance of Taiwan, there are a variety of answers that I might give. It's a touchstone of American credibility for both our allies and others. It's a debt we owe to the people of Taiwan for having ignored their interests as we cut strategic bargains [with Beijing]. But my current answer to the question is that how the Taiwan Strait issue is resolved is an important test—perhaps the most important test—of what kind of great power China will be and of how the U.S. will play its role as the guardian of the international system.

Arguments like these are sometimes misread as justifications for containment, attempts to use Taiwan to prevent China from increasing its national power and status. In reality, while some advocates of containment do include Taiwan in their strategic thinking, a policy that supports Taiwan's efforts to craft a relationship with the PRC that serves both sides' interests is not anti-China. On the contrary, it is a policy aimed at upholding a system of international institutions and interactions in which countries and peoples are empowered to choose their own ways of living, free from coercion, violence, and intimidation.

Nor does the current U.S. policy militate against China's long-term goal of unification. The United States has never taken a position as to how the cross-Strait relationship ultimately should be resolved. Instead, the

United States holds that any outcome—including both unification and independence—is acceptable, so long as the two sides arrive at that outcome through a peaceful, mutual, and noncoercive process. Washington has made it clear that Beijing should not bully Taiwan, and Taiwan should not provoke or insult the PRC. During the Chen Shui-bian administration, U.S. officials forcefully reminded Taiwan's leaders that they expect Taipei to respect Beijing's bottom lines and to avoid giving gratuitous offense or acting unilaterally. When cross-Strait tensions eased under President Ma Ying-jeou, U.S. officials were quick to express encouragement for the warming trend.

While the world has an interest in seeing Taiwan's future decided peacefully and democratically, it does not have an interest in blocking Taiwan from forging a permanent peace—even to the point of unification—with mainland China. Today, few Taiwanese believe Beijing is prepared to offer a unification proposal that would preserve their democratic system, but if the PRC were to offer such a deal in the future, Taiwanese might well support it. And if they did, nothing in such an arrangement would be inconsistent with the interests of other nations, including the United States.

In 2002 Nancy Bernkopf Tucker published an article in the *Washington Quarterly* entitled "If Taiwan Chooses Unification, Should the United States Care?" In it she enumerated the costs unification might have for the United States. She also described the difficulty Washington would face if it tried to block a unification deal that enjoyed wide support in Taiwan. In the end she concluded the United States could not and should not intervene to obstruct a mutually acceptable unification deal. Her analysis is still persuasive today:

> The United States rightly remains opposed to the use of force to unify China. So long as unification can only be achieved through coercion, Washington should and will prevent the success of an unprovoked attack. Further, Washington's commitment to Taiwan's democracy means respect for the choices made by Taiwan's people. They have so far sought nothing more than affirmation of their political autonomy, even in the face of rapid economic integration with mainland China. The U.S. abandonment of agnosticism to dictate an answer, whether unification or independence, would be a great betrayal as well as a dangerous gamble after all these decades of stalemate, struggle, risk, and reform. The United States has much at stake in the Taiwan Strait. Washington would not serve its strategic interests, secure the goodwill of Taiwan's people, or win the hearts and minds of the mainland Chinese by trying to impose a solution to the Taiwan Strait dilemma.

Taiwanese treasure their democratic achievements and their personal freedom. They also love their island homeland. Still, most recognize and acknowledge their Chinese roots. It is not inconceivable that the two sides could negotiate a form of unification that protected Taiwan's political system and honored its unique position in China's past, present, and future. A loose confederation would not please hard-line unificationists in China or hard-line independentistas in Taiwan, but it might satisfy moderates on both sides. The proposals that have been put forth to date invariably attracted heavy criticism, so it is probably premature to delve too deeply into the details of what a successful deal might look like. Maintaining peaceful interactions between the two sides, interactions that enhance their mutual interests and build cross-Strait confidence, is the most sensible near-term goal.

The United States and other countries have no interest in encouraging conflict in the Taiwan Strait; on the contrary, given the deep interdependence among the PRC, Taiwan, and the global economy, instability in the Strait would be a catastrophe for everyone. At the same time, though, lasting peace and stability cannot be built on a foundation of might-makes-right. It was twenty-five hundred years ago when the envoys from a massive Athenian strike force confronted the leaders of Melos—a Lacedaemonian colony that was resisting Athens' growing power—and demanded their surrender. Thucydides records their words in *The Peloponnesian War* (the translation is Richard Crawley's):

> For ourselves, we shall not trouble you with specious pretences—either of how we have a right to our empire because we overthrew the Mede, or are now attacking you because of wrong that you have done us—and make a long speech which would not be believed; and in return we hope that you, instead of thinking to influence us by saying that you did not join the Lacedaemonians, although their colonists, or that you have done us no wrong, will aim at what is feasible, holding in view the real sentiments of us both; since you know as well as we do that right, as the world goes, is only in question between equals in power, while the strong do what they can and the weak suffer what they must.

These words—especially the phrase about the strong and the weak—are famous; they are practically a mantra for the Realist school of international relations theory. Less well-known, but equally telling, is the Melian leaders' reply:

> As we think, at any rate, it is expedient—we speak as we are obliged, since you enjoin us to let right alone and talk only of interest—that you should not destroy what is our common protection, the privilege of being allowed in danger to invoke what is fair and right. . . . And you are as much interested in this as any, as your fall would be a signal for the heaviest vengeance and an example for the world to meditate upon.

Today the privilege of invoking "what is fair and right" is substantiated in international norms that condemn aggression, force, and coercion and encourage negotiation, cooperation, and compromise. As the Melian leaders pointed out, every nation wants to be able to appeal to a shared moral code when it is threatened, and that makes ignoring the code, when one's power allows, a risky undertaking, one that stirs up resentment and—when the time is right—invites revenge.

China's leaders and people are rightfully proud of their accomplishments. The PRC's fast-growing economic power and international influence give Beijing both the means and the will to prevent outsiders from intruding and interfering in matters it defines as "core interests," including Taiwan. But this capability does not predetermine the choices Beijing will make regarding Taiwan. The PRC has great latitude in how it handles its relations with Taiwan; its options are limited only by the two sides' creativity and flexibility. And because the issue is so important to China, it stands to reason that the PRC should use its full measure of options to ensure a happy outcome. International norms and the interests of the international community demand that other states encourage both sides to make the most of their opportunities for peaceful resolution and to discourage coercion and violence. It is important to do so even when relations between Taiwan and the mainland are at their best, because paying attention to Taiwan only when it is playing the "troublemaker" rewards risk-taking and punishes prudence.

One final sense in which Taiwan matters to the world is that it stands as a perpetual reminder of what is possible in international relations—both for better and for worse. Taiwan offers proof that development—both political and economic—is possible, but its experience shows how fragile states' independence really is. It reveals that the autonomy most nations take for granted ultimately rests on the forbearance of the strong or on wobbly balances of power that, when they shift, leave states defenseless. In one sense, Taiwan is extremely unlucky: thanks to Chinese nationalists on both sides, it lost its chance at full independence. In another sense, though, Taiwan is lucky: unlike the many countries that have seats in the UN but are at the mercy of political and economic forces that make life miserable, Taiwan is wealthy and successful, and protected, for now, by powerful friends. Taiwan is able to mobilize others to support its survival, if not its sovereignty.

Taiwan's people have a long history of reinventing their homeland. They have reinvented its culture and identity, its economy and society, its politics and status. These reinventions represent adaptations to global forces—economic and geopolitical—pressing on the island and they arise from islanders' ambition, determination, pragmatism, and optimism. The qualities that drove the island's economic and political miracles also made it possible to build the world's tallest skyscraper in Taipei. Those traits enabled Taiwan to navigate its complex relationship with the People's Republic of

China for six decades; with luck, cleverness, and encouragement, they will continue to do so.

While the challenges facing Taiwan are real, Taiwanese have many strengths and resources to bring to bear on those challenges. Taiwan matters, to China, to the United States, to the world—and above all, to its own people. It is not an object of others' destiny, but the subject of its own history; it is not a means to others' ends, but an end in itself. Regarding Taiwan in this way does not foreclose any outcome in cross-Strait relations, but it does call on others to support outcomes that affirm and uphold Taiwan's dignity and democracy.

SOURCES

Most of the quotations in this chapter come from interviews conducted in 2010. I've also quoted Nancy Bernkopf Tucker's article, "If Taiwan Chooses Unification, Should the United States Care?" published in the *Washington Quarterly* in 2002 and Thucydides, *The Peloponnesian War*, as translated by Richard Crawley. Crawley's translation is available at the Internet Classics Archive at MIT: http://classics.mit.edu/Thucydides/pelopwar.5.fifth.html.

Epilogue

Taiwan's democratization had many cheerleaders, but it could have used a few more sympathetic skeptics to warn Taiwanese just how difficult democratic politics can be. Since the financial crisis of 2008, Taiwan has fallen into step with democracies in North America, Europe, and Asia that suffer from a post-industrial syndrome characterized by slow growth, rising inequality, stagnant wages, persistent underemployment, and political gridlock. The syndrome's underlying causes are the same everywhere: Globalization, technology, and pro-business policies have redirected wealth away from the working and middle classes in advanced countries and toward developing countries (including China) and the rich. Politicians in developed countries seem powerless to preserve collective prosperity in the face of these challenges. Taiwan faces all of these problems, but with a unique twist. The result is a troubling slide toward political and economic insecurity.

Ma Ying-jeou won a second four-year presidential term in 2012, but the victory was a far cry from his triumph four years earlier. The election was closer, and where the 2008 race represented the enthusiastic ratification of a popular leader, for many voters the 2012 election felt like a weary slog to choose the lesser of two evils. Ma had no post-election honeymoon—the day after the election he was back at work battling an endless succession of daunting problems. Charges that Ma and those around him lack empathy, creativity, and tactical savvy may have merit, but leaders from Washington to London to Athens to Tokyo are struggling with similar burdens, so it can't all be his fault.

Taiwan shares the political and economic dilemmas facing other developed countries, but it also faces a unique challenge: fending off the PRC's insistent demands for unification. The struggle for a comfortable future is ubiquitous, but in Taiwan, the struggle for prosperity is entangled with a battle for national survival. Thus its domestic politics has come to focus— almost obsessively—on cross-Strait relations and mainland China's influence on Taiwan.

For decades, Taiwanese identified the Republic of China—the China within Taiwan—as the obstacle to a free and democratic Taiwan. Today, most Taiwanese see the People's Republic of China—and, increasingly, its agents on the island—as the greatest threat to Taiwan's democracy. At the same time, though, Taiwanese recognize that the island's economic future lies in its ability to capitalize on mainland China's huge labor force and market. The tension between political and economic survival—and the impossibility of resolving it—drives a relentless, exhausting churn in Taiwan's public life.

After the 2008 economic crisis Taiwan's recovery outpaced other developed countries, but it still fell far short of the high levels Taiwanese had come to expect. Spillover from the PRC's huge stimulus in the wake of the financial crisis helped Taiwan avoid the worst of the recession, but its economy is hypersensitive to global demand trends, so the slow recovery in export markets was a drag on Taiwan's domestic revival. With sales and profits low, Taiwan firms struggled to fund the investment required to keep abreast of developments in information technology and stay ahead of the new product curve.

Cross-Strait business remains a key driver of Taiwan's economy, but the relationship changed after 2008. After focusing on the mainland as a manufacturing platform for twenty years, Taiwan firms found themselves running up against the limitations of that approach. With wages increasing and profit margins shrinking, some Taiwan-based firms adopted new strategies, including automation and relocating production to lower-wage countries—even back to Taiwan. More and more, Taiwanese companies are looking to the PRC as a market rather than a base for export manufacturing. The golden age of cross-Strait manufacturing seems to be drawing to a close.

While the prediction that cross-Strait economic integration would hollow out Taiwan's domestic economy has not come true, moving final assembly and other manufacturing functions to the mainland did affect employment patterns on the island. As in other developed countries, lower-skilled jobs have disappeared, and the addition of high-skilled positions has not kept pace with the growth of the work force. As in other advanced economies, overall job creation remained slow and wages stagnated, especially after 2008. Meanwhile, the return on capital increased relative to wages, which exacerbated the familiar pattern of growing income inequality.

After decades of rapid wage growth, rising living standards, and relatively equal incomes, Taiwanese found the post-2008 trends intolerable. They pressed the government to reverse them, but solutions to these problems are scarce, and the ones the Ma government proposed—such as a tax on stock transactions—encountered political resistance. Confidence in the Ma administration's ability to manage the economy ebbed, while realistic alternatives remained scarce.

Many business leaders argued the best way to boost Taiwan's economy would be to double down on cross-Strait economic interactions, but proposals to relax restrictions on PRC access to Taiwan's economy stimulated concerns about the PRC's growing influence on the island. Mainland China is a rich potential source of investment capital and human resources, but Taiwanese fear they will pay a price in their political independence if they allow Chinese to acquire too large a presence in the local economy.

Taiwan's lackluster economic growth and rising income inequality contributed to a growing sense that the beneficiaries of cross-Strait trade and investment were selling out the interests of the society as a whole; disputes over economic policy thus ripened into pitched ideological battles. All of these trends converged in 2012 in a massive political movement that came to be known as the anti–media monopolization campaign.

Between 2008 and 2012, Taiwan's Want Want Holdings company made a series of media acquisitions, first in publishing, then in television. In 2012, an investor group led by the Want Want chairman's son launched a bid to buy the assets of the Next Media company, which includes a major daily newspaper, *Apple Daily*, and a top-selling magazine. (Next Media is best known to western audiences for hilarious animated shorts on topics ranging from Tiger Woods' marital problems to Italian Prime Minister Silvio Berlusconi's fall from grace.) Want Want also owns two other leading dailies, the *China Times* and *Want Daily*. The Next Media purchase would have put about 50 percent of Taiwan's media under Want Want's control.

Want Want has massive interests on the mainland: Its founder and chairman Tsai Eng-meng is an avowed unification supporter and Chinese Communist Party apologist (he has defended the crackdown on Tiananmen Square protestors in 1989 and once told the *Washington Post* he hopes to witness the unification of Taiwan and the PRC). Most Taiwanese see a strong pro-China bias in Want Want publications. Even journalists who work for Want Want–owned news outlets acknowledge their pro-Beijing slant. A *Want Daily* reporter based in the PRC told me his editors spike stories they think show the PRC in a negative light.

Want Want's bid for Next Media sparked a massive outcry from democracy activists and unification opponents. The prospect that an avowed pro-unification tycoon could buy up half the island's media crystalized the fears of many that a small but well-funded cabal of pro-China businessmen are conniving with Beijing (and some Taiwanese politicians) to engineer Taiwan's surrender to the PRC. The protesters took media consolidation as their target, arguing the state had an interest in protecting competition in the media sector and preventing monopolization of public discourse by a handful of voices. Want Want's aggressive response to the protests—including slandering student activists, a charge one of the group's papers admitted to—only reinforced the protesters' case and buttressed their claim that Want Want's expansion threatened free speech in Taiwan.

After months of controversy, including a protest in early 2013 that attracted more than 100,000 people, Taiwan's media and anti-trust watchdogs, the National Communication Commission and Free Trade Commission, indicated they would view the purchase skeptically. At the same time, the DPP geared up to propose legislation limiting media consolidation—an idea that attracted support from other parties as well. With the prospects for a successful merger dimming, the Want Want-linked investor group withdrew its offer, and the deal died in March.

Media consolidation is a problem in many countries, but as with so many other issues, the fight against Want Want was especially intense because of the cross-Strait dimension. Opposition to the deal was driven more by fear of Beijing's growing influence than anything else. That same fear has slowed implementation of the cross-Strait Economic Cooperation Framework Agreement (ECFA) signed in 2010 and infuses debates over issues as divergent as the treatment of mainland-born spouses and the conflict over islands in the East China Sea.

Those who lean toward the DPP tend not to trust Ma or his party to put Taiwan's interests first—even when Ma's actual policies challenge Beijing. As tensions between Beijing and Tokyo over the disputed Diaoyu/Senkaku island chain escalated to worrying levels in 2012 and 2013, Taipei strongly defended the claim that the islands belong to the Republic of China—a declaration that irritated both regional powers. Even so, the DPP criticized Ma's response, which the Democratic Progressives thought was too close to the PRC position. Meanwhile, KMT supporters continue to paint the DPP as reckless and provocative.

Between the parties' caricatures of one another stands a stark reality: The PRC is growing stronger by the day, economically, politically, and militarily. Despite its myriad problems, there is no question that China is far more powerful than Taiwan, and the gap between the two will continue to grow. For Taipei, that gap means it is more important—and more difficult—than ever to manage relations with the mainland in a way that preserves the island's political autonomy and economic prosperity and reflects the Taiwan people's continuing preference for the status quo.

Phillip Saunders, a China specialist at the U.S. National Defense University, calls Taiwan's approach to this dilemma the "Scheherazade Strategy." Like the legendary Persian storyteller, Taipei has perfected the stalling tactic known as jawboning. Scheherazade's stories postponed her execution one day at a time; likewise, each round of negotiations over economic minutia postpones the moment Taipei will be compelled to enter negotiations about its ultimate status. Perhaps, like Scheherazade's royal husband, Beijing will be so charmed and seduced by all the chatter that it changes its mind about Taiwan's fate. Or perhaps, as the PRC hopes, the extended courtship between the two will win the hearts of Taiwanese and dissolve their resistance to unification. Either way, a happy ending could ensue.

No matter what happens, a simple truth remains: Taiwan matters. As citizens in a self-governing, democratic society with a distinctive identity and culture, Taiwanese deserve to shape their own future. With confidence, self-respect, and a little help from friends, they can.

Bibliography

Adrian, Bonnie. *Framing the Bride: Globalizing Beauty and Romance in Taiwan's Bridal Industry.* Berkeley: University of California Press, 2003.

Andrade, Tonio. *How Taiwan Became Chinese: Dutch, Spanish, and Han Colonization in the Seventeenth Century.* New York: Columbia University Press, 2008.

Blumenthal, Dan, and Randall Schriver, "Strengthening Freedom in Asia: A 21st Century Agenda for the U.S.-Taiwan Partnership." American Enterprise Institute and Armitage International, 2008.

Brown, Melissa. *Is Taiwan Chinese? The Impact of Culture, Power, and Migration on Changing Identities.* Berkeley: University of California Press, 2004.

Campos, Jose Edgardo, and Hilton L. Root. *The Key to the Asian Miracle: Making Shared Growth Credible.* Washington, D.C.: Brookings Institution, 1996.

Chao, Linda, and Ramon H. Myers. *The First Chinese Democracy: Political Life in the Republic of China on Taiwan.* Baltimore: The Johns Hopkins University Press, 1997.

Chen Ming-tong, and Jih-wen Lin. "The Origins of Taiwan's Local Elections and the Changing Relations between State and Society" ["Taiwan difang xuanju de qiyuan yu guojia shehui guanxi zhuanbian"]. In *Basic Level Elections and Socio-Political Change on Both Sides of the Strait* [*Liang an jiceng xuanju yu zhengzhi shehui bianqian*], edited by Chen Ming-tong and Zheng Yungnian. Taipei: Yuedan Publishing Company, 1998.

Chen Shui-bian. *The Son of Taiwan: The Life of Chen Shui-bian and His Dreams for Taiwan.* Translated by David J. Toman. Taipei: Taiwan Publishing Co., Ltd., 2000.

Chen Wen-chun. "The Political Culture of Taiwanese Students: High School and University Students' Attitudes and the Future of Taiwan's Democratization." *Guoli Zhongshan Daxue Shehui Kexue Jikan* 1, no. 3 (Spring 1998): 29.

Chen Yu-hua. *Buyiyang de Nuren* [*Uncommon Women*]. Taipei: Hsienjue Publishers, 2000.

Cheng, Tun-jen. "Democratizing the Quasi-Leninist Regime in Taiwan." *World Politics* 41:4 (1998).

Ching, Leo. *Becoming "Japanese": Colonial Taiwan and the Politics of Identity Formation.* Berkeley: University of California Press, 2000.

Chiu, Chien-chung. "The Improvement and Production of Rice in Taiwan." *Taizhongqu Nongye Gailiangchang Yanjiu Huibao* 05: 121–132 (1981): 123. http://tdares.coa.gov.tw/htmlarea_file/web_articles/tdares/219/5-15.pdf.

Chu, Yun-han. "Taiwan's Politics of Identity: Navigating between China and the United States." In *Power and Security in Northeast Asia: Shifting Strategies,* edited by Byung-Kook Kim and Anthony Jones. Boulder, Colo.: Lynne Rienner Publishers, 2007.

Chu, Yun-han. *Crafting Democracy in Taiwan.* Institute for National Policy Research, 1992.

DeGlopper, Donald R. *Lukang: Commerce and Community in a Chinese City.* Albany: SUNY Press, 1995.

Dickson, Bruce J. *Democratizaton in China and Taiwan: The Adaptability of Leninist Parties.* New York: Oxford University Press, 1998.

Fell, Dafydd. *Party Politics in Taiwan: Party Change and the Democratic Evolution of Taiwan, 1991-2004.* New York: Routledge, 2005.

Gold, Thomas. *State and Society in the Taiwan Miracle.* Armonk, N.Y.: M.E. Sharpe, 1986.

Greene, Megan. *The Origins of the Developmental State in Taiwan.* Cambridge: Harvard University Press, 2008.

Hood, Steven J. *The Kuomintang and the Democratization of Taiwan.* Boulder, Colo.: Westview, 1997.

Hsueh, Li-min, Chen-kuo Hsu, and Dwight H. Perkins. *Industrialization and the State: The Changing Role of the Taiwan Government in the Economy, 1945–1998.* Cambridge: Harvard Institute for International Development, 2001.

Hughes, Christopher. *Taiwan and Chinese Nationalism: National Identity and Status in International Society.* New York: Routledge, 1997.

Jordan, David K. *Gods, Ghosts and Ancestors: Folk Religion in a Taiwanese Village.* Taipei: Caves Books, 1985.

Keliher, Macabe. *Out of China: Yu Yonghe's Tales of Formosa.* Taipei: SMC Publishing, 2003.

Kerr, George H. *Formosa Betrayed.* Great Britain: John Dickens & Co Ltd., 1965.

Kerr, George H. *Formosa: Licensed Revolution and the Home Rule Movement, 1895–1945.* Honolulu: The University Press of Hawaii, 1974.

Lai Tse-han, Ramon Myers, and Wei Wou. *A Tragic Beginning: The Taiwan Uprising of February 28, 1947.* Palo Alto: Stanford University Press, 1991.

Lau, Joseph S. M., ed. *Chinese Stories from Taiwan: 1960–1970.* New York: Columbia University Press, 1976.

Li Hsiao-feng. *Forty Years of Taiwan's Democratic Movement* [*Taiwan minzhu yundong sishi nian*]. Taipei: Independence Evening Post, 1987.

Lynch, Dan, "Mr. Ma's Taiwanese Identity." *Far Eastern Economic Review* (March 2008).

Moody, Peter. *Political Change on Taiwan: A Study of Ruling Party Adaptability.* New York: Praeger, 1992.

Phillips, Steven E. *Between Assimilation and Independence: The Taiwanese Encounter Nationalist China, 1945–1950.* Palo Alto, Calif.: Stanford University Press, 2003.

Rigger, Shelley. *Politics in Taiwan: Voting for Democracy*. London: Routledge, 1999.

Ross, Robert. "The 1995–1996 Taiwan Strait Confrontation: Coercion, Credibility, and Use of Force." *International Security* 25, no. 2 (Fall 2000): 87–123.

Rubenstein, Murray, ed. *Taiwan: A New History*. Armonk, N.Y.: M. E. Sharpe, 1999.

Snow, Edgar. *Red Star over China* (revised edition). New York: Grove Press, 1968.

Szonyi, Michael. *Cold War Island: Quemoy on the Front Line*. Cambridge: Cambridge University Press, 2008.

Suisheng Zhao. "Strategic Dilemma of Beijing's Taiwan Policy." In *The "One China" Dilemma*, edited by Peter C. Y. Chow. New York: Palgrave Macmillan, 2008.

Teng, Emma Jinhua. *Taiwan's Imagined Geography: Chinese Colonial Travel Writing and Pictures, 1683–1895*. Cambridge, Mass.: Harvard University Asia Center, 2004.

Thornton, A., J. S. Chang, and H. S. Lin. "From Arranged Marriage toward Love Match." In *Social Change and the Family in Taiwan*, edited by Arland Thorton and Hui-shen Lin. Chicago: University of Chicago Press, 1994.

Tien, Hung-mao. *The Great Transition: Political and Social Change in Taiwan*. Palo Alto, Calif.: Hoover Institution Press, 1989.

Tucker, Nancy Bernkopf. "If Taiwan Chooses Unification, Should the United States Care?" *Washington Quarterly* 25:3 (Summer 2002).

Tucker, Nancy Bernkopf. *Strait Talk: United States-Taiwan Relations and the Crisis with China*. Cambridge: Harvard University Press, 2009.

Vogel, Ezra. *The Four Little Dragons*. Cambridge: Harvard University Press, 1991.

Wachman, Alan. *Taiwan: National Identity and Democratization*. Armonk, N.Y.: M. E. Sharpe, 1994.

Wachman, Alan. *Why Taiwan: Geostrategic Rationales for China's Territorial Integrity*. Palo Alto, Calif.: Stanford University Press, 2007.

Wade, Robert. *Governing the Market: Economic Theory and the Role of Government in East Asian Industrialization*. Princeton: Princeton University Press, 2003.

Weinstein, M., T. H. Sun, M. C. Chang, and R. Freedman. "Co-Residence and Other Ties Linking Couples and Their Parents." In *Social Change and the Family in Taiwan*, edited by Arland Thorton and Hui-shen Lin. Chicago: University of Chicago Press, 1994.

Winckler, Edwin. "Institutionalization and Participation on Taiwan: From Hard to Soft Authoritarianism?" *The China Quarterly*, 1984.

Wu Rwei-ren. "Fragment of/f Empires: The Peripheral Formation of Taiwanese Nationalism." *Social Science Japan* (December 2004): 16.

Wu, Joseph Jauhsieh. *Taiwan's Democratization: Forces Behind the New Momentum*. New York: Oxford University Press, 1995.

Wu, Rong-I, and Chung-Che Huang. "Entrepreneurship in Taiwan: Turning Point to Restart." http://www.mansfieldfdn.org/programs/program_pdfs/ent_taiwan.pdf.

Index

About the Author

Shelley Rigger is the Brown Professor of East Asian Politics at Davidson College in North Carolina. Her first trip to Taiwan was in 1983, and she has visited the island regularly since 1991. She has been a visiting researcher at Taiwan's Chengchi University and a visiting professor at Fudan University in Shanghai. She earned a PhD in government from Harvard University and a BA in public and international affairs from Princeton. She is the author of two books on Taiwan's domestic politics, *Politics in Taiwan: Voting for Democracy* and *From Opposition to Power: Taiwan's Democratic Progressive Party*, and has published many articles on Taiwan's domestic politics and Taipei-Beijing relations. Her monograph "Taiwan's Rising Rationalism: Generations, Politics and 'Taiwan Nationalism'" was published by the East West Center in 2006.